ESSENTIAL DARKROOM TECHNIQUES

ESSENTIAL DARKROOM TECHNIQUES

Jonathan Eastland

BLANDFORD PRESS
POOLE · NEW YORK · SYDNEY

Series Editor: Jonathan Grimwood
First published in the UK 1987 by Blandford Press
Link House, West Street, Poole, Dorset BH15 1LL

Distributed in the United States by
Sterling Publishing Co, Inc,
2 Park Avenue, New York, NY 10016

Distributed in Australia by
Capricorn Link (Australia) Pty Ltd
PO Box 665, Lane Cove, NSW 2066

British Library Cataloguing in Publication Data

Eastland, Jonathan
    Essential darkroom techniques.
    1. Photography — Developing and developers.
    I. Title
    770'28'3   TR295

ISBN 0 7137 1651 7

Typeset by Asco Trade Typesetting Ltd, Hong Kong

Printed in Great Britain by Purnell Book Production Ltd
Member of the BPCC Group

Contents

Acknowledgements

Without the tireless assistance, advice and co-operation of a great many people within the photographic industry, this book would probably not have been completed. In particular, my grateful thanks to the following who supplied photographs, test samples of materials and data:

M.J. Elsdon of Photo Technology Ltd, manufacturers of Photocolor processing chemistry; Pat Wallace in the press office of Polaroid (UK) Ltd for her enthusiasm and unstinting help; Keith Malone at Johnsons of Hendon Ltd, distributors of Durst darkroom equipment; Peter Sutherst in the Kodak Customer Relations department; Martin Reed at Silver Print Ltd, Gulliver's Wharf, London; Ian Dickens of Olympus Optical Co. (UK) Ltd; Graham New of Nova Darkroom Equipment; Paterson Products Ltd of London; and Tatung (UK) Ltd, for their assistance with the Einstein computer on which this book was written.

A special thank you to my friend and assistant Andy Rose for holding the fort and keeping the whip poised!

All photographs are the copyright of Jonathan Eastland, except where credited otherwise.

JONATHAN EASTLAND 1987

Introduction

The more perceptive enthusiast will have noticed that most technological advances in the photographic industry in the past two decades have been manifested mainly in the area of electronic wizardry. Cameras are less bulky, lighter and, with few exceptions, mainly electronically controlled. Darkroom equipment and accessories are less 'Heath Robinson' in appearance and sprout various electronic or easy-to-use devices in profusion.

But it is ironic, particularly in this area of work, that those of us who cannot afford the quite substantial investment required for the purchase of motorised processing drum units and sophisticated auto-focus, auto-colour-balance enlargers are, by the very nature of the chemistry processes required, forced to revert to the simple open-tray system for print-making and a sealed light-tight plastic or stainless tube for film developing. The only other requisites for this part of the operation are a clock and thermometer. Neither the method nor the basic apparatus has changed significantly from that used by the pioneers of popular photography a hundred years ago.

While the optical quality of lenses improved rapidly during photography's history, it is only in very recent years that there has been any significant improvement made in the resolving capability of film stock, and in particular to the field of colour-negative work. And, in order to transfer the two-dimensional negative film image to positive paper, the chemical processes used today are only marginally faster than they were a decade ago.

In ten years' time – and probably much sooner than that for industry – photography as we all know it today will have changed immensely. There will still be cameras, of course, and perhaps even interchangeable lenses. But the medium used to capture the image will almost certainly be a CCD – a charge coupled device, a computer microchip which converts incoming light into electronic signals which are then stored on a floppy disc not so dissimilar to those already in use with desk-top micros.

Several top names in photography and electronics have been hard at work to improve the Still Camera Video System since Japan's Sony Corporation first introduced the *Mavica* in 1981. Canon have also been to the forefront in this field with the launch in 1986 of their own SVS. Their new six-piece system is aimed mainly at the professional market and comes with a massive price tag way beyond the reach of the average amateur enthusiast. However, once technology in chip design can produce quality electronic images on a par with conventional photographic materials, ordinary film and paper may well be headed for the museum display cabinets.

Current CCD technology allows the storage of some 400,000 pixels – tiny squares or dots that form the picture. This is a lot less than the 35 mm film format which, comparatively speaking, holds some 18 million pixels. Both Nikon and Sony have been working together on lens and television design to produce a new generation of ultra-sharp image hardware. Independent lens manufacturer Tamron already has a little black box on the market which converts conventional film images for television viewing. When the chips are down – and Eastman Kodak will doubtless be first with their newly developed 1.4 million pixel CCD – and dry print-making technology is compatible, the first area to feel the effect will almost certainly be the high-street and in-store developing and printing industry.

Electronic picture gathering (EPG) equipment and techniques will spawn a whole new area of photography, and in some ways, I must say, I am quite looking forward to the day when I can use my computer as a darkroom for those occasions when prints are required in a hurry. I somehow doubt that the quality of electronically produced stills image will ever quite compare with the conventionally produced metallic silver-based photograph, and for the latter there will always be a demand by perfectionists. The computer darkroom will, however, be able to offer a choice, and the hardware necessary is already available off the shelf.

I mentioned Tamron's Fotovox earlier. This box of tricks allows the photographer to view conventional negatives and slides on a television monitor. Polaroid, who have for some time been able to supply the 'Palette' for the production of computer graphics onto film, recently introduced a new version which incorporates an SX-70 camera, allowing prints to be made directly from the screen using Polaroid materials. This basic hardware, called a 'Freeze Frame Video Palette', is capable of producing perfectly usable computer-enhanced prints on normal Polaroid print film. The computer image-enhancer reduces the 'rasta line effect' normally associated with television and there are some expensive enhancers that can change the colour of the subject or any part of it.

For most newsprint and magazine reproduction a few hundred thousand pixels less will make very little difference in general run-of-the-mill reproduction. If the Polaroid Corporation could modify their Palette so that conventional medium-format cameras with interchangeable backs could be used, obtaining an ordinary negative, slide or Polaroid of an SVS-originated image would open many new possibilities for the creative photographer. But, who knows, by the time this hardware is available in the discount superstore, someone will have produced a miniature dry paper copier capable of producing hundreds of originals from either source in a matter of minutes.

Well, that is about as far as this book will delve into the future of electronic image-making. For the time being at least, conventional photography is here to stay and the following chapters are designed to guide the hobbyist through what appears to be a minefield of conventional processing magic to obtain the best results with the least amount of fuss and bother.

If a densitometer is mentioned, it will only be in passing to illustrate its function in more scientific areas. For all practical purposes, amateur and working photographers have long since adopted the maxim that if it looks right it will be all right. For those interested in publishing, the book will discuss the best and most economic ways of producing prints for reproduction which are of high quality. We will look at processing techniques in the light of experience. Some eyebrows may be raised in the darkest corridors of camera club activity, but I can assure the reader that everything you read in the following chapters will have already undergone some practical precedent. It was either found to work, or not, as the case may be.

In the last sentence lies the clue to the key of success in opening this black magic box; it is simply that it is only with the benefit of practical experience that I am now satisfied as to why anything in the darkroom works at all.

Like thousands of others, my interests in photography were sparked off at an early age. In the quest for enjoyment and rapid transition to the finished print, I spent ill-affordable funds on materials, chemicals and equipment. Only a passing glance was given to manufacturers' instructions and the texts of books devoted to this side of the operation. I had subconsciously divided the art of photographic image-making into two separate operations, one of which appealed enormously as much for its fashionable connotations as for its end product. The actual process of making the paper image was always fraught with errors and mishaps because of my impatience. Consequently, the net result was that, while I felt confident in my ability to compose and shoot the picture, little was understood as to why the effort expended during half a night of labouring in a darkened bedroom frequently produced the most atrocious results. For that understanding I had to wait a long, long time, during which miles of film and paper made its way painfully into the rubbish bin.

Some photographers profess to know nothing of the chemistry of their craft and, what is often surprising, to want to know even less. I suppose that some professionals can get by without ever wetting their hands in a darkroom, but I fail to see how any craftsman can hope to produce consistently creative work that is of professional quality without some understanding of the mechanics and chemistry of the medium.

There is nothing at all bewildering about darkroom practices. If one were to follow the processing and print-making instructions packed with each product, even the individual coming in cold from the outset could produce results. As much as anything, darkroom techniques are just that and nothing else; a variety of methods by which certain chemicals are applied to a variety of supporting media. All we need to know in order to succeed with a certain amount of style is the order and degree of finesse by which each method is applied. Do not worry overmuch if at first you don't succeed; practice, common and creative sense, and buckets of determination are all that are required to achieve good results.

1
Darkroom Design and Layout

Everyone has their own idea of what is ideal for a particular room, whether it be the bathroom, bedroom or kitchen. Likewise, no two darkrooms are ever the same. What all should have in common, however, is a demarcation between 'wet' and 'dry' areas.

In most homes, by far the biggest problem facing the photographer about to set up a darkroom is not where the real or imaginary divider between wet and dry should be placed but how much space is available for use as a whole. Strictly speaking, a darkroom is no longer necessary for film processing or for printing. Daylight developing tanks can be easily loaded in a changing bag. Acceptable enlargements can then be made using a daylab. Print-making in the conventional way requires a more elaborate and light-tight working area. This may be an area set aside in a bathroom, bedroom, garage, outside workshop or under-stair cupboard, in fact anywhere where adequate space can be found to set up an enlarger and the minimum of trays, tanks and washing facilities. Excellent quality enlargements have been made in the field using nothing more sophisticated than two plastic buckets and a folding enlarger erected inside a black plastic tent. Slightly more sophisticated, fully framed rectangular tents are available through some mail-order suppliers both in Europe and the USA. Some larger models available through suppliers in the USA are equipped with collapsible-framed wet and dry benches. The advantage of a darkroom tent is that it only need remain erected for as long as is necessary. When the space is required for another purpose, it can be quickly dismantled and stowed away or erected just as swiftly in another area. The disadvantages are that no permanent water or waste services can be connected and all water for mixing and washing usually has to be imported by the bucketful.

PLANNING THE DARKROOM

The permanent darkroom is more complicated and, if it is to run efficiently, needs almost as much attention to detail in the planning as the field darkroom lacks in facilities.

The first requirement is to try to establish as far as possible what the darkroom's primary function will be, i.e. whether it will be used for producing mainly colour prints, colour transparencies, black-and-white or all three. Second, it will pay dividends to ruminate on further acquisitions of hardware: a second enlarger, possibly of larger format and requiring significantly more height and

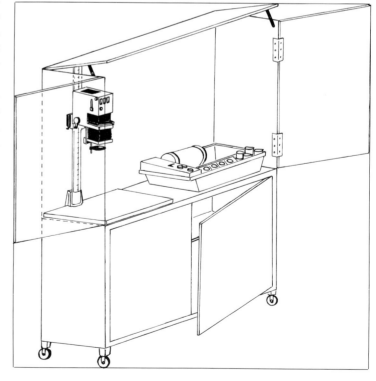

Detail of mobile darkroom.

New York. Nikon F2, 200 mm Nikkor on Tri-X rated at ISO 400. The film was machine-processed in a Kreonite processor for an effective EI800 which made the negative extremely dense. The skyscraper was burned-in heavily. Agfa Record Rapid, grade 3.

baseboard space than the one in current use; automatic print dryers capable of higher throughput; deep tanks; motorised drum processor; steel cabinet film dryer; and so on. You may decide that you need none of these things immediately, but if the photographic bug is deeply rooted, rest assured that there will be innumerable additions to the basic inventory from time to time. All of them will need a working space, so it is just as well to make some allowance at the outset.

Professional darkrooms need similar considerations. Where the area is to be used by more than one operator, some consideration should also be given to the way in which those operators prefer to work. In one example, where a team of so-called specialists were employed to design and build a darkroom for the London base of an international news agency, not one of the photographers or darkroom operators were consulted regarding the location of basic equipment, at what height it should be most conveniently placed, or even what type of equipment was preferred. The net result was that both photographers and printers were given a new working area that rapidly proved to be an ergonomic disaster. It took weeks of rearrangement together with the installation of preferred machinery before the place could be made to work efficiently.

The only benefit was the huge amount of space allocated to the darkroom, and although in this case it was rather more than was necessary for even peak traffic periods space should always be a prime consideration. Even the lone freelance with a more or less continuous workload will find that space to move around the working area with relative safety and ease, space on which to dump sheets of negatives as far from wet areas as possible, space to step back so as to regard the easel image in comfort and space to be able to wander from the wash tank to an enlarger, or a light box, or to a bench on which half-a-dozen damp dry prints are laid out for inspection, is a great asset.

Such acres of space are frequently at a premium, however, and perhaps the most that one can hope for is a spare room which is easily divided into a functional wet and dry area with the least amount of conversion. Studios employing a full-time darkroom technician and assistant will need proportionately larger areas, but I hasten to add at this point that, in so far as the concept of this book is concerned, multi-personnel work areas are beyond its scope and will therefore not be discussed at any length.

Just how much space will be required will also depend largely on the personality of the individual concerned. Those with a fairly meticulous disposition, who cannot work efficiently at anything unless tools and materials are well ordered, may easily be able to withstand what others might consider an element of claustrophobia. Just how small will depend on the physical size of equipment, how much of it there is, and where it must be placed in relation to the operator. One photographer I know works within the confines of a 6×4 ft (1.8×1.2 m) box in which the centre piece is a revolving office stool. An enlarger and assorted shelves of paper and smaller equipment line one side of the box, while dishes, an auto print processor and wash tank are laid out opposite. The back of the door serves as a hanging rack for a home-made film dryer and a safelight.

Photographers are sometimes found in much smaller work places, but not ever having had that experience myself I would imagine that too little space would severely restrict not only output, but also any inclination to attempt much that was adventurous.

Those of us who prefer what appears to others to be a slap-happy aproach to work often produce our best while buried under a mountain of totally irrelevant material. My own darkrooms have become progressively larger over the years. This has been partly due to necessity – the acquisition of more equipment – but also because I enjoy working in that atmosphere of apparent confusion. I need acres of space around an enlarger baseboard, for negatives, boxes of filters, dodging utensils, masking frames, pens, notebooks and all the paraphernalia that seems to accumulate. I hasten to add that this confusion is all of my own making and so long as it remains that way I am perfectly content to continue working. When a stranger invades the darkroom and tries to make order out of mess, I am then at a loss to know where to begin again. Having a larger darkroom helps. I can keep my mess around my own work station while others create theirs around a second or third. Surprisingly, the wet area is nearly always fairly orderly, though I must admit that my patience is hardly ever extended to cover the totally unnecessary practice of whitewashing the walls with hypo.

Small darkrooms encourage the photographer to be more disciplined; large ones have the opposite effect, especially when more than one person has simultaneous access. It is essential, therefore, when planning your place of work, to pay attention to the detail of layout.

Traditionally, the following spaces are most commonly allocated for work when a temporary darkroom is considered the more practical: utility; kitchen; bathroom.

If the work area is to be of a permanent nature the following are usually considered: attic; spare room; bedroom; garage; garden chalet; other exterior.

Older houses often have far more in the way of protected space than most modern buildings, but even so, when the temporary darkroom is preferred, that bathroom almost invariably tops the list. Why this should be so is something of a mystery to me, especially if materials and equipment are to be stored in the same room after each use. Aside from the immediate advantage of a hot and cold water supply and adequate waste system, bathrooms are not ideally suited to the photographer's needs. Accumulating moisture, condensation and steam produced by other users when the place is not used for processing or print-making will soon damage paper supplies and rust equipment which is left unprotected.

However, as a very temporary measure until some other facility is found, all that is required is some kind of support for an enlarger, a large sheet of heavy-duty black plastic which can be taped to any window to keep the light out, a safelight and three plastic dishes that will fit easily into the bathtub.

One of my first encounters with a darkroom took place in a friend's house. Some clever handiwork had produced an efficient and very suitable mobile bench which resembled an oversized walk-in wardrobe. I was so impressed that I used the idea, slightly modified, while living in various rented accommodations. Provided the mobile is custom-made to fit into an existing bathroom and there is space available to store it outside when not in use, the problems recounted with regard to moisture etc should be easily overcome.

The most common fault in picture-taking at the film/negative stage is camera shake. This may be induced by the camera operator or some other phenomenon. However slight the shake appears to be on the negative, it will always be enhanced when the final print is made. Unless firmly secured, enlargers often suffer from the same malady.

Except for office buildings where the floors are generally constructed from reinforced concrete, both old and new homes tend to be built with wooden floors on wooden joists. Any mobile or portable enlarger bench must be secured as firmly as possible in order to help reduce the possibility of shake being set up through erroneous exterior vibrations while prints are being exposed. The portable cupboard bench poses some problems in this direction and, while the emphasis will be on portability to a large extent, none of the solidity of a fixed bench should be sacrificed to that cause. If construction is to be in timber, use a minimum of 2 in (5 cm) square prepared wood for the main frame uprights, working bench chassis and supports for the under shelf. The back can be clad with pegboard, and sides and cupboard door fronts with thin 3-ply or hardboard pinned to light door frames. The actual working surface should be as heavy as possible; a high-density chipboard is ideal provided it is fitted with a plastic laminate working surface and is properly edged to prevent any moisture from penetrating the core. 15-mm plywood, also with the upper surface covered, will be suitable. For little extra expense, however, including the time expended in fitting the laminate top, it would be more efficient to have a 'post-formed' top custom-made to fit the proportions of the chassis. Post-formed worktops are basically comprised of chipboard with a rounded leading edge onto which has been heat-sealed a plastic laminate top and bottom. Paying a little extra for a made-to-measure enlarger bench will pay dividends.

As I have already said, attention to detail in the planning of any darkroom is of the utmost importance and cannot be stressed too heavily. Slightly more investment than was originally envisaged into better quality building materials will always benefit the operator in the long term. But if you are working to a rigid budget, there are ways in which funds can be pruned on some items.

Because photography is such a popular leisure pursuit, the price of some items of equipment may seem to some to be inordinately high. In other words, 'Where is the value in that?' I would prefer to see rather more spent on essentially functional equipment, which because of its construction will stand the test of time, than on some item which is designed to appeal purely for aesthetic reasons.

Darkroom safelights are a good example of how industry caters for the amateur market. It is essential, as we shall see later, to have a faultless safelight system, but this can be organised easily and cheaply for most printing requirements and graphic arts materials use with simple wall-mounted light fittings and a handful of pygmy bulbs. These are the tiny 15-watt fairy lights which are often found decorating restaurant tables, large Christmas trees and so on. One such light placed strategically and shrouded by a baffle can be mounted above the mobile bench on an extending arm which is locked into place when the bench comes into use with a bolt and butterfly nut.

In larger, permanent darkrooms, pygmy lights can be positioned around the room so that they will throw light over relatively safe areas. Red bulbs are most suitable but you must ensure that the socket end of the bulb is properly shrouded as there is usually a paint defect which allows small amounts of white light to be transmitted.

Other budget-saving utensils include measuring jugs which are invariably cheaper to purchase from the catering departments of large department stores or specialist plastics outlets which cater for industry and agriculture. Here, too, you will often find items which are more than suitable as semi-deep tanks, developing trays and wash tanks.

Hardware stores can usually provide ordinary domestic dish-stacking racks of the plastic-coated wire-basket type. These can be hung on clips under the enlarger work surface, and are useful for storing things such as tanks or the dozens of empty film cassettes and medium-format spools that some photographers hang on to for no special reason. A useful film-drying hanger can be easily adapted from one of those wall-mounted kitchen-towel holders with several swing-out arms. When not in use, the arms can be folded down out of the way or swung back against a wall.

So far, I've assumed that most photographers will require a bench large enough to tackle both black-and-white and colour processes using wet tray methods. The portable described will certainly have enough working space for most techniques to be executed. Those photographers who are equipped with auto drum processors for colour print-making and film-processing may reasonably decide that a smaller portable unit will be more practicable for the space available. There is also the question of where such a unit could be stored when not in use.

The major disadvantage of any temporary set-up within the living area of a home is that, while the photographer is working, other members of the household are subjected to certain restrictions. 'Bathroom off limits' is definitely an inconvenience to most people even when the frequency of blackout is so low as to be almost never! For the photographer, psychological factors concerning the preparation for a print-making session may diminish the enthusiasm more than somewhat. Combine the two attitudes and you have a cast-iron case for considering a more permanent working area. I hasten to add, however, that, while attitudes are often a governing factor as to the ultimate choice, temporary darkrooms will work well for those who are happy with them. Ingenuity and improvisation are the essential keys to successful working in any temporary set-up.

For those interested only in the processing of reversal materials for projection purposes, a darkroom as such is not essential. Provided that film can be loaded onto spools either in a changing bag or some completely light-tight cupboard space, processing can take place in a very small area in broad daylight. The most commonly active location seems to be the kitchen sink, usually after dishes from the evening meal have been cleared away and the rest of the household is glued to some favourite television soap opera. With today's chemical technology, reversal processing is no more difficult than colour-negative or black-and-white and requires only that temperatures are maintained accurately throughout the process. But more of that later.

And so to more permanent fixtures: the walk-in darkroom large enough to swing a cat in; or, if not, one with at least an apparent feeling of practically usable space.

There are several tasks which need special consideration when planning the layout of a proper working area; these are as follows, but not necessarily in order of preference.

1) Decide the ideal wet and dry bench height from the floor in relation to operator convenience.
2) Decide the ideal dry bench height in relation to maximum elevation of the enlarger and the most convenient easel height from the floor.
3) Will the wet and dry be adjacent with the divider or on the opposite side of the room?
4) Check the convenience of the main services, i.e. incoming water, waste, and electrical ring-main supply take-off point.
5) If there is no existing window opening into the atmosphere, check the construction details of the building for allocation of a suitable ventilation system.
6) Ensure the soundness of the floor joists before importing heavy autoprocess equipment/metal-cased dryers etc.
7) If using attic space, check that the roof is sound, and not leaking in your selected area.
8) Make general checks all round for signs of damp, and remedy these if found in any area.

Once you have given some thought to the relevant items above, you can begin to plan alternative layouts. If you plan to make a fairly substantial investment into building a customised darkroom, try assembling a small cardboard model of your plans. Each unit should be made to scale as far as possible, as this will give a very good idea of the amount of 'moving' space which will be left when all fittings are in place. It also allows for major and minor detail changes to be made to plans before any building commences. It's essential that when complete your darkroom allows you freedom of movement between benches, enlargers, drying cabinets and any shelving which is likely to project into the actual working area.

Commercial darkrooms are invariably fitted with some kind of elaborate light trap entrance which allows operators to come and go at will without hindrance to anyone who may still be working. Off-the-shelf light trap doors of the revolving type are available at huge cost, and because of their size are totally unsuitable to the average home. A little ingenuity, again using a cardboard model, will soon show that it is perfectly possible to have an adequate light trap entrance which occupies very little space. This can be done using a double curtain technique, or by having a fixed baffle which is constructed from hardboard on a light studding frame.

It is assumed that anyone considering a permanent set-up will have access to the choice of spaces already mentioned. There will be numerous advantages and disadvantages attached to all, and these, along with everything else, must be weighed in for debate. For example, attractions of an attic or loft darkroom mainly centre around privacy and seclusion. The same thing goes for the basement to a large extent, but if there is a choice my money would almost certainly go below stairs rather than in the roof, unless I had already undertaken major conversion work in the attic/loft.

In older houses, main services are available in the loft, but few houses have roof spaces which are fully insulated from cold and heat. Any darkroom built into an uninsulated roof space will suffer from an excess of heat in summer and freezing cold in winter. Basements tend to remain at a fairly even temperature all year round, do not require cooling in summer and consume little power for heating in winter. Add to this the fact that mains water, waste and power services are usually immediately to hand, and little work needs to be done to make the space light-tight, and you have a good case for using the basement.

Spare rooms on the first, second or even third floor will be ideal, provided they are of adequate size. Ambient room temperatures can be easily controlled by thermostat where hot air, conventional central heating or air conditioning is installed. In more temperate climates, heating can be arranged where no fixed installation is present using portable electric convector or oil-filled radiators fitted with a time clock. This will help to keep the space at an even temperature and prevent unnecessary power waste.

When the appropriate space has been selected and before any new construction takes place, a thorough check of the state of floors and walls should be made. If plasterwork or floorboards are in need of repair, this should be carried out immediately with careful attention being paid to any possible sources of dust being properly sealed.

In older properties, dust will be a frequent problem in the darkroom unless it is dealt with at the outset. First of all, remove all traces of the existing floor covering; remove any nails which protrude and secure any loose boards. Replace those which look as if they may be rotten. This is always the best time, too, to inspect underfloor wiring. If it is at all suspect, have a qualified electrician

do the work. This solves two potential problems: one is the risk of electrical fire caused by circuit failure; the other is the necessity or temptation to install the darkroom wiring circuit yourself without really knowing what you are doing, and then having to satisfy any insurance company inspector that the work you are planning to carry out meets specific insurance provisions. It is usually worth checking both house-cover policy and house-contents policy to ensure that, if you *do* do the work yourself, cover remains in force.

Once you are satisfied that the floor is stable and any work which needed doing under it has been completed, the task of sealing can begin. Use sheets of hardboard pinned or stapled in place over the whole floor area. Alternatively, spend more funds on high-density chipboard. This material is a better insulator and, if thick enough, will provide a solid work base. A proprietary vinyl floor-covering should be used next, although there is no reason why some other material, such as cork tiles or industrial linoleum, should not be used. A degree of comfort in any darkroom is essential, especially when there is a likelihood of long hours being spent standing. In this case, a cushion-floor-type vinyl floor-covering is to be preferred. When measuring the area to be covered, make an allowance for a few extra inches all the way around the room perimeter. The covering can then be folded upward and stapled to skirting boards. This will help facilitate the cleaning of the floor and will also prevent any dust finding its way upward from under the floor. Seal the edges of vinyl where it is stapled to the skirting board with waterproof carpet tape.

It is essential that all dust sources are eliminated at the outset. Attic/loft and basements will cause more problems in this area than most others if not efficiently dealt with in the beginning. One basement darkroom I worked in for a number of years had a flagstone floor laid over the bare earth. It had been a wine cellar before my occupation, and, while most of the seams between each flag had been filled with cement and the floor painted with an industrial sealant, it caused never-ending problems. Had I put down a layer of concrete over the flagstones and then sealed it, I doubt it would have been such a niggling thorn for so long.

THE WORKING LAYOUT

Now that most of the groundwork has been done, you can begin to think about the most practical and convenient layout. Remember that you are the prime operator. If anyone else is invited to work in your darkroom, it will be as a guest only. All detail should therefore be aimed at providing you with facilities which suit your own needs and not those of others.

There are several schools of thought regarding darkroom design, very few of which could ever be described as being 'the best' or 'better than'. Much will depend on the amount of space available, whether you are left- or right-handed, whether you prefer to stand or sit when working, *et al*. It is assumed, however, that work produced will be of an exacting standard and will cover all aspects of photo-processing technique.

The layout illustrated here can be adapted without too much difficulty for use by disabled people. Where possible, darkroom sites should be situated on lower floor levels and proper provision made for access by wheelchair if necessary. This will mean that the entrance and/or exit will have to be wider than normal and ramps may be needed where a step up or down is sited. Bench heights must be naturally accessible by anyone seated and should not be so deep that the back cannot be reached from a sitting position. Most off-the-shelf enlargers are designed for use by people who are not incapacitated. Operation by wheelchair-bound photographers may prove difficult if the equipment is placed on a side bench. To overcome this problem, the enlarger should be mounted on its own custom-adapted table and placed as near to the centre of the darkroom space as is practicable. Assuming there is adequate aisle space to allow ease of movement, the disabled operator should now be able to operate all the controls by moving around the equipment. Because most modern enlargers are of lightweight construction it will be an added advantage to have both table and enlarger baseboard fixed in position so that the equipment remains secure in the event of accidental collision.

Electrical switch boards and all electrical appliances must be properly grounded and placed well away from wet areas. Operating switches will be placed within easy reach of the chair-bound person, and all ceiling-hung lights will be more practically operative when fitted with ceiling-mounted pull cords.

Still on the subject of power, it is worth elaborating further on alternative installations. Mains power to the darkroom should be independent of the main household domestic supply. There are good reasons for this. One is that if the darkroom supply is connected to the domestic ring main there is always the possibility that a user other than yourself may overload the system and blow a main fuse. If you know that some equipment in the darkroom is liable to draw a lot of power at any time, the chances of the system being overloaded during hours of peak consumption will be higher. To avoid such disasters, a direct feed line from the incoming main supply of the house to the darkroom could be fitted.

Suggested darkroom layout.

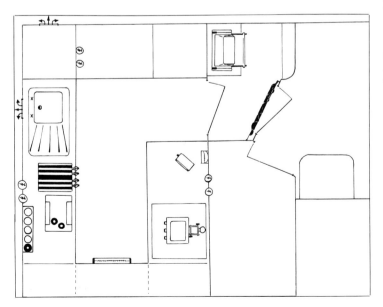

In most households, the electricity supply coming in from the street is fed through a meter to a junction box or a fused switch box. There should be a spare untapped line from which a 30-amp cable can be run directly to the darkroom where it should be connected to a 30-amp trip switch before feeding directly into another fused switch box. Separate circuits from each fuse are then set up around the various workstations. If faults develop at a later stage it should be relatively easy to isolate the trouble. If everything should be shorted at once, for whatever reason, all the fuses in the box will blow but the trip switch will cut off the main supply. The normal domestic supply should not be affected.

There are many different types of electrical fittings available to the home owner and home electrician. It should be emphasised, again, that if you are at all unsure of what is required consult a competent and fully-qualified electrician with a view to having the work done properly. If you feel confident that you can do the work yourself, select only the most suitable fittings for the nature of the work. All cable should be sealed in conduit. Most sockets of the standard three-pin variety are quite unsuitable in the wet bench area due to their vulnerability to water penetration. Legrand Electric Ltd manufacture a range of weatherproof fittings which are widely available throughout Europe through wholesale distributors, but you may be able to obtain a catalogue of their wares by writing direct to their head office in Dunstable, Bedfordshire, England.

Some of their sockets are fitted with sprung, hinged covers and large rocker switches instead of the fiddly things most of us are used to. These are ideal for use in the darkroom. If power sockets are required near the wet area, make sure that they are secured to a batten on which the power supply cable is fed through conduit and clamped with the correct fittings. The batten on which sockets are placed in this area should be not less than 30 in (75 cm) above the bench. Those darkrooms with central wet benches should have the power supply connected to any appliance via an overhead cable which leads back to a dry area. NEVER operate switches or sockets with wet hands; keep the hand which is not in use away from wet trays and metal objects in the immediate vicinity.

In an average room space measuring 10 × 8 ft (3 × 2.4 m), the most convenient layout will have wet and dry benches sited opposite one another. Ideally, bench width should be in the region of 30 in (75 cm) which will allow a 3 ft (1 m) aisle between the two. Narrower benches provide inadequate space for practical working around the enlarger when larger-than-average prints are being made, and less space on wet benches for processing trays of proper size. To prevent undue splashing of chemicals, my own arrangement utilises two trays for developer, stop and fix. The smaller of the two contains the chemical, the larger outer catches the drips, but can also be used as a warming bath when required. For most black-and-white work, dish-warmers of the electrical type are unnecessary and, in my view, quite dangerous unless of professional-quality construction.

I have an automatic agitator which is a custom-made unit in which the electrics are housed in a watertight fibreglass box. The mobile top, which also acts as a dish-warmer, is fitted with lugs into which varying sizes of stainless steel trays may be fitted. Only small amounts of liquid are necessary for developing purposes. However, while this machine is of immense help when producing large quantities of prints, I actually find it easier to control temperature and action using the dish water-jacket method described in the previous paragraph. As soon as the temperature of the developer begins to drop significantly, the contents of the outer dish are discarded and fresh warm water added. In summer, there is hardly ever a need for the water-jacket, except when processing colour materials, and in winter, provided the developer solution is no more than lukewarm to the touch, perfectly acceptable results will continue to be obtained.

But back to the layout plans, and back once again to the cardboard cut-outs. Bench height will depend largely on whether the operator prefers to stand or sit, but in any event would not normally exceed 36–7 in (91–94 cm) in height. Check that, at this height, the ceiling height will allow a full height extension of the enlarger head. Some large-format enlargers have an immense range, but need a lot of space upward in order to achieve full working height. I have a 5 × 7 in (13 × 18 cm) format MPP which when fully extended stands well over 6 ft (1.8 m) above bench height. The smaller the format, the less operating height required, but it is always worth checking dimensions before going ahead with bench construction.

You could use an alternative layout, in which more space is assumed and central feature of the work area is a wet bench with integral sink unit and running water. Many larger professional darkrooms with multiple operators are laid out in this fashion too, but, in my mind, if space is available, it provides one of the most comfortable working layouts. All dry areas are kept to the sides of the room and a central, ceiling-hung safelight provides more than adequate illumination over the main working area. For professionals working alone there are added bonuses over the conventional layout. For example, if you are in the middle of developing prints and the phone rings, you can continue to attend the print from any side of the bench while answering the call. Other multiple tasks, such as washing and drying, are made easier, and usually the layout allows for more convenient storage space.

2
Hardware and Equipment

Special attention should be paid to plumbing, waste services and equipment selected for sink spaces. Unless your brazing and tinning techniques with copper pipe are 100 per cent, the services of a professional plumber will be well advised. The last thing any photographer wants in the darkroom is a leaky or dripping pipe. If, because of the budget, you have to do this work yourself, use brass compression joints and *ptfe* tape, or bos white and hemp strands. Underground alkathene plastic pipe is perfectly suitable for the cold water supply, easy to fit and does not require any special bending; use compression joint bends for rounding corners etc. Provided the water temperature is not boiling, it is possible to use this material for the hot supply too, but copper would be safer.

Brass taps of the garden variety with long spouts are ideal. If you include one which has a threaded spout (on the cold supply) you will find this very useful for attaching a length of wandering hose.

One of your most important choices will be the sink. Some wet benches are basically just one long trough with a deeper trough housing the waste exit at one end. Trade photographic magazines which specialise in professional equipment frequently carry advertisements for darkroom sinks. These are constructed using polypropylene or glass fibre and are available off-the-shelf, at a price. Some manufacturers offer a customising service. The ordinary kitchen sink unless of stone porcelain or high-grade stainless steel (18–8), is virtually useless. Inferior-grade steel stains easily and if constantly splashed with hypo will soon begin to rust. This is not to say that the humble kitchen sink is out of place in a darkroom. I've managed to get by with one for years. However, it is worth hunting around for a sink large enough to take at least a 12 × 10 in print; better if you can find a flush-mounting stainless bowl that can be let into a fibreglass base.

Polypropylene is commonly found in industry and is used for a variety of products including storage bins and trays. Farmers, growers, and dairy producers invariably use them and would know where such products could be obtained if you cannot find a local distributor. Lists of plastics manufacturers are to be found in the telephone directory and they are always worth investigating before committing funds elsewhere. Brass and stainless waste fittings are always available from builders' merchants; a hole-cutter of the right size on the end of an electric drill and a little silicone sealant is all that is required to make a perfectly usable darkroom sink.

Much of the furniture, i.e. base units, shelving and so on, will be custom-made using materials already described. Free-standing floor units are quite suitable if they are to be used only as cupboards. Dry benches should be firmly secured to the wall using battens and firm uprights screwed to the floor. Some kitchen wall-cupboards are inexpensive and can be fitted above the ends of a dry bench to provide clean storage space for stocks of paper, spare bulbs and anything else you want to keep out of harm's way.

Much money is often unnecessarily spent on items of equipment which cannot possibly have any effect on the final print quality. A fairly long list of essential items follows with brief details as to preferred type. If trade names are included, it is because I have found these particular products to be robust, accurate and functional. Much automated equipment has been omitted for the simple reason that much of what is currently available is far too expensive for what it is, gives

Tri-X rated at ISO 400 and developed in D-76 diluted 1 + 1. Lens was a 105 mm Nikkor used wide open with available window light. Continuous but slow agitation in daylight tank. Paper, Kentmere Bromide, grade 3.

Ships. Printed from a 35 mm negative shot on OM1 with Zuiko 180 mm f2.8 on HP5 through orange filter. ISO 320 and developed in HC110. Printed on Agfa Record Rapid grade 3. It was burned-in at the top, edges and bottom.

no great advantage and invariably only consumes excessive power. The enlarger is dealt with separately in Chapter 3.

SAFELIGHTS

Efficient safelights are essential in any darkroom. Not only must accidental fogging of sensitised materials be prevented at all times, but the operator must be able to see clearly around the main working areas without suffering the slightest eye strain. Safelights come in all shapes and sizes, from the small 5 × 7 in wall-hanging type which facilitates easy filter change, to huge overhead sodium types and plug-in globes of varying colour.

Ordinary coloured lightbulbs of the bayonet coupling variety used by the thousand along the promenades of seaside resorts are invariably of too large a wattage (power) to be considered 'safe'. 15 watts is the safe maximum for smaller work areas. They can be fitted directly to a suitable wall-mounted socket or used in photographic safelights. This type of bulb, known as a 'pygmy', is available through most electrical wholesalers and, provided they are fitted with a black baffle at the base to cut out the small amount of white light which escapes through the unpainted portion of the bulb, make ideal safelights for most black-and-white and lithographic film processes. I have used these lights in tandem with conventional safelights in my own darkrooms for many years with no adverse effect and vastly-improved working vision. It should be emphasised, however, that it is important for every photographer to check thoroughly the safelight level before any serious work is begun in a new darkroom.

All safelights should be placed a minimum of 5 feet (1.5 m) from any area where sensitised materials are likely to be left exposed, i.e. the wet bench area, and in the immediate proximity of the enlarger. Once you have placed all lights strategically, carry out this simple test.

Turn all safelights on. Take two sheets of black-and-white printing paper of approximate grade 0; with emulsion face uppermost, place one sheet on the enlarger baseboard, the other in a clean, unfilled developing tray in the wet bench area. Take several coins and place three or four over each sheet of paper. Leave the darkroom for one hour. On returning, tear off a small corner from the sheet of paper left under the enlarger. The missing corner is a marker to tell you which area of the darkroom it came from. Mix a small amount of fresh developer and process both sheets of paper for double the recommended time. Stop and fix normally. Rinse both prints for a few seconds, drain and turn on normal room lighting. If your safelights are really 'safe', the base white of the processed paper should be as white as its own reverse side. Check this by simply folding a third of the paper over so that you can see both the reverse and emulsion side simultaneously. If the emulsion looks at all grey, even vaguely dirty white, thoroughly check the emulsion side for evidence of coin shapes. If you can see them clearly, you have a safelight problem which must be attended to before any further work can be carried out. If both sheets of paper are pure white, without any trace of coin shapes or visible tone differential, work can proceed. If you are in any doubt as to the whiteness of the paper base after processing, take both sheets of paper into daylight for a further check.

Irregular and darker patches on the paper usually indicate that something other than safelights are at fault. Check all window seals and any existing outer wall ventilation bricks or cavities. Stray light entering from the latter is not always immediately visible to the naked eye; turn off all lights, including safelights, and just stand in the room for two or three minutes while your eyes become accustomed to the darkness. If there is any stray light entering the room, your eyes will soon spot the reason why. When you have remedied the fault, try the coin test again.

SAFELIGHT COLOUR

Safelight colour will be determined by the type of material being handled and work about to be done.

Dark green is the colour commonly associated with the development of panchromatic film, but not as an inspection lamp. It gives a very low level of illumination barely sufficient to enable the operator to see anything worth seeing. It is much better if you start out by learning how to do everything in complete darkness by touch. Use the glow of the green to see whether sheet film being dish-developed is properly fixed. Remember, *do not* use the lamp for inspection of film undergoing development. Pan film is sensitive to all colours of light.

Light amber and red can be used for general illumination when ordinary fibre-based bromide and resin-coated black-and-white papers are processed. Red can also be used when processing orthochromatic film such as that used in the graphic arts trades. If you are at all interested in producing line negatives on lith film for special effects, a very effective method of processing this film is to use a transparent tray for the developer. Development of the film takes place over a sheet of flashed opal glass or plastic substitute through which a dark red safelight is shone from a distance of some 4 feet (1.2 m). Reduce the intensity of the light if you have to bring it closer to the developer dish.

Dark amber is used for the processing of colour negative papers, print film, Kodak 'Panalure' paper (used for making black-and-white prints from colour-negative materials) and some positive reversal printing papers. Always check the paper manufacturer's instructions regarding safelight usage before opening material.

Nearly all manufacturers of sensitised materials quote the *Wratten* safelight filter type by number when specifying safe operating levels. Wratten filters are an exclusive Kodak Ltd registered trade name; a typical designation on a black-and-white paper packet would read, 'Open only in darkroom. Use Kodak Wratten Filter Series OC', or '... Series 2', and so on.

Working photographers refer to most lights used in the darkroom as being yellow, red or green. Do not use coloured domestic bulbs without a neutral density screen or

baffle which are either yellow or green in colour. Only red can be considered safe for some of the processes already described.

Black plastic tanks and nylon reels from Paterson Products. Tanks can be used for film and paper processing.

HARDWARE ITEMS

The following items can mostly be obtained from a local hardware store.

1) Industrial rubber gloves, for the mixing of some dry powder chemicals.

2) Overalls or apron, for protection against chemical staining of clothing.

3) Cotton tea towels, four at least; rotate two at a time. Very useful for wiping utensils, benches etc.

Paterson Products archival print-washer tank and basket.

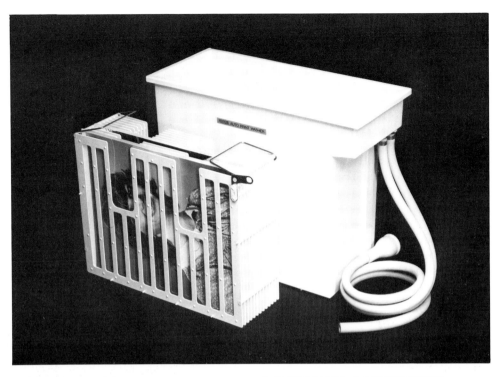

4) Floor mop, of the squeegee sponge type with a lever. Essential.

5) Plastic buckets, two. One for the floor and spilled chemicals, the other to be kept solely for mixing of powder chemicals.

6) Plastic funnel, large, for the transfer of chemicals etc after use/mixing. The funnel can also be used in conjunction with coffee-making paper filters obtainable from food stores. This arrangement is ideal for filtering sediment and emulsion particles from used chemicals before re-use.

7) Waste bin and liners. Go for the largest bin that can be reasonably housed. Small ones fill too quickly and spill over, creating messy crystallised chemicals which eventually add to the dust problem.

8) Kitchen stool, very useful if long sessions are spent under the enlarger.

9) Graduated mixing vessels, in 1 and 2 litre sizes available from hardware, catering and some department stores. Graduations should be in fl oz as well as cc and ml.

10) Stirring rods, two required as a minimum. Some say glass is best, but I use Chinese chopsticks which are of tough plastic and do not break.

DARKROOM ACCESSORIES

The next list of items is best purchased through a photographic dealer. The darkroom accessory market is a minefield. It is worth spending money on the following items.

TIMERS

Smiths darkroom timer. They make a whole range. You need a mechanical type with wind-up spring rated in seconds and minutes from 1 to 60. You simply set the time required, press a large lever on the side of the timer and away it goes. When time is up, the bell rings in a short but fierce burst. Most mechanical clocks and timers are unaffected by chemical contamination. My experience with modern electronic types has been somewhat less than perfect.

Stag twin range mechanical timer with in/out power transfer and on/off switch. I have had one of these switched timers in my darkroom for some fifteen years. They can be adapted for a number of uses, but as an enlarger timer the Stag is hard to beat for reliability and accuracy. Professional electronic time switches with built-in exposure measuring devices from a variety of sources abound. The section on printing (Chapter 7) will endeavour to teach those who want to learn how to judge exposure to within half a second of accuracy.

THERMOMETERS

Mercury thermometers are very accurate but often difficult to read, especially in subdued lighting. Alcohol types such as those made by Paterson are better and sufficiently accurate to within half a degree. Electronic Temperature Instruments supplied me with one of their first photographic digital thermometers. The unit is small enough to fit in the palm of a hand and is powered by a small 9-volt dry cell. A wandering lead with metal probe attached records the temperature of liquids which is displayed using liquid crystal figures. After years of using an ordinary stick type, I found the digital read-out faster and much more accurate. It also enabled me to conduct other tasks while reading the instrument from a distance – something I could not do with the ordinary type. For this convenience, there is a price to pay. Sadly, I am now temporarily without the unit, having dropped it twice into developer. All attempts to revive it by drying in the hot-air cabinet have failed. Its only fault seemed to be that the wandering lead was not really long enough for this kind of work. Ideally, the instrument should have hung on a wall bracket so that the only mobile component, the lead and probe, could be dunked in whatever container was in use more or less anywhere on the bench.

DEVELOPING TANKS

One of the best small tanks I ever owned was a Rondinax daylight loading and developing tank. The film cassette was inserted into a small chamber in the top of a light-tight bakelite box which contained a 35 mm plastic spool and cutter. After cutting off the film leader, the film end was clipped to a rubberised canvas tail from the centre of the film spool. With the lid in place, the knob on the

Marrutt RC35 film-drying cabinet. Ideal for a small darkroom. (Courtesy Creative Advertising.)

outside of the tank was wound slowly to feed the film onto the spool. When tension prevented further winding, the film end was cut using the internal knife blade and, lo, one film ready for processing. I later managed to find another similar tank for larger-format film. Such tanks are a boon to the photographer who has no safe place to load ordinary tanks, and to the reversal enthusiast who has no need of enlargers and a full-blown darkroom. One other benefit was that they used very little chemistry and relied on constant turning of the film spool knob to give a 'lick and dip' development.

Popular tanks for the miniature and medium-format user are made by Paterson.

same knack, but is very easy once accomplished. Brooks tanks and spools are among the best stainless marques. They are manufactured in sizes to take from one 35 mm/120 to up to 8 × 35 mm or 4 × 120.

Sheet film is preferably developed in open tanks using cutfilm hangers. Kodak make a very good range and Combi make a range of sheet film developing tanks marketed under the trade name of Combi-Plan.

WATER FILTER

An in-line filter in the main darkroom water supply is to be preferred, but if this is not possible for any reason a filter of the charcoal or micronyl type which can be placed between tap and wandering hose is ideal. Water filters will help to eliminate many of the problems associated with negatives which become contaminated by hard water supplies, by rust and other foreign matter which often finds its way into liquid processing chemicals. All solutions should be filtered before bottling and on re-use, as explained earlier.

FILM-DRYING CABINET

Investing huge funds into camera equipment and not in the darkroom is something of a contradiction in terms of both respect for one's own ability and the quality of the final product one hopes will emerge from photographic endeavours. Dust, scratch marks and, worse, film-drying marks are the bane of any self-respecting photographer's life, and yet, certainly in the amateur field, very little is available to encourage the concerned enthusiast to eliminate most of the causes of poor-quality prints.

'Hang the film on a line', is an oft-quoted instruction in much text that has been written on the art of film processing. Does the author mean a line in the garden? The garage or outhouse? I sometimes wonder. If you want prints that are as free as possible of any contamination, they must be dried in an almost sterile compartment. Special gloves for handling are available too, believe it or not.

Brooks Stainless steel tanks. (Courtesy Pelling & Cross.)

Colleagues who use them regularly tell me they are very good, but I could never get the hang of loading the spools without some unfortunate mishap. I find the stainless variety better, more economical and allow film to be loaded or removed and loaded again while the spool is still wet. Colleagues who do not use these tanks tell me that the spools are difficult to load, so I suppose it is very much a matter of personal preference. I can only say that I have never had one serious mishap with a stainless spool or tank. The loading procedure is an acquired knack which will come after about an hour's practice using a gash piece of film loaded into an old cassette. Loading medium-format film requires the

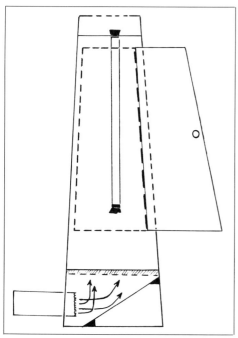

Plans for a home-made
full-length film drier
using thin plywood faced
with melamine and
1–2 kw fan heater.

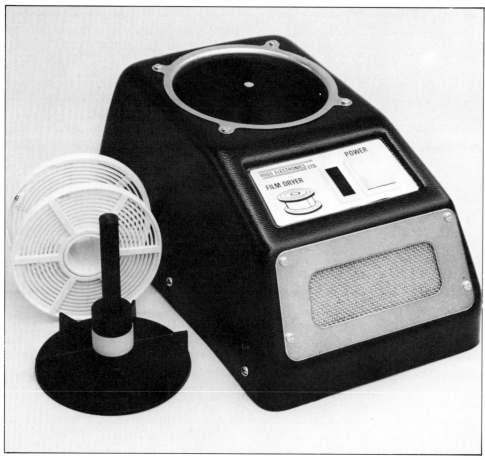

Single spool film-drier
made by Ross Electronics
Ltd, and distributed by
John Boxall
(Photographers) of
Cuffley, Hertfordshire.
Drying time is between
20 and 30 minutes.

Two Durst RC print-driers. (Courtesy Johnsons of Hendon.)

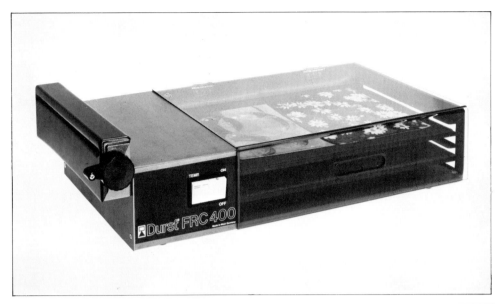

The investment required for a commercial film-drying cabinet is quite high. Nevertheless, if you can afford one, it is a great luxury to have around. Those of you with a little carpentry experience should not find it difficult to build a cabinet, using thin sheets of plywood for the main carcass of an upright box, whose depth measurement is large enough to enable an oblong slot to be cut at the bottom for the insertion of a small fan heater. Ventilation holes should be cut in the top of the box to allow air to escape.

A cheaper alternative to the commercial drying cabinet is a hot-air clothes drier of the wall-hung variety. The unit houses a high-powered fan blower, a switch for 'high' and 'low' heat settings and a time switch to operate. A zipped translucent bag is hung by poppers around the machine. Film can be hung from the folding clothes rack. I use one of these machines in my own darkroom and can give it nothing but praise. The air intake grill can be fitted with coarse foam filters to keep out any dust. It will dry a dozen or more full-length 35 mm films in a few minutes at very little cost. It is also extremely useful for drying resin-coated (RC) papers, the techniques for which are described in Chapter 5.

PRINT DRIER

There are many different marques of resin-coated printing papers. The better-quality types are invariably more expensive than lesser-known ones, not only because of the range of papers available but also because of the quality of materials used in manufacture. One of the most noticeable defects in cheaper papers is the lack of quality finish when the paper has been dried after processing. Some, for example, never seem to stay flat once they have been dried. Buckling of the polyethylene base is a common fault often caused by an excess of washing and overheating in drying. Delamination of the corners is another fault usually manifested through the same causes. Quality papers seem to be more durable in this respect.

How best to dry RC papers has beset amateurs with problems ever since the material was introduced. Ordinary fibre-based papers caused fewer problems, partly, I suspect, because convention had been well established. The sandwich technique between layers of blotting paper, though long-winded, gives extremely flat and stable prints. The flat-bed drier is still one of the most commonly used items of equipment for fibre papers, but is absolutely useless for drying RC paper.

Rotary glazing machines are few · and far between. Commercial processors having switched almost entirely to RC papers, the market for rotaries is now confined to a very small portion of the amateur field. Photopia used to market a small rotary glazer for fibre prints, but even these are no longer available, although I understand that one company is contemplating the manufacture of a new model to cater for the resurgence of interest in fibre-based papers for black-and-white work. Just occasionally, rotary machines are to be seen advertised in the second-hand columns of the trade press at knockdown prices. If you have the room for one of these machines, and are a fibre paper fanatic like me, such opportunities to buy should not be overlooked. A highly-polished drum in good condition will glaze a gloss fibre print and give it a finish that will make even the best-quality RC print look dull by comparison. The Kodak 15 in (38 cm) Velox dryer is an ideal size for most smaller darkrooms.

RC paper users have a greater choice of print driers, and all at widely contrasting price levels. The Ilfospeed RC dryer uses sponge-covered rollers and infra-red heat lamps to dry the print. The machine is fast, producing a wet-to-dry print in seconds rather than minutes. De Vere and other makers also make similar machines. The price tag for one of these machines is relatively high compared with the investment required for the hot-air blower type.

The cheapest hot-air drier consists of several plastic-covered wire shelves rather like vegetable racks which are inserted into a metal box, at one end of which is installed a drier of similar specification to an ordinary room heater. These machines are available from a number of retail and mail-order outlets specialising mainly in equipment for the amateur market. Such driers are quite adequate when only a few prints at a time are required. Each print needs to be turned every few seconds so that it dries evenly, and to do this comfortably no more than two 10 × 8 in prints at a time should be inserted. The main problem with all these machines is that the hot air does not circulate evenly, and, worse, prints take an age to dry unless they have been properly squeegeed first.

There are, of course, a number of things which can be done to remedy these faults. One is that a bigger investment could be made into an air blower type that incorporates its own roller squeegee. Another would be to adapt an old washing machine mangle so that it is fixed near the wash tank. As prints are removed for drying, they are passed one by one through the rollers. A sheet of plywood covered on both sides and edges with Formica laminate and stood vertically at an angle to one side or at the back of the sink will make a useful platform on which wet prints can be wiped with a length of squeegee blade. This is certainly the cheapest method.

My own method utilises the base and part of the roller system from an obsolete stabilisation print maker. These machines work on the 'lick and dip' principle. By removing the two sets of dip rollers and by adjusting the position of the remaining sets, a very efficient motorised squeegee enables large quantities of prints to be throughput to the film-drying cabinet. Prints are hung by a corner using rubber-edged clips obtainable from a hairdressing supplier. Because the down draught from the blower circulates the air more efficiently, up to twenty 10 × 8 in prints can be dried in a matter of minutes, giving a very high gloss finish and with no tendency to curl because of over-heating. A degree of ingenuity is required from the photographer

Durst Comask masking frame and rotary print trimmer. (Courtesy Johnsons of Hendon.)

unable or unwilling to spend what amounts to excessive funds on professional drying equipment.

MISCELLANEOUS ITEMS

By now, the darkroom inventory will be almost complete. There are numerous miscellaneous items not discussed at length which will still be essential and these are listed as follows.

1) Film hanger clips – should be weighted and in stainless steel.

2) Polythene storage bottles – at least 4.5-litre capacity, for liquid chemical storage.

3) Filing cabinet – of suitable size for storing negatives.

4) Negative files – loose-leaf type for miniature and medium-format negatives if not stored singly in glassine envelopes.

5) Scissors – Wilkinson straight-edge type for various tasks. Both short and long are useful.

6) Print tongs – for handling prints in open trays. Use rubber gloves if preferred.

7) Dust blower – compressed aerosol can type, or large soft dusting brush or anti-static

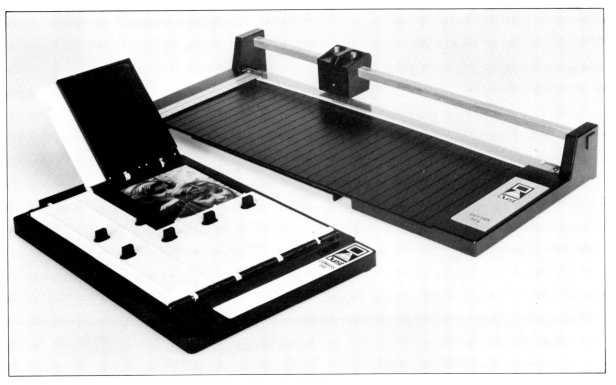

brush or all three. Lens cleaning cloth is also useful. *Do not* use paper tissue of any description if you value negatives and lenses.

8) Rotary cutter – for print trimming.

9) Dry-mounting press – or domestic iron together with a supply of mounting tissue. Sheets of self-adhesive paper can be used, as can aerosol contact adhesive available from graphic arts centres. A supply of mounting card, available from art shops, and a mount cutter will be needed.

10) Dodgers – various shapes of dodging aids for the purpose of 'burning-in' and 'holding-back' certain portions of prints are essential. Experience will show which shapes are the most useful and frequently used. Many professional printers use their hands only, and it would be as well to start learning how to accomplish this technique at the beginning of your printing career. In my experience, the only really useful aid, apart from hands and fingers, is a 4-inch square piece of black card with a circular hole cut in the middle. It helps if the hole, which will vary in size from approximately a quarter of an inch (6 mm) in diameter to a little under half an inch (12 mm), has a furred edge. It may be necessary from time to time to cut out shapes from black card which can be utilised as custom dodgers which fit the subject.

11) Spotting brushes and inks, surgical scalpel – all for retouching prints.

12) Stanley knife or craft knife – fitted with retractable blade, for general-purpose use.

Not all of the items listed above are essential for general printing, but, if you hope to produce good-quality work, you will find that everything has a specific use and that doing without will only make life tiresome. As time passes, your inventory is bound to increase, not just because of new developments which take place from time to time, but because inevitably there will be some items not listed here which you may find essential for certain types of work and because it is always pleasant to have the odd luxury, even if its use is only occasional.

3
The Enlarger

Some photographers know instinctively what format, type and marque of camera equipment they want to buy without having to spend hours mulling over reports or advertising propaganda. A great many others are prepared to investigate the market thoroughly before making a decision. Rather less attention seems to be given to the one piece of equipment in the darkroom which will show whether the camera you chose is any good, or not. One only has to look at the plethora of enlargers on the market to decide that whoever was responsible for the design work probably was not a photographer or a practising darkroom technician.

The vast majority of amateur units available through retail outlets are mass-produced, are too light and rely on cheap and sometimes badly finished components, the consequence of which is that most photographers have not much hope of producing finished work which is truly representative of their camera's worth. Happily, this sweeping generalisation does not apply to every marque, but there are many machines on the market which are neither worth the asking price nor fit for serious use. If the same consideration given by photographers to their choice of camera were given to enlargers and their lenses, I am sure that the general quality of work would improve.

CHOOSING AN ENLARGER

When choosing an enlarger, the following points might be considered.

BUDGET

If you are planning to invest in new equipment, weigh up whether the extra price you will pay over a second-hand item in mint condition is going to be worth the warranty and the packaging. Diligent searching and inspection of used goods will often turn up just what you wanted, or better still more, for a lot less than the cost of new equipment. I do not mean to advocate the adoption of this policy for everything and there are some items of equipment which I would not give a thought to purchasing in used condition. However, if you have time and enthusiasm to chase advertisers, there are some good bargains to be had.

OPERATION

Simplicity, ease of and accuracy in operation (SEA, for short) are the three main requirements of an enlarger. To achieve these facilities, the manufacturer must work to fine tolerances. A good enlarger is the result of precision engineering coupled with an understanding of operational requirements.

LIGHT SOURCE

There are three main types of light source used in enlargers. These are known as 'diffused', 'condenser' and 'cold cathode'. The first two utilise conventional tungsten lights, or halogen sources, which are then either diffused through a sheet of flashed opal glass, or plastic in many cheaper models; or the light rays are gathered by optical condensers to provide an even spread of light over the negative format. General-purpose enlargers capable of handling negative sizes from the larger medium formats down to miniature often have only one set of condensers to accomplish this feat. To achieve correct magnification of the image, differing focal length lenses are inserted in the lens panel. The printed image from smaller formats invariably suffers.

The flashed opal diffused illumination is preferred by some photographers because it has the apparent effect of reducing visible film grain in the print. Diffuser-type enlargers are often difficult to focus correctly and *apparent* print sharpness is sometimes inferior. They are not good if your negatives are slightly shaken or unsharp for any reason, but useful for high-key and female portrait work where subtle and flattering results are required.

Cold cathode light sources provide even illumination across the negative format without the use of condensers, resulting in enlargers considerably smaller in size, format for format, than those utilising conventional tungsten sources. Cold cathode enlargers are, however, mainly available only for formats of 5 × 4 in or larger. The light source is constructed of thin opal glass tube moulded into a square or rectangular grid. Some enlargers of this type are fitted with mercury vapour-filled tubes, others utilise light-corrected fluorescent tubes. Cold cathode sources are not always compatible with colour printing materials and often have a peculiar effect on some variable-contrast black-and-white papers. There are listed fluorescent specialists who can make light tubes to colour and size specification. Custom-made tubes are usually expensive. Cold cathode advantages are few, the main one being that the lamp house does not get very hot, which allows some larger-format negatives to be printed using glassless negative carriers. The disadvantages are that the nature of the light makes the baseboard image difficult to focus when negatives are dense.

Many enlargers on the market today use low-voltage lamps in conjunction with sophisticated electronic circuitry and a reflex system of mirrors and single convex condenser lenses to project the light source. This enables manufacturers to design smaller, more compact machines. The penalty is that they are often lighter and therefore do not have the rigidity of older 'heavy metal' lamphouse models. It is therefore essential to ensure that your enlarger will be mounted on a firm and solid base which cannot be subject to vibration.

Durst were one of the first manufacturers to introduce the reflex lamphouse over two decades ago. Two of their modern enlargers are illustrated on these pages. For the average amateur, their range represents excellent value. One of the best enlargers made in recent years were those manufactured by MPP – Micro Precision Products. Sadly, the company ceased manufacture some time ago but their range included three superb models for large – and medium – format work, as well as a general-purpose machine which easily converted from a medium-format enlarger to one capable of taking miniature formats by the simple changeover of condensers, negative carrier and lens. Nearly all of the black-and-white and colour prints made for this book were produced on MPP equipment.

Range of enlarging easels. (Courtesy Pelling & Cross.)

Durst 605 colour enlarger. Cutaway shows light source and dial-in filter mechanism. (Courtesy Johnsons of Hendon.)

Well-engineered instruments of similar specification to MPP products are produced by Gamer-Congreve Engineering. Gamer enlargers are hand-made and are available in both 35 mm format and general-purpose configuration. Gamer have been making enlargers for many years and their equipment is much admired by those photographers I know who use it.

FOCUS

Two methods of focusing are available: automatic and manual. In the first mode, the enlarger is set up at a predetermined level of magnification and accurately focused. Thereafter, the head of the enlarger can be racked up and down the column to any level of magnification and the negative will stay in focus at any stage. I have never yet had the pleasure of using an automatic system which actually worked efficiently or accurately, though I am not intimating that because of my bad luck there are no automatic machines available which can be trusted. Provided that your eyes are in excellent order, there is nothing to beat the positiveness of a manual device. Focusing on most manual enlargers is adjusted using a single rack and friction wheel device which moves the lens panel as required to give the sharpest baseboard image. Sharpness of the image can be checked using a grain magnifier while simultaneously operating the fine focus control. The latter method is slower in operation, although once you are used to a particular enlarger and use it frequently, I doubt that the operational time difference between the two methods would be very noticeable. I know that when I am using an automatic I spend more time checking and re-checking the focus than I would when using my own manual machines. Then there is also the price differential, and this will have to be taken into consideration by the investor with a limited budget.

NEGATIVE CARRIER

Just as flatness of the film plane in a camera is of critical importance to negative sharpness, the degree of flatness of the negative at the enlargement stage will have a profound effect on print sharpness. The choice of carrier type in enlargers is twofold – glassless or glass sandwich. Both have drawbacks in some respects. In the case of the latter, the negative is positioned in a carrier comprised of two sheets of optically flat glass. This provides four *extra* sides of medium through which the light must be projected and onto which all kinds of foreign matter may cling. Dust, being what it is, has a habit of turning up all over the place; in so doing, it invariably causes a great deal of heartache to the concerned print-maker and costs hours in terms of time spent removing it and retouching prints affected by it.

Glass carriers are preferred for larger formats where, if no heat shield is present in the enlarger, heat generated by tungsten source

Durst AC707 black-and-white enlarger.

illumination will cause minute buckling of the negative. This phenomenon is usually particularly noticeable when using medium- or large-format negatives which have a very thin polyester base. Any undue warping of the negative will make it difficult for the printer to focus the image evenly across the print easel. Because of its physical size in relation to larger formats, miniature film tends to be more stable and less affected by heat.

Larger formats, on the other hand, require less magnification to achieve larger print sizes and, therefore, any dust or foreign matter accumulated on a glass carrier will be less noticeable in the resulting print than on a same size print made from a smaller negative enlarged through glass.

One other phenomenon which is manifested when using glass carriers, particularly if the glass is non-optical in quality, is *Newton's Rings*. This is a series of concentric coloured rings which appear on the print, and is the result of the glass carrier sandwich being forced apart by the slightest pressure exerted usually on the top plate when a negative buckles under an excess of heat. The change in shape of the negative is sufficient

to cause uneven contact with one or other, or both, glass plates, resulting in an unsightly mark on the print, which may at first appear to have the characteristics of a water mark on the negative, produced in the film-drying process.

Anti-Newton's Ring glass, such as that used in projection quality transparency mounts, can be used in some enlargers which are fitted with diffuser type light sources. However, the etching is usually too coarse, resulting in a mottled print effect. The correct material for enlarging purposes is very finely etched, like the fine, clear matt screen in a single lens reflex camera. Newton's Rings can be eliminated by ensuring that your enlarger is fitted with a heat shield glass

Durst C35/Photocolor II package, ideal for starter kit for beginners. (Courtesy Johnsons of Hendon.)

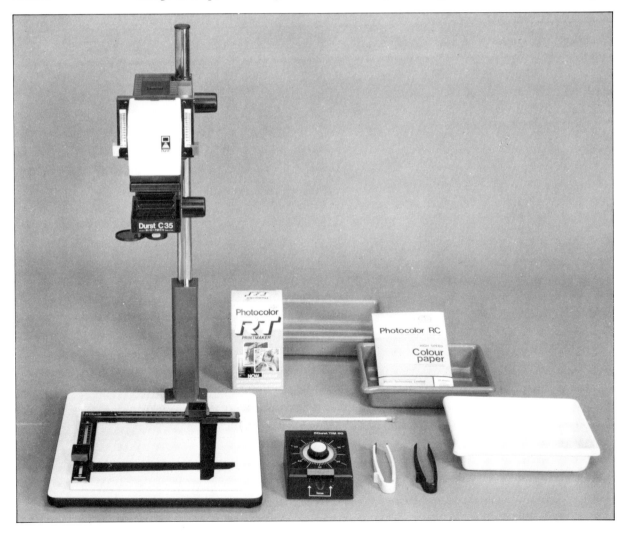

above the condensers or between condensers and negative stage. It should not be in contact with the negative and should be sufficiently distanced not to cause further problems with the focusing of dust particles.

When all the evidence is weighed, a fairly strong case supports the glassless theory, especially for the small- and medium-format user. With larger formats, glass carriers are more or less mandatory. Most auto-focus enlargers are fitted with glass carriers as a matter of course, as are many enlargers on the amateur market. In practice, there is no question in my mind; glass*less* carriers get first choice every time.

DISTORTION CONTROL

If you own a camera with 'movements', i.e. one which has a rising, tilting, horizontally movable front lens panel and similar film plane movements, you will know just how useful this can be in helping to produce distortion-free negatives of some subjects. Such movements are particularly useful in architectural, product and close-up photography. Special lenses are available for both miniature and medium-format cameras, but they are expensive, and, unless you have a regular use for them, are not normally considered essential items of equipment. An enlarger equipped with swings and tilts at the negative and lens panel stage can very often be used on those odd occasions when it is necessary to correct, say, obvious vertical distortions of buildings taken on a camera without the means to remedy the fault.

Distortion correction using the enlarger is not an alternative to correction made at the time of the original exposure in the field and the degree of success to which it is possible to make adequate corrections in the darkroom will depend largely on the versatility of the equipment. The enlarger lens panel, negative carrier and easel should all be capable of independent movements, not only in one direction in an arc moving from left to right, but also back and forth when the equipment is used facing the operator in its normal bench-mounted position. If this is not possible, some means of rotating the negative is necessary. This is a feature sometimes found in large-format enlargers and some more expensive professional small-format equipment. Those without can only be made to produce correct results with difficulty.

However, it should be emphasised that it is not essential that any enlarger be fitted with any of these refinements if some small degree of correction is to be accomplished. Simply by raising or lowering one end of the print easel, moderate distortion can be significantly reduced. A pile of books or block of wood supports the attitude of the easel in this fairly primitive but traditional method.

MAGNIFICATION

To quantify image magnification numerically the following formula is used:

$$\frac{\text{Lens to paper distance}}{\text{Lens to negative distance}}$$

In purely lay terms, the maximum magnification possible by any enlarger when used in its normal bench-mounted mode will depend entirely on the height of the column when measured from the baseboard. Nearly all enlargers are capable of being used in different modes; the head can be swung through 180 degrees to allow floor projection to take place. Some have heads which can be swung through 90 degrees to allow horizontal projection and some are equipped with columns which are extendable. In the normal course of events, magnification figures for off-the-shelf enlargers vary between 8 and 19, for 35 mm formats, to 6 and 19 for medium formats. This information assumes enlargers manufactured for specific negative formats. The figures for general-purpose machines will vary according to column height, negative format and focal length of lens used.

COLOUR HEAD

There are several advantages to having an enlarger fitted with a filter drawer or integral dial-in Dichroic filter head. For colour work, colour balance filters are essential in both negative and reversal printing. They are also very useful when using the enlarger to make duplicate positive film transparencies and also for variable-contrast black-and-white paper printing. If you specialise mainly in black-and-white work and like the 'Poly-contrast' or 'Multigrade' papers available, a dial-in filter facility gives the operator more subtle control than the standard filter pack normally used in conjunction with a filter drawer.

For regular colour work, the use of individual gelatin filters which must be switched back and forth in a drawer inevitably slows the operational process of print-making to such a degree that work can become very tiresome. The other advantage associated with a colour filter head is that some enlarger manufacturers incorporate electronic circuitry in the head which enables the printer to assess the correct colour balance and exposure for every print, regardless of size. With such facilities, work can progress at a fairly rapid rate, though I am none too certain that working blind in this fashion actually teaches the uninitiated very much about techniques of colour printing. The manual insertion of separate filters and inevitable calculations with regard to test exposures does have benefits in this respect.

The only significant advantage of enlargers fitted only with a filter drawer are in the cost department, and it may well be that funds saved in this area can be added to the cost of a really high-class enlarging lens.

LENSES

You will need lenses of differing focal length for different negative formats. There is really very little to say about the lens, except that, aside from the general features of the enlarger already mentioned, it is the singly most important feature of any enlarger. A lens of only adequate quality will only produce adequate-quality prints. Fast, wide-aperture lenses are not important or practically very useful unless the negatives you produce are constantly over-developed or over-exposed, or both, in which case an extra stop may help in viewing the projected image; it will do little for print quality. With normal negatives, the print exposure time becomes so short as to be impracticable for generous management.

4
Fundamentals of Black-and-White Photography

The successful origination of prints from negatives in black-and-white or colour work, and from reversal materials (transparency), will depend always on the quality of the intermediary. Quality of the negative is defined in broad terms as being 'normal', 'dense' or 'thin'.

A normal negative is one in which the subject matter has been rendered sharply in a range of tones exactly matching the tonal values of each colour of the subject. Such a negative will have adequate density in the highlight (dark) areas and visible detail in the shadow (light) portions, with clear distinctions of the range between these brightest and darkest areas, permitting a relatively short exposure to paper in order to obtain a clear, bright and fully developed print within a specified time.

Dense negatives are the result of over-exposure and/or over-development, and are easily identified by their lack of contrast and delineation of tonal values. Dense negatives yield flat, greyish prints in which there is no apparent real sharpness and in which film grain is more evident than from an equivalent 'normal' negative.

Thin negatives are identified by their overall translucency and inability to produce sharply-defined, bright, clear prints with a full range of tones from the purest white through to black. The cause is invariably one of under-exposure and/or under-development. The most common fault is under-exposure.

FILM AND FILM EXPOSURE
Understanding the fundamentals of film exposure is of paramount importance to any photographer who hopes to produce consistently good results from the darkroom. Problems with over- and under-development

can sometimes be rectified, but if too little exposure in the origination has caused certain elements of the subject matter to remain unrecorded on film, there is very little that anyone can do to remedy the fault.

Three common methods of assessing exposure in the field are:

1) use of a hand-held light meter;
2) use of in-camera meter;
3) use of film manufacturers' recommended exposures.

The latter are to be found on a sheet of instructions packed with each film, or marked with simplistic symbols on the packet.

By following the detailed instructions packed with each item, anyone could be prevailed upon to make adequate exposures. However, without some kind of understanding as to how light affects film and how variation in exposure can be utilised to produce constantly predictable results, the photographer without this knowledge will spend much of the time working blindly. As we will see in due course, exposure variation is not enough in itself. Varied development techniques as well as the use of different developers coupled with exposure techniques must all be practised, and the results of each experiment indelibly printed in the mind for future reference.

If this sounds at all complex, let me assure the reader that it is not. Exposure and development variations follow established guidelines which are flexible enough to allow for individual experimentation. Once the basic knowledge has been mastered, the only limitations on what can and what cannot be achieved will depend largely on the ingenuity and imagination of the photographer.

Firstly, let's consider the mechanical

aspects of photography and print-making in its simplest terms in relation to the one phenomenon which makes the process possible – light.

The human eye is capable of absorbing a brightness range – the difference expressed as a ratio between the lightest part of the subject and the deepest shadow (darkest) – of as much as 10,000 : 1. Most film, and this includes all colour film, is limited to between 2,000 : 1 and 200 : 1. The print has an even smaller capability, as little as 20 : 1 and a maximum of 60 : 1. The reader will see immediately that an enormous gulf exists between what the human brain can easily differentiate in tonal terms and the capabilities of film and paper stock. The photographer should never lose sight of the fact that the brain sorts information on a subjective level, i.e. it is subject to instantaneous change by whichever set of emotions and senses are stirred into action at any given time. The camera, exposure meter, film, paper etc, are all ingredients of a mechanical recording process; it is an objective process which cannot think and is therefore only capable of producing what is asked of it.

FILM TYPES

A huge array of film types from different manufacturers is available to the photographer. Familiarisation with as many different brand types as possible will allow the photographer to select instinctively types which are more suitable for specific tasks and eventually to standardise on two or three emulsion types for most work.

In black-and-white, *panchromatic* is the most commonly used emulsion. Pan type films are sensitive to all colours of the spectrum and to ultra-violet light. Each subject colour is recorded on the film as a grey tone and its density will depend largely on the brilliance of light reflected by the colour of the subject. Unexposed and exposed but unprocessed film should be handled in total darkness.

Other types of emulsion are *orthochromatic*, which is insensitive to red light and can therefore be handled under a red safelight. It is sensitive to blue, green, yellow and ultra-violet. Red-coloured subjects photographed using this material appear dark, while blue subjects appear lighter. Ortho film is mainly available in sheet form. Agfa make it in 35 mm format. Ortho film is ideal for document-copying and can be used for some industrial subjects.

Infrared film is a panchromatic emulsion in which the sensitivity to red has ben extended into the invisible, electro-magnetic spectrum where infrared radiation from the subject matter is used to expose the film. Subjects which do not emit sufficient quantities of infrared radiation may be photographed using a dark red filter or infrared filters in conjunction with normal light sources, such as flash, tungsten and daylight. The following filters are useful in obtaining accurate results with infrared film: Wratten 15, 29 and 88a (orange, dark red and black).

Infrared photography is used extensively for forensic and scientific purposes, and the photography of important historical documents, paintings and other works, usually to help establish fraud and to uncover works and details normally hidden to ordinary vision.

Chromagenic black-and-white film is a relatively new introduction. Ordinary panchromatic and other silver halide emulsions produce the image through the action of light on the halides which is converted to metallic silver in development. Chromagenic film produces a dye image through the use of colour couplers. In development, the couplers are activated by chemical residues from developed silver. The more exposure to light, the more silver produced, the more chemical residue and thus more dye. A bleach-fix bath after development simultaneously removes the residue of silver and stabilises the image.

Chromagenic films have enormous exposure latitude and fine grain characteristics. Their brightness range acceptance level is also much higher than panchromatic film. Chromagenic film normally rated at ISO 400 can be exposed for values of as little as 50 and as much as 1600 ISO on the same film

without recourse to extended or curtailed development techniques. One other plus factor is that for the photographer normally engaged in producing colour negative material, the same chemical process (C-41) can be used for processing black-and-white stock.

FILM SPEED

Each film pack should contain both directions for correct exposure given certain lighting conditions and instructions for development using tested formulae. In-camera exposure will vary according to film speed which is ascertained according to its light sensitivity. Film speed is now designated with the universally accepted numerical ISO measurement which to a very large extent has replaced the earlier ASA and BS measurements. The German DIN equivalent is still used in conjunction with ISO.

Film is normally categorised as slow, medium or fast. The lower the ISO measurement the slower the film, the higher the faster, and so on. In very simplistic terms, this information will give the photographer some idea of each film's exposure range of practicable shutter speeds and lens aperture settings for given lighting conditions. To the more knowledgeable photographer, ISO figures will also be indicative of other film characteristics, including ability to delineate fine subject detail, acutance, contrast, grain characteristic and tonal range.

DEFINITION

The ability to delineate fine subject detail, commonly called definition, is dependent on two main factors. One is the grain structure of the film. Minute particles of silver salts comprised of a mixture of halogens (silver bromide, silver chloride, silver iodide and silver nitrate) are scattered over the supporting gelatin base of the film. Grain structure and density is varied in manufacture providing the basic slow, medium and fast; fine-, smooth- and coarse-grained emulsions. All of these characteristics are subject to further

Generally speaking, it is much more difficult to achieve *impact* with colour. Here, use is made of the mainly monochromatic colours of each subject and combined with an unusual viewpoint (left) and use of long-focus lens (right). In black-and-white, neither picture would have worked.

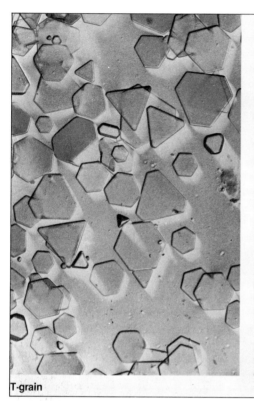
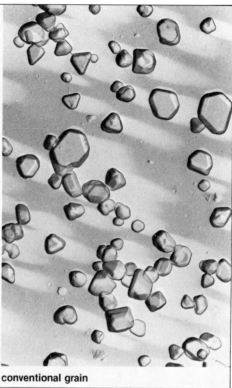

T-grain   conventional grain

When magnified nearly 6,000 times with a scanning electron microscope, silver halide grains such as those used in Eastman Kodak Company's Kodacolor VR1000 film (left) appear flat and table-shaped. These contrast to the pebble-like silver halide grains found in conventional photographic film (right). The new 'T' grains maximise the absorption of incoming light, resulting in a more sensitive 'faster' film. (Photo by kind permission of Kodak Ltd.)

change during the course of exposure and development.

Acutance is the measurement of film sharpness, but can normally only be accurately measured under a microscope using a densitometer. In practice, the term 'high acutance' is given where the demarcation line between light and dark subject tones is very narrow. When film is exposed there is a tendency for extraneous light to be scattered over the emulsion surface, which causes a slight fluffing of the tonal separation zone. Its effect is less noticeable in finer-grained film than in high-speed, coarse-grained emulsions.

Grain pattern and acutance are both subject to over- and under-exposure as well as over- and under-development. Both are also subject to physical change if unsuitable developers are employed to realise the image.

Grain structure in the final print is nearly always the most noticeable phenomenon apart from overall sharpness. A fine-grained film will not necessarily yield sharp pictures as a matter of course. It will, however, invariably show more subject detail where the zone of sharpness is apparent. Coarse-grained, high-speed films are capable of acute apparent sharpness, but format for format are less capable of high resolution than slower-speed emulsions.

In black-and-white work, the varying effect of granular structure has long been used by photographers for special effect. In recent years, the characteristics of coarse-grained colour emulsions have been exploited to create the Pointillist effect favoured by artists at the turn of the century. Certain high-contrast film developers, high-speed print and lith film developers can all be used to increase the apparent effect of grain in most emulsions, but are particularly successful used in conjunction with fast emulsions.

The ability of film to produce sharply defined images is dependent on several factors. Grain structure is one. Thickness of the supporting film base is another; the thinner the better. Accurate exposure and accurate development using the time and temperature

Film grain and vaseline used on a filter during exposure have both been used here to enhance the effect of solitude; HP5 rated at 650 ISO and developed in HC110. Print on bromide grade 3 paper.

method is equally important. Film contrast and tonal range are other factors.

Slow-speed film is generally recognised to be capable of high definition, but not necessarily of acute sharpness. Slow-speed, fine-grain film has high contrast which effectively compresses tonal range. The opposite is true of high-speed, coarse-grained emulsions. When matched to suitable subject matter under 'ideal' lighting conditions, both types will produce sharply defined images. But

sharpness is a subjective phenomenon and there will often be instances where apparent sharpness may be more effectively reproduced using low-contrast emulsions in conjunction with high-contrast printing papers. The greater the contrast between tonal values and the fewer values contained, the greater the effect of sharpness.

BRIGHTNESS RANGE

To return now to the ability of film to

record a given range of brightness, the reader will, I hope, begin to understand that some emulsions are capable of recording an extended range while others effectively diminish it. Most black-and-white pan film is capable of recording a range of 1,000 : 1, but, in practice, the figures are very much reduced. The brightness range of the subject to be photographed is measured by a meter and expressed as a range of 'f' stops. If the brightness range exceeds the capability of the film in use, and/or the print range, some tonal rendition will be lost or disguised.

With this information, the photographer can now be more selective in terms of which tones are more important to the final print. Further, by varying exposure and development technique in tandem with different emulsion speed, the photographer is given more precise control over the rendition of images on film and paper. Details of zonal processing controls are given in Chapter 6.

CONTRAST

To fully appreciate and understand how both density and contrast may be controlled during development, how film speed is arrived at and how exposure should be calculated to give a *desired* result, the working photographer should be equipped with at least a basic understanding of the theory used in laboratory evaluation of emulsions.

SENSITOMETRY

Laboratory investigation into the sensitivity

Fine-grain emulsions, such as Ilford's Pan F, are ideal for recording images where detail in the subject is more important than any atmospheric effect created by visible grain in the print.

This picture is typical of the kind of scenes which not only work better in colour, but which are extremely difficult to expose for properly when using 35 mm format black-and-white, unless the subject is to be used for an entire roll of film. Cluttered scenes, such as this, extend the tonal range of black-and-white emulsions almost to the limit, and some sacrifice must be made in highlight areas in order to retain detail in the shadows. This is where compensated development techniques come into their own.

of emulsions is known as sensitometry, and is mainly concerned with investigating the effect of exposure and development. The results of experimentation are plotted using logarithmic values of exposure against density levels to form a graph in the shape of an inclined and expanded letter 'S'. Thereafter, this is called a characteristic curve, and from it relevant information regarding contrast, actual film speed and rate of development may be gleaned.

The configuration of the curve is important. It has a 'heel' which slopes sharply into a straight line portion before tailing off at the 'shoulder' into a reverse curve. It is the 'straight line portion' and gradient which

In practice, knowledge of how the characteristic curve of a particular emulsion can be changed with exposure/processing technique is especially useful to the black-and-white worker. In this shot, the film is almost being asked to achieve the impossible with a real brightness range of approximately 1000 : 1 being compressed to 100 : 1 on the negative and considerably less in the print. Meter readings of both darkest and lightest areas were taken and averaged. Exposure selected enabled detail in mid-tones to be retained while unimportant losses were effected at top and bottom end of the range.

are of most interest to the photographer, although there are also factors regarding the demarcation line between fog level and zero exposure density contained in the heel portion of the graph.

The gradient, or slope, of the straight line section is expressed using the Greek letter 'γ' (gamma), and this is found by establishing a point (a) on the exposure base where film density is measured as 1. At the point (b) on the exposure base where an imaginary line drawn from log E vertically to intersect the straight line portion of the graph corresponds with $E = (a) + 1$, a new density reading is taken. The density readings at (a) and (a) + 1 are subtracted from one another; the result is the 'γ' figure which indicates the contrast range of the emulsion.

The contemporary photographer, equipped with very sophisticated state-of-the-art electronic cameras in which exposure metering is almost foolproof, may wonder why any of this knowledge regarding 'curves' and sensitometry is necessary.

It is necessary for two fairly obvious reasons. The first has to do with statements made in earlier paragraphs regarding mechanical recording devices which cannot think for themselves. Even the computer used to produce the text for this book had to be given constant instruction with regard to the layout and construction of sentences. It could only replace mis-spelled words on command. A modern camera needs the same kind of constant attention if it is to produce the result required by the operator; otherwise, when it is operated using settings for average conditions, it will produce only average results.

If this seems like a contradiction of manufacturers' claims that certain cameras only need to be pointed in the right direction before they can render optimum results on film, rest assured that it is. A modern, electronic auto-everything instrument will be able to produce perfectly adequate negatives and/or transparency material at the touch of a button. What it will not do is to render the subject matter in a way envisaged by the photographer which is outside the scope of normal meter settings. For this, some readjustment of input information to the camera microprocessor is necessary. New settings may be made easily on the basis of the blind leading the blind, but results will be unpredictable and for the most part of no value to either photographer or viewer of the work.

In the laboratory sensitometric test, a sheet of cut film is exposed to a point source light of known intensity at a fixed distance. No camera, lens or enlarger is used – the film is exposed direct to the light source.

The sheet of film is exposed in a series of steps in much the same fashion as one would make a print test strip under the enlarger from a negative. The exposure time for each consecutive step should be double that of the preceding one and a unit of time chosen that will give an exact and convenient relationship to its logarithmic value. When the exposure sequence is completed, the sheet of film is then cut into four equal strips, each one containing the series of stepped exposures.

The development stage comes next. Using a known developer of working strength and held at a constant temperature, the four strips are immersed and then extracted one by one for fixing at predetermined intervals. When washed and dried in the normal manner, the technician will have four strips of film on which varying exposure has been subjected to varying development times. Using a densitometer, the density of silver deposit at every exposure stage is measured and then plotted against the logarithmic values of exposure. The resulting characteristic curve will indicate which development time produces the better contrast range where the density of the darkest (highlight) portion of the strip along the straight line section of the graph is just printable – the level of maximum correct exposure – and where the density of the lightest (shadow) is such that it is visibly different to the base translucency of the film, or, in other words, the level of minimum correct exposure for a given development. The piece of film is known as a step wedge. Wedges can be made at home or purchased direct from film manufacturers in varying densities and contrasts.

Who needs a step wedge? In everyday photography, the step wedge has little use, unless the discerning photographer aims to try to maintain a collection of negatives which are of uniform density and contrast. The negatives may depict a range of subject matter and exposures may have been made over a long period of time, but if exposure and development of film stock is geared to a constant gamma, many problems normally associated with printing difficult negatives will be eliminated. In this case, it may be helpful to have access to a variety of step wedges.

DENSITY

Density of the negative in ordinary photographic terms is usually applied to the whole negative, rather than to a single portion of it. One which is literally too dense will be almost opaque, allowing insufficient light transmission through any of its parts for practicable print-making. One which is classified as too thin will be so translucent that there are no areas of opacity in the highlight areas and no detail at all in the shadow areas. Both types will be equally difficult to print successfully, even though in the last resort a chemical reducer or intensifier may be used to make either negative more acceptably workable.

ASSESSING FILM SPEED

In practice, standardised exposure meter settings geared to recommended film speed ratings will give an average exposure assessed for the whole scene and this is where the unwitting photographer will rapidly be led astray. The majority of in-camera meters are not equipped to deal with maximum correct or minimum correct exposure and if the brightness range of a subject exceeds the film/developer capability something, somewhere, will have to be sacrificed. Perhaps the most common failing in this area is the landscape or seascape picture in which the blue sky and fluffy white clouds of reality are lost for ever in tonal compression.

A simple and interesting experiment which will establish the correct average film speed (ISO) for a desired tonal range under known lighting conditions can be easily executed with the most basic of facilities. Items required are; camera, film, developing tank, timer, thermometer, chemicals to process.

Load a preferred film, or one which you intend to become a basic standard, into the camera. On either the in-camera meter or a hand-held, set the manufacturer's recommended ISO speed rating. Assuming a 36-exposure roll of film, divide the film into six parts of six frames each. Use a note pad to keep a record of the frame numbers and the exposure given to each. One page for each of the six parts is ideal.

Set the camera on a tripod or firm support and frame a previously selected subject. Do not attempt to make close-up or selective meter readings of different parts of the subject. It should be well lit with side or frontal lighting. Try to make a mental note of what you can see in the light and dark parts of the subject; in particular whether the eye can accommodate detail at extreme ends of the brightness range. Set a shutter speed of say 1/125th of a second and set the metered 'f' stop. Make an exposure. Consecutive frames in the first sixth should now be exposed at metered values which are higher and lower than the first exposure but which give the same exposure, i.e. the second exposure could be at 1/250th second at f5.6 if the first was at, say, f8. Third, fourth, fifth and sixth exposures will follow suit until the highest shutter speed is reached. If this is accomplished on exposure 4, 5 will begin with the lowest shutter speed practicable, i.e. 1 second or 1/2 second or less.

The next six frames should be exposed at ISO-N (Normal) − 1 full stop. Set the camera ISO indexer to the next lower numerical setting to the one previously used. Expose the first frame of the next sixth at the most suitable metered reading, say 1/125th second @ f8. The next two frames should be given + and −1 full stop and the next two + and − 2 stops. Place the lens cap over the

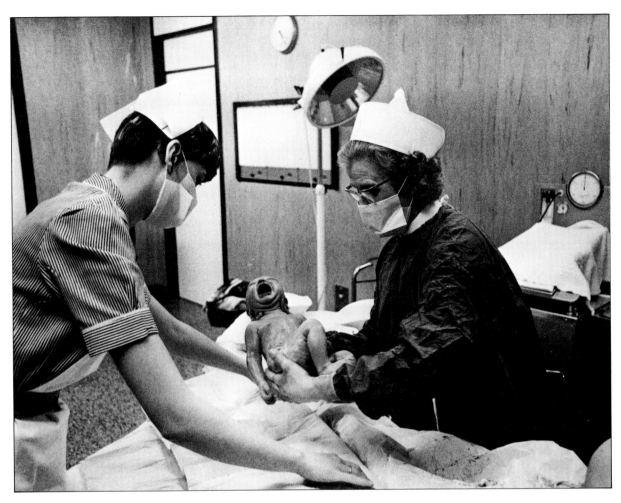

'Fast' films (high ISO No.) are necessary when working under low levels of available light. Tri-X rated at EI1600 and developed in full strength D-76 allowed some flexibility in the choice of higher shutter speeds to stop movement. Interestingly, there is very little compression of the brightness range in this scene printed on a grade 2 bromide.

lens for the sixth frame and expose the frame blank. Repeat this procedure for the next sixth at ISO-N + 2 full stops.

The second stage of this experiment with the remaining 3/6ths of film require the exposure procedure to be repeated exactly as in the first stage. When complete, take the film into the darkroom. Prepare the developing tank and processing solutions. Ensure that developer, stop bath and fix are all at the same temperature which should for preference be 20 °C (68 °F). It will be helpful to have more than one loading spool and a spare tank, but if this is not available follow this next procedure.

Ensure that a pair of scissors is to hand. Cut off the film leader and trim the film end for spool loading. Extinguish all darkroom lights. Take the film cassette in one hand and,

with forefinger and thumb of the other, catch a firm hold of the exposed film end. Pull the film firmly but slowly until it is fully extracted but still attached to the cassette spool. Grip the leader end between your teeth, then slide thumb and forefinger down the edges of the film until an approximate midway point is reached. Stop here and carefully bring up the cassette until you can retrieve the leader end with the same hand, keeping thumb and forefinger of the other hand firmly clasped to the film edges. You will have now effectively folded the length of film in half.

Allow the cassette and leader end to fall, while still retaining a firm grip with the other hand on the middle section. Take the scissors and cut the film at the midway point. Take the loose length of film and place the

From a nine-negative test to establish acceptable contrast and tonal range, using normal speed rating/exposure and compensated development exposure.

HP5 ISO 400. Hand meter reading of skin tones and highlight areas in jumper f8–11. Normal development.

HP5 ISO 400. TTL reading through 200 mm Zuiko lens gave f6.3. Normal development.

HP5 ISO 400. Hand meter reading of shadow area under left arm gave f5.6. Normal development.

HP5 EI320. TTL reading f5.6. Hand metered reading of face f8. Aperture set f5.6, development compensated less 25 per cent. Straight print from negative.

leader between your teeth while rewinding the other length back into the cassette. Load the loose length onto the developing spool and place it in the tank.

If you have two tanks, load the cassette length also. If not, the following developing sequence will have to be repeated.

Begin the developing sequence and start the timer as soon as all developer is poured into the tank. Development time should be that recommended by the manufacturer for the film used. Begin pouring the developer away 10 seconds before the time is up. Stop bath, fix, and then wash for 10 minutes, drain and dry.

The second developing sequence using fresh developer can now begin. The development time should be cut by 30 per cent.

When this length of film is washed and dried, you should have two sets of 3×6 frame exposures. Compare them with the notes of metered exposures. You will see that in the first set of six, which were processed normally, each frame should be of almost identical contrast and density. It may vary slightly depending on the accuracy of your equipment. These six frames will show that changes in the numerical value of exposure effect no difference in contrast or density when the value is equal to an optimum figure expressed by the metering system. In other words, the same amount of reflected light reached each frame irrespective of the change in exposure combinations and the duration. If it could be assumed that both shutter speeds and aperture functions of the camera were accurate, any further variation in contrast and density would have been caused by a phenomenon known as reciprocity failure, about which there is more in Chapter 9.

Compare these negatives now with the second batch of six where ISO-N − 1, and then again with the third batch. Compare all three batches with the second length of film which was given significantly less development. Without comparing notes against the exposed frames, try selecting what appears to be an ideal negative of the subject matter. Inspect it closely under a powerful magnifying glass. See if you can detect clear differentiation between tonal values. Is there a highlight within the highlight and is there sufficient printable detail in the deepest shadow areas? All these values should be readily identifiable, even to the untrained eye.

CONTROLLING DENSITY AND CONTRAST BY DEVELOPMENT

There are various other experiments which the photographer can conduct, but, in order to obtain full value from any of them, a large-format camera employing cut film is more suitable than the miniature. Cut film allows greater flexibility in developing individual frames as well as giving a clearer indication of what is happening to the negative. If no large-format equipment exists, a way round the problem is to load short lengths of bulk film into spare 35 mm cassettes, enough for say 3 or 4 exposures on each length. To gain a more precise result, include a standard grey scale in the picture, as well as a piece of white card about the size of an enprint (5×4 in) on which are written film type and exposure details.

Details on the card may read as follows:

HP5 ISO = 320
EXPOSURE = +2 STOPS

Use a felt-tip marker and ensure that the letters/figures will be large enough to be legible for inspection by eye and for printing. To be effective, any test requires a minimum number of negatives which have been over- and under-exposed by 1 and 2 stops, and under- and over-developed by as much as 30 per cent and 50 per cent respectively, as well as normal exposure and development. At the very least, seven negatives will be required, and one of these will have been exposed and developed normally. Ideally, nine are required which will give three of normal exposure at differing levels of development, three of at least one full stop less than normal exposure and three of at least one stop more than normal exposure and processed with percentage reductions and increases as above.

Using a normal grade of glossy or semi-matt paper, make nine enlargements from each one of the negatives. There should be sufficient density in the brightest highlight of the thinnest negatives to make printing on a normal grade of paper perfectly possible. Do not attempt to use a different grade of paper, unless the new grade is used for printing all negatives. Development should adhere rigidly to the recommended time and temperature technique and, provided exposure is correct for the degree of magnification used, a very useful set of prints will result.

From the first experiment, select the negative containing the best contrast range and make a 10×8 in enlargement, again on glossy or semi-matt paper of normal grade, or of a grade matching the one used to print

Studio lighting can be controlled by the photographer to give a predetermined effect on selected emulsion and developer combinations. A large format and diffused lighting rendered detail in brightest highlight areas and deepest shadow.

the nine negatives if this was different from normal. When all prints are dried, lay them out on a viewing area for inspection.

It should be understood that these tests are designed to help the photographer establish a range of exposure and development techniques that will give the most desirable print result for personal preference. The preferred effect of tonal rendition and contrast tends to differ wildly according to each photographer's taste. The subject matter itself is of great importance and in most cases will dictate to a large extent the tonal composition of the final print. In scientific or laboratory experiments very little, if any, allowance is made for the taste factor. Here, tests are designed to establish only a correct range of values for given circumstances.

LIGHTING

When possible, tests should be carried out using different types of light: tungsten, flash and daylight. Using tungsten and studio flash, the photographer will frequently be afforded more control over lighting and exposure and, because many of the factors involved will be constant, more control over the processed result. With direct on–camera flash, and frequently in normal daylight conditions, exposure will be affected by a variety of elements which are beyond normal control.

Here are two examples of flash techniques where full control over lighting and exposure was only possible in the studio shot.

The second picture was shot to a client's visual brief and required an atmosphere that would have been difficult to achieve without the use of tungsten lighting. Neither of the final results, however, would have had the same effect had 'normal' exposure and development techniques been employed. Both pictures were given more or less than the recommended 'normal' exposure, and more or less than the recommended 'normal' development.

There are several exposure and contrast problems associated with ordinary on/off-camera flash techniques. In some instances, the negative is in fact a good one, with a full range of tones in the straight line section and of a contrast which allows for controllable printing exposures on a variety of paper grades. Any less original exposure would

The darkest area of the tree required f2, the lightest area of the van on the corner required f32. Straight print from negative.

result in a thin negative, given normal development. Increased development would effectively compress the highlight areas and result in a negative that is simply too dense to print easily. How can this be so?

Part of the answer has to do with basic equipment which is, in many respects, inadequate for the task at hand. Most single lens reflex cameras used today are equipped with a focal plane shutter. Most older cameras of bellows type, twin lens reflexes and some medium-format SLRs like Hasselblad and Rollei are equipped with leaf shutters – a series of blades which open and shut concentrically as in the Compur shutter type.

Both types of shutter can be synchronised to bulb or electronic flash. In the leaf type, the shutter is opened to make full use of the peak output of the flash cycle. In the focal plane type, the shutter is opened towards the end of the peak. This timing factor in syn-chronisation creates a somewhat uneven negative exposure when a focal plane type shutter is used with electronic flash. The difference is less noticeable with bulb flash.

More important is the fundamental difference between the duration of bulb and electronic flash. Because of the bulb's longer flash duration and greater illuminary power, a reciprocity factor is introduced which helps to expose silver halides more efficiently. In negative comparisons using normal exposures and standard development, the bulb flash negative will show better exposure of shadow detail, which results in an altogether richer print. To obtain similar results from an electronic flash of equal power, a slight adjustment to exposure and development is required. For this reason, it is useful to conduct a series of tests using electronic flash to discover the most suitable exposure/development combination.

5
Basic Black-and-White Processing Techniques

So far, I have assumed that the reader will have at least a basic working knowledge of the procedures required to develop film and paper, and that some equipment will be available. If this is not the case, three wide-rimmed and fairly deep soup dishes, plus a watch, table and jugs to hold solutions, will enable cut film and medium-format roll film to be developed and fixed. A room which can be completely darkened will also be necessary. This is a messy procedure so be sure to wear an apron and cover the floor or carpet with newspapers or, better, a sheet of polythene.

Proceed as follows. Mix developer and fixing chemicals to make a maximum of 8 fl oz (230 ml) working strength solutions. Raise the temperature of each solution by immersing its container in a bowl of hot (not boiling) water. Test the temperature using a finger. When the liquid is no longer unpleasantly cold but barely lukewarm, remove the container(s) from the water-jacket.

Slightly warm the three soup dishes in the same bowl of hot water. If you have chemicals to make stop bath, use the same procedure to bring up the working temperature. Otherwise, use water. Lay out the three dishes on a table or bench so that they are about 12 inches (30 cm) apart. Into the left-hand dish, pour the developer, the stop or water into the middle and the fix into the third, on the right. Make a mental note as to the positions of each dish in relation to the table or bench edge.

Assuming a roll of medium-format 120 film to be processed of known type and speed, consult the developer recommendations for a development time at 20 °C (68 °F). The time will be given in minutes and seconds. Calculate the total time required in the developer in seconds, which you will have to

count to yourself in units of a thousand. Take the film roll in the left hand and, with a pair of scissors, cut the exposed paper seal. Peel off and discard, keeping a firm grip on the film so that it doesn't unravel. Extinguish all room lights. Check that no stray light is entering the room.

The next stage is decidedly tricky and requires a certain agility on the part of the operator. Still holding the film roll in the palm of the left hand, place the thumbnail between the backing paper and the bulk of the roll. With the right hand, grasp the end of the backing paper and peel away slowly until you feel the edge of the film itself click over the thumbnail. Drop the backing paper and continue to pull the film out and away with the right hand. It is important to do this in one straight movement. You will find the end of the film attached to the backing paper with a length of sticky tape. Keeping the film straight, gently tear it away from the paper using your thumbnail as a cutter. If you cannot accomplish this, move the hand towards the mouth and tear off the film from the backing using your teeth.

It is an essential part of the technique to keep the film straight at all times before immersion into the developer. Move to the dish containing the developer, raise the left hand skyward and place the right-hand end in the dish. Keeping sufficient tension on the film, slowly bring up the right hand, allowing the left to follow in a downward direction. Start counting in steps of 1,000, 2,000, and so on as soon as the process has begun. When the left-hand end of the film has travelled through the developer, reverse the process and continue it back and forth until you have counted the entire developing sequence. By this time, your arms will ache but the film will have lost much of its spring and will be far more

This picture works better in colour because there are small areas of colour to relieve the monotony of large areas of black. In black-and-white the picture would be better shot from an angle where there is more sidelighting and reflected light from nearby stalls to enhance shape and add detail.

manageable. Drain at the end of the sequence and then transfer to stop bath and finally to the fix. When this is completed turn on the room light.

'Do I really need to know all this?' I can hear the cries from anguished photographers everywhere. You don't have to know, and, furthermore, if you have to ask, the chances are you would never consider giving it a whirl anyway. Very little effort is required by the photographer of the 80s in order to accomplish a great deal. After all, basic items like processing tanks are relatively inexpensive and they make life so much easier.

But (and there's always a but, always a debate to be had in any creative arena) photo-processing may be a kind of technical skill and it is certainly often considered in that light today. There was a time, however, when the pioneers of photography hardly knew what they were doing. They found out largely by feel. Knowledge of the subject was gained empirically. Their efforts, their trials and tribulations, their apparently nicotine-stained fingers spurred scientists and technicians to investigate further and give us what we have today. Just becuase there is a wealth of technical information available to us in books, magazines and instruction sheets does not mean that we should all sit back and do only what we are told to do. Not all of us are scientists or technicians, and if we were we probably would not be very creative or have too many hopes of being so. To get the most out of this medium, you have to know how it reacts, and what it feels like slithering around in an open dish full of slimy developer.

I am not suggesting that you now discard your tank for the soup dish. But everyone should have a go at some stage in their photographic career. Not only will it help the photographer to understand the physical properties of modern emulsions, but in a

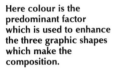

Here colour is the predominant factor which is used to enhance the three graphic shapes which make the composition.

peculiarly inexplicable way it will help to broaden one's knowledge and understanding of the silver image, and it may, as with a painter mixing a palette, give a little pleasure.

Pleasure, of course, is one of the least likely of emotions to be experienced when things begin to go wrong; and go wrong they will given half a chance. Darkroom mishaps usually start with an unruly film which refuses to be spooled no matter what one does. As I mentioned earlier, spool-loading is an acquired knack and, if you have never had occasion to load film before, be warned; a lot of practice with outdated or duff film prior any real darkroom work will be of immense benefit.

LOADING TECHNIQUES
Here are a few tips on loading techniques to make life less exasperating.

1) Always use fresh film stock in your camera. Try to expose all of it as quickly as possible. Even a week in the camera in a partly wound-on state will make the film base less supple. Avoid storage of a loaded camera in close proximity to heat. Keep out of car glove compartments; avoid extremes of temperature.

2) Process the film as soon as possible after exposure. If this is within a day or so of loading, the film will remain manageable.

3) 120 roll film is the more difficult to load onto a spool due to its size and thinness compared with 35 mm. Old roll film has a tendency to reverse-curl when pulled away from its backing paper. This can present problems with automatic processing machines where roller feed tension is slightly slack. Film may not be properly processed.

With small tank nylon spools of the Paterson type, carefully follow the next few steps.

1) Hold the roll of film in the left hand, palm uppermost (see diagram). Cut the paper preventer with your thumbnail or a scissor blade.

2) Hold the film as shown and gradually but carefully pull the paper backing away from the body with the thumb and forefinger of your right hand.

3) Stop when you feel the film base protrude over the left thumbnail. Move two fingers around the back of the roll to keep the backing paper tight against the roll. Tear off the loose end with your right hand.

4) Now clasp the roll with the slightly protruding film base with the backing paper between the thumb and index finger of your right hand. The backing paper affords some protection of the film as you unravel a further half-inch (13 mm).

5) Take the spool in your left hand, the film gate uppermost, and clasp it in the palm of the hand. Using your thumb and index

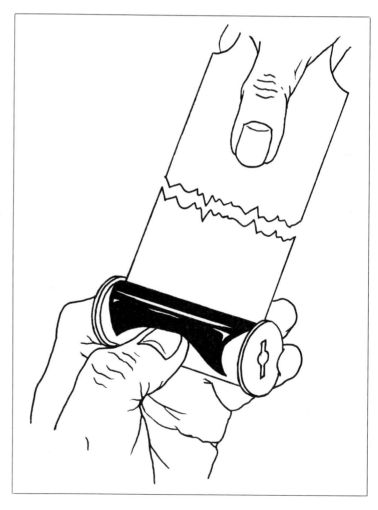

finger, manoeuvre the film into the gate and pull forward until a full rotation is nearly complete.

6) With a hand on each side of the spool, now allow the film to drop between your body and hands. Begin an alternate back-and-forth winding motion to feed the remainder of the film onto the spool.

7) This action should be carried out smoothly and with gentle pressure on the spool towards the centre. Too much pressure will buckle the film and cause it to jump out of track. You will feel when the secured end is approaching. When there are only a few inches to go, stop winding and, with the spool pressed against your abdomen and held in place by your arm, use both hands to tear off the backing paper.

8) Resume winding until the film is secured on the spool. Place it in the tank and secure the light-tight lid.

Some tank manufacturers supply film-loading guides for their nylon spools. Jobo is one, and Kindermann is another. If practice is fruitless, insert a scrap of backing paper between the film tracks before loading commences. The paper acts as a guide for the film end, but it must be removed before processing. An alternative is to use a length of card or very thin plastic sheet cut and sanded with wet emery cloth.

Always ensure that nylon spools are perfectly dry before loading with fresh film. The slightest trace of dampness can sometimes make a film stick in the tracks. Inadvertent use of force to shunt the film on will only result in near disaster, or worse. The only course of action is to remove the film, rewind all of it except the leader back into the cassette, and thoroughly dry the spool. A small electric hairdryer is a very useful darkroom tool for this and other purposes.

Roll film can be salvaged even after the paper backing has been discarded. Keep a squarish cardboard box (a shoe box will do) permanently in the darkroom for these emergencies. A black polythene packet from a box of paper is used to drop the film into, in its naturally and loosely coiled state. Fold over the end of the bag and place it in the box. Cover with the lid. Now you can turn on a safelight, or even a white light if the situation demands.

With stainless steel spools, the film take-up starts at the centre of the spool where the film end is inserted under a spring clip. The procedure for handling the film is the same as in 1–4 above. Then, proceed as follows.

5) Hold the spool in the palm of the left hand with the thumb over the spring clip, and finger underneath. Marry the film end in your right hand to the thumb of your left. Use the thumbnail of your right hand, still holding the film firmly, to press down on the spring clip and insert the film.

6) Ensure that the film is centralised.

7) Continue to hold the spool in your left hand and using the thumb and forefinger of your right, protruding over the ends of the film spool, as a guide, begin winding slowly. The exact amount of tension must be kept on the film to allow it to find its own way between the grooves.

8) Use the same procedure at the end, above, to release the film from the backing paper.

9) Place the loaded film in the tank and secure the light-tight lid.

Some stainless manufacturers also supply loading guides, but once you have acquired the knack these can be dispensed with.

With 35 mm film, loading is simplified due to the fact that there is no backing paper to contend with. With nylon spools, follow the same procedures as above. Always shunt enough of the leader around the spool grooves before attempting to wind on. Let the film cassette hang between the body and spool. Pull out about 12 inches (30 cm) of film at a time at first and wind on firmly but slowly.

When using stainless spools, follow the same procedure for loading the spool as for roll film. Use your thumb and forefinger as a film guide, keeping the cassette firmly clasped under the palm with the little finger to hold it in place. As you wind on, the film will leave the cassette easily.

Some 35 mm film cassettes need a bottle opener to remove the tin cassette end. Special wall-mounted darkroom openers are available. However, you should not need one of these cassette wreckers if you practise the habit of not winding the leader into the cassette after the film has been exposed in camera. Wait until you feel a slight increase in tension as the film nears the end of the rewind sequence, then give an extra sharp half-wind or so. The leader will be off the take-up spool but will not have disappeared out of sight. The habit helps to make light work of loading a spool in the dark.

Because some cameras have a take-up spool system which winds the film on emulsion outward, any delay in rewinding it back into the cassette after exposure invariably causes a 'reverse-curl' effect which makes darkroom handling more than just a nuisance. To overcome this malady, extinguish the darkroom lights, pull the entire length of film from the cassette and snip off the end, keeping a firm hold on it once this is accomplished. Now load the film onto the developing spool starting with the film *end*. It should feed on without further difficulty. Stainless spools do not need to be bone-dry to load. They can easily be loaded, unloaded and reloaded when dripping wet. Practice is the key.

SHEET FILM

This is best processed in a tank of the type mentioned in Chapter 2. Stainless sheet film hangers which have four small spring clips in each corner and a hanging rail are preferred for larger tanks. It is possible now to obtain spools of similar type to roll and miniature film types which allows 5 × 4 in sheet sizes to be processed in cylindrical tanks.

I find it easier to clip the film into a stainless hanger and dish-develop in total darkness when all that is required is an occasional negative. Less solution is required and the dish needs only a gentle rocking motion to ensure adequate agitation. When I have more to process, I use a three-litre box tank

Confronted with this everyday situation, the photographer working in black-and-white would almost certainly want to up-rate whatever film stock was in use. Fast (ISO 400) emulsions could easily be used at their manufactured ratings, but more atmosphere, depth and contrast with the added advantage of higher shutter speeds to help eliminate shake would be possible with higher EI values (See Table 3).

which I made up some years ago from sheets of opaque black perspex. A few hours spent with a sharp electric fine-toothed saw and a tube of *Weldite* enabled me to make seven of these tanks which, at the time, were required for colour reversal processing. Plastic holders for sheet film should be avoided if possible as they stain quickly, become brittle with age and are liable to fracture which could cause irreparable damage to film.

Except for some graphic arts process film, all sheet film whether it be colour or black-and-white has a series of notch codes in one corner. The number and, in some cases, shape of the notches indicates the type of film. When they are at the top right-hand edge of the film, the emulsion faces inward — toward the user. These are manufacturers' guides to help with dark slide-loading as well as film-processing. Notch codes are particularly valuable when using the open-dish method, and are useful for checking that the film is not lying emulsion-side-down where it is liable to be badly scratched by the dish surface.

Agitation of all film during the development and fixing sequences is vitally important. With sheet film developed in a deep tank on hangers, the procedure should be as follows.

1) Lower the hangers into the tank and knock smartly on the tank bottom or side to dislodge air bubbles that may adhere to the emulsion surface when the film is left to stand.

2) Agitate the film back and forth through the developer for between 5 and 10 seconds every minute, or every two minute until time is expired.

3) To avoid the risk of air bubbles before development starts in a tank or dish, use a tank of pre-heated, filtered, water in which the film sheets are immersed for about half a minute. Remove air bubbles as in (1) above.

When using a dish to develop sheet film, make sure the dish is at least twice the area of the film. Using a same-size dish creates film handling problems with increased risk of damage to one or both film surfaces. Use a dish that is large enough to hold a litre of working solution and one that you can easily move a hand in. Insert the film into the liquid by raising one side of the dish slightly; hold the film by, say, the top right-hand corner and place the bottom edge of the film, emulsion uppermost, on the raised side of the dish. Simultaneously level the dish, lower the film to a flat position, and allow developer to wash over it. Once it is covered, gently knock the bottom edge of the film against the dish side to dislodge air bubbles. To agitate, work by gently raising each corner of the dish in rotation in a continuous action.

There is a theory that uniform agitation can cause development marks on the film. Whether it be miniature or roll film on a spool, sheet film developed in a dish or tank, I have never come across this phenomenon. Development marks are usually caused by the following.

1) Insufficient agitation, especially during development times of less than 5 minutes.

2) Agitation periods spread too far apart and inadequate.

3) Incorrect entry of film into developer when using dish techniques. This often causes large air bubbles to be trapped under film which has been immersed emulsion-side-down. The problem is nearly always apparent when too small a dish is used.

4) Miniature and roll film processed in cylindrical tanks can show uneven development marks caused by insufficient liquid to cover the spool. Always use at least twice the amount stated for each roll of film in larger tanks.

5) To dislodge air bubbles in cylindrical tanks, bang the bottom of the tank against the bench in several sharp taps. If the facilities for dunking film in a pre-wet are available, make use of it.

6) Cylindrical tank agitation should follow the inversion/rotation procedure. Invert the tank, and, when the first spool has reached the new bottom, begin rotation and right the tank to its normal standing position. Small plastic tanks have an insert which allows

Larger-format negatives are capable of great detail; see the enlarged section of the first picture. In the picture opposite a small section enlarged would lose detail due to the enlarged grain structure.

clockwise rotation of the film spool during development. The tendency is always for the operator to spin the spool too fast. Don't. Only enough movement is required to change the position of the film in relation to fresh developing agents.

Remember:

1) too much agitation increases grain, contrast.
2) too little agitation decreases contrast; causes irregular development marks.
3) less agitation towards the end of the development sequence can increase edge acutance.

PROCESSING STEPS

The standard processing method for black-and-white film is as follows and assumes the use of the time and temperature method according to film and/or manufacturer's recommendation.

1) In total darkness, unless a daylight-loading tank is used, load film into tank and secure lid.
2) Pre-heat all solutions, including wash water, stop bath and fix, to the selected temperature.
3) Pre-heat tank for a few seconds by holding it over bowl of hot water.
4) Set timer to required time.
5) Pour developer into tank. Start timer.
6) Tap tank bottom against bench to dislodge air bubbles. Agitate vigorously for the first 15 seconds.
7) Agitate as directed.

Mother and child. Nikkor 105 mm f2.5 lens and Tri-X. Window light would have given an acceptable exposure but with too many shadows. I used bounced electronic flash for the main exposure, over-exposed by one stop, and cut development by approximately 10 per cent to give a fairly high-key effect.

8) Allow 10 seconds before the end of development to pour away the developer. Discard if using diluted one shot solution.

9) Pour in stop bath and agitate vigorously for 15 seconds. Then pour away to container.

10) Fill tank with fixer; agitate for the first 15 seconds and thereafter every 2 minutes.

11) When fix time has lapsed, pour fix away to container and fill tank with wash water.

12) White light may now be used to inspect the film in its wet state.

13) Re-spool film and immerse in hypo (fixer) clearing agent for the time directed.

14) Commence 20–30 minute wash cycle, or at least 45 minutes if no clearing agent is used.

15) Using a clean large jug containing at least 1 litre of filtered water, add photo-flo solution. Immerse film on spool and dunk several times. Remove spooled film by pulling off the spool while still in solution. Hold the film firmly at both ends, upend it and allow surplus water to drain off. Use a weighted clip on the lower end and hang in a dust-free compartment to dry.

VARIATIONS ON THE BASIC PROCEDURE

Following the above procedure will normally result in accurately developed and dried negatives. There are, however, variations on this procedure which will help to improve results.

TEMPERATURE

Allow film to reach the ambient darkroom temperature by leaving it to stand for up to 20 minutes. Darkroom temperature should be maintained, as far as possible, close to 20 °C (68 °F). This is especially necessary when the film is rushed in for processing from a cold exterior. If exposed film is stored in the refrigerator, remove and allow to stand for the same period as above before processing.

WATER-JACKET

A water-jacket for working solutions can be made from a garden tub of the windowbox variety. Four containers can easily be stood in water, which should be changed only after the solutions have reached working temperature. Polythene and stainless containers absorb heat rapidly. Rigid translucent plastic containers take longer to heat contents.

PRE-HEATING

Always pre-heat the tank either by holding the base over a steaming pot, or by pouring in a little warm water; swill and discard once the tank is warmed.

PRE-WETTING

Pre-wetting of the film in filtered water of the correct working temperature reduces the risk of air bubble formations and development streaks; it also makes the film emulsion surface more miscible.

LOADING

Two methods of loading standard cylindrical tanks with developer solution are as follows. (a) Insert the spooled film(s) into the tank and pour in the solution. When a large quantity of developer is needed to cover the maximum number of spools, the process can take up to 30 seconds before the top film in the tank is completely covered. There is always a risk that this and other film may receive only partial development. A better method when more than two rolls of film are to be processed is (b) Fill the tank with developer solution. Load the spools onto a stainless hanger. Dunk in one go, seal the tank and start the clock.

AGITATION

Agitation will vary with different film types and developers. Ensure that the manufacturer's instructions are understood in this respect. Too much agitation, especially of the vigorous, continuous kind, can have the effect of increasing both film speed and grain, leading to excessive clumping of the silver halides.

Agitation techniques can be improved with time. After printing negatives from each consecutive roll of film, you will begin to see that there is a fine line between too

Limitations of both equipment and the medium in use must be clearly understood from the outset. In these two portraits, one is a disaster (left). A face full of character like this deserves more than the slap-happy approach to composition, background detail and, most of all, in this case, exposure and development technique. This picture resulted from a two-minute session in which everything possible was not done to make the most of the subject. Meter readings were taken from the palm of my hand and transferred direct to camera. There was filter and no compensation in development. In the right-hand picture, the following day, the same 6 × 6 camera was used with a 150 mm lens fitted with a medium yellow filter. Assistance was volunteered by onlookers to hold up a plain white backcloth which obscured direct sunlight and presented a clean backdrop. Meter readings were taken from the shadow area of the face and factored for the filter using EI 320. And finally, film, PH5, was given compensated development in HC110.

much and too little agitation; too vigorous and too gentle. Medium-speed films like Plus-X and FP4 will benefit from controlled agitation during the first two thirds of development while an absolute minimum is given in the last third, with virtually none at all during the last minute and a half. This procedure allows edge acutance between contrasting tonal values to be more sharply accentuated.

DEVELOPMENT TIME

As we have already seen, extended development increases overall contrast of the negative. As soon as a specified development time for given film speed (ISO) (i.e. for the actual exposure given which would record all required tones from the subject) is increased, significant blocking of the highlights begins to take place. The longer development is allowed to continue, the more apparent will be the highlight blocking. Shadow areas will simultaneously become more dense, giving a negative the appearance of one which has been over-exposed in the first instance. With high-contrast emulsions, it is important to establish at the outset exactly what development will be given for the selected film speed which may be different from that recommended by the manufacturer.

STOP BATH

There are two schools of thought regarding the use of a stop bath. This is invariably a solution of mild acetic acid diluted with water to make a working strength as indicated. Most photographic stop bath solutions contain a coloured dye additive which changes colour when the chemical stopping power of the solution is expired.

An acid stop bath immediately arrests the action of developing agents and when known development time and temperature techniques have been proven over a period of time a stop bath is to be recommended. Glacial acetic acid without indicator is available from most druggists. In its purest form (approximately 99.5 per cent), glacial acetic acid is corrosive and harmful to sensitive skin. The fumes are flammable and should not be inhaled. Open the container in a well-ventilated room and prepare to make a dilute solution which will then be diluted further for normal photographic use.

This is achieved by mixing the concentrate in a 3 : 8 ratio with water to make a 28 per cent pure solution. The working stop bath is mixed in proportion by adding 1 part of diluted acetic acid to 13 parts of water.

If no acetic acid is available, a similarly weak solution of metabisulphite can be used.

To make an indicator stop bath, add several drops of bromothymol to the working solution. This will give the stop bath a yellow colour which in darkrooms using the amber/ yellow safelight will appear colourless. When sufficient alkali is transferred from the developer, the indicator will turn dark blue or purple, at which point a fresh stop bath must be made up.

As any acid bath immediately neutralises the developer action, it may not always be preferable to use this method. Too strong an acid stop bath may also damage the emulsion by creating localised pinholes which will appear on the print as tiny dark spots. I quite frequently use plain water of the right temperature. This allows greater latitude in development techniques especially when I am using a rapid-acting general-purpose developer. Kodak's HC110 has a very syrupy consistency which even when diluted to a working strength has a tendency to stick to the emulsion surface. By further dilution in a water stop bath, I have found that the development action is continued as chemical agents are still absorbed in the swollen emulsion. Very weak development action seems to have the effect of enhancing subtle shadow detail without significantly increasing negative contrast.

FIXING

Several water washes are used before employing the first of two fixes. Using two fixer baths ensures complete fixation of each film without running the risk of using an exhausted solution. Both baths are dilutions of the stock solution to which a hardener has been added. I test the first bath before each processing session begins by dunking snipped-off film leaders and checking the clearing time. The first fix is used for two thirds of that time and is then followed immediately by the second fix for the remaining time. This is nearly always extended by a minute over the instructed time. As the first fix bath is exhausted, it is replaced by the second and a new batch is made up to replace that.

Film which has not properly cleared will have a slightly milky veil over the emulsion and if left will ultimately turn brown as the negatives age. The veil can be removed by further fixation as soon as the symptoms are recognised on removal of the film from the fix. However, because partial fogging will have taken place if the film was exposed to white light, resulting prints may show faint effects of solarisation.

Sodium thiosulphate was at one time commonly used as the solvent ingredient of most 'hypo' solutions. Hypo itself is an abbreviation of 'hyposulphite of soda' and has long since been discarded in the annals of photo-processing history. Modern rapid fixers use a closely related ammonium thiosulphate solvent to the working solution to which is sometimes added an emulsion hardener, usually potash alum.

Provided the strength of working solutions does not greatly exceed the quantities given by the manufacturer, a film left completely immersed in a fixing solution for up to double the recommended time will come to no harm. However, rapid fixers will attack and dissolve metallic silver salts if negatives are left immersed for extended periods. The symptoms of an over-fixed negative are noticeable bleaching of the shadow (thin) areas and, if left long enough, a reducing effect on highlights resulting in a negative that may look as if it was under-exposed by several stops.

Stale fixer, which has absorbed all the silver it is capable of dissolving, may still be able partially to clear unfixed film, but, no matter how long the film is left immersed, complete clearance will not take place. The negative may look as if it has cleared, but time will produce a darkish brown stain caused by silver-sulphur compounds that form in an over-extended fix solution. This is another good reason to use a second fixing bath. A silver recovery unit uses electrolytic action to recover silver deposits from exhausted fixer. To make economic use of such a machine, the fixer throughput needs to be of reasonable quantity, say a minimum of 20 litres per month. This allows a constant recovery of silver from only partially exhausted solutions, and these can then continue to be used as fresh stock.

WASHING

To achieve archival permanence of negatives, washing must take place in running water, or several changes of water for a minimum period of 45 minutes. If no running water is available, vigorous washing action of the film by hand is necessary in one change of water every two or three minutes for the first 15 minutes. Thereafter, water changes may be less frequent. The use of a plastic bucket into which a short hose rests over the rim is useless. The hose must be placed in the bottom of the bucket and weighted if necessary to facilitate a proper cleansing circulation. To cut down time significantly, a hypo clearing agent is used after the initial rinse following the final fix. If this procedure is carried out properly, washing times can be reduced to 20 minutes for archival permanence, and to as little as 5 minutes if negatives are only required to be kept for a year or two. I have some negatives from a variety of news stories that were given only a quick dunk in clearing agent and then rinsed before drying, which are still perfectly usable some ten years later.

Rapid processing techniques used by some newspaper darkrooms and freelances leave much to be desired in the washing department. I once watched, horrified, as several of my films from a particularly important event were developed, fixed, rinsed and dried in barely more than five minutes. As soon as I had retrieved them from the editor, I hurried home to give them a thorough wash. Since then, I have learned that it is of course perfectly possible to develop and fix a film in less than two minutes using high-speed developers and rapid fixers. Some time, however, is always required to remove all traces of chemical from the film, if negatives are to be kept for several decades.

FILM DRYING

Methods of drying a film will vary dramatically. Commercial premises will use some kind of drying cabinet like the ones illustrated or described in Chapter 2.

To take the worst kind of example first, where rapid drying, or drying to a point where the negative can actually be used, the following methods are effective. Make up a fairly strong solution of methylated spirit diluted 1 : 6 parts of water. Remove the film from the fix and, keeping it spooled, rinse briefly in clean water. Shake and dunk in meths solution. Take hold of the leader end of the film and, once free of the spool, pull sharply in a vertical direction, allowing the residue of meths to drain back whence it came. Attach a weighted clip to the bottom end of the film and an ordinary clip hanger to the top end. Hang the film. Using a dry chamois leather cloth, or a fine cotton, well-washed and clean handkerchief, carefully wipe the non-emulsion side of the film. Begin at the top and work downward in a single movement. Repeat until all traces of water have disappeared. The emulsion side should now have had sufficient time for excess liquid to drain. Using a hair drier with a snout, begin drying the film by gradually passing the snout down the length of the film on the non-emulsion side. Do this several times before turning the film around and working in the same fashion on the emulsion side. As it dries, the film surface will begin to flatten and eventually buckle in concave fashion, emulsion inward.

When speed is of the essence, at the risk of imparting particles of dirt, scratch marks and dust to the wet and slightly soft gelatin base, use a clean tea towel to wipe both sides of the film free of moisture in a simultaneous downward action. You may have to do this more than once. Proceed with the hair drier as previously described.

If your drying cabinet is efficient, dunking the film in a meths solution, draining and then hanging it under a medium heat setting will dry a film cleanly within a few minutes. When I have time to spare, I prefer the following method.

Wash the film as described. Fill a litre jug with fresh, clean water which is raised to a temperature of 20 °C (68 °F). Add one or two drops of domestic liquid detergent and mix evenly. Do not make a froth. Keeping the film spooled, dunk several times in the detergent rinse without actually removing it from the container. Take hold of the end of the film and, once clear of the spool, pull it out sharply in a vertical direction. Holding the film upright, grasp the bottom edge with your free hand. Keep the film straight, slightly relax the tension and then snap it back sharply in a series of flicks. This action will remove a great deal of surplus water. Weight the end of the film and hang it up. Allow the film to drain for a further 5–10 minutes before applying a medium, evenly distributed heat.

Proprietary wetting agents, as detergent additives are known, are just that. Kodak's *Photo-Flo* and other similar agents are refined detergent solutions which make the final rinse water more miscible and thus reduce the risk of foreign matter adhering to the film surface, particularly in hard water. Provided a disciplined technique is adopted in this last and most important part of the processing cycle, negatives should be pristine when finally dry. Rubber squeegee tongs for wiping film should be avoided whenever possible, even when thrust into one's hands by well-meaning colleagues or friends who swear and declare by them. I do not think I have one negative which has ever been squeegeed which is not damaged in some way, usually with a set of immaculate and deeply etched tramlines.

Film which is drying should always be hung in a dust-free atmosphere. Do not attempt to change the position of a film once the drying cycle has begun; it will cause subtle changes in density where one part of the film may have dried more quickly than another. Moving film around during the cycle also increases the risk of dust sticking to a partially dry emulsion with dire consequences.

Excessive heat has a tendency to increase the size of negative grain as well as distorting the film base. Using the above methods, there is no reason why film should not be dried effectively and quickly with little risk of contamination.

6
Advanced Black-and-White Processing Techniques

I said earlier that much of the knowledge gained by the pioneers of photography came through trial and error, and when one photographer discovered a technique which suited his own visual personality others soon followed suit; usually with a lot less effect unless in the course of so doing they inadvertently happened on another technique which gave them a different but equally dramatic result.

Throughout the course of photographic history, photographers have been developing (excuse the pun) style and technique best suited to their own needs and ends. Like artists with a brush, I doubt there have been two photographers who are masters of their craft who have produced works so alike that they could not be told apart, either in the style of original photography or in the mechanical process which originates the print.

Some painters have publicly scorned photography as nothing but an optical gimmick which produces, through some obscure chemical process, the likeness of a person or thing which all photographers would love to be able to paint, but cannot. I do not intend to delve into the enormous canyons of debate here about whether photography is an art, an art form, or a form of art. I would hope that most thinking photographers are certainly aware of the limitations of the medium and, more importantly perhaps, are aware of what they are endeavouring to communicate to the viewer through it. After all, if you had wanted to be a painter, doubtless you would be wielding a brush and palette instead of a camera.

But be that as it may, in order to present the viewing public with images which demand a second glance, the concerned photographer must rely heavily on his/her own ability to be able to identify, select, compose, expose and process the silver image in such a way that it achieves the desired effect. There are innumerable clichés which are often used to describe 'great works of art', but in photographic terms they are not relevant. In photography, it is the picture with impact that will make the viewer stop and take a second and possibly longer look.

Impact in a picture is achieved in several of the ways described above: by being selective about the choice of subject matter as it relates to the photographers' own points of reference, by being selective about the composing of elements of that subject, by being selective about the choice of format and means used to transfer the image to film, by being selective in choosing the tonal elements of the negative and in following a similar procedure in making the final print for public presentation. None of these selections are made on a purely objective basic, even though the knowledgeable, the emotionally detached and the concerned photographer may be influenced to a larger or lesser degree by objective circumstances at the time the exposure is made. In the final analysis, the selection of elements which comprise and render the *pictorial* image (as opposed to the *technical* one) are based on a subjective analysis. The interested viewer receives the information in a similarly subjective way, emotions being stimulated by whatever impact the picture contains.

If one assumes that some of these most important requirements are met, the degree of impact of a print on the viewer will depend almost entirely on presentation. But the ease with which a black-and-white or colour print may be made today is certainly no guarantee that the desired effect on the viewer will be achieved; in all probability, it will not.

In order to make prints which stand out from the run-of-the-mill mounds of turgid grey bromides, a much deeper understanding of how exposure and development can affect the negative is required. Moreover, if your eyes have been somewhat blinkered by an onslaught of trade advertising blah-blah about how good your pictures will be if so-and-so camera and such-and-such lens is used, what you present in terms of the two-dimensional print will almost certainly be something of a compromise. If, on the other hand, you know exactly the limitations and advantages of various formats, the precise characteristics of certain taking lenses and the lengths to which those characteristics can be exploited, you will have already achieved a great deal in progressing toward making a print that epitomises the fullest capability of your equipment, knowledge and imagination.

CONSIDERATIONS OF FORMAT

The question of which is the most suitable format for the serious hobbyist has long been debated and will no doubt continue to be, both in these and in the pages of other books and magazines. I make no excuses for devoting a little space here to a topic which some readers may feel has no place in a book which is essentially darkroom-orientated.

The considerations of format are important not just for the usual reasons of economy, versatility and the psychological aspects of ownership, but as well for aesthetic and technical values of the end result. Furthermore, its consideration here is all the more important because, in a sense, the darkroom is where photography begins and ends. In time, what one learns about processing is as much a result of what is known about photography generally, as the application of certain chemical techniques.

Let us assume for a minute that you did not purchase the camera you now have, whatever format it may be, and that you are still considering from the vast selection currently available. If you knew that 83 per cent of film produced by Kodak was colour-negative material and that only 5 per cent was black-and-white, you would be right in thinking that the vast bulk of that 83 per cent was gobbled up by cameras utilising the 35 mm format. The chances are that the reason you are using a 35 mm format camera for the bulk of your work has to do with the marketing techniques of both film and product manufacturers. The consideration of the cost of equipment will be a secondary factor, but equally important will be the 'value' factor in terms of versatility in use. The limitations of the format itself will not become readily apparent until you have (a) had a great deal of use from your 35 mm instrument and (b) had the chance to compare its results with those from something utilising a larger format. This should not be construed in any way as a denigration of the format; there is, after all, bountiful evidence of its superb performance in many fields of photography. Nevertheless, the key to whether it will produce the kind of results you might hope for is right there in that word *performance*.

So perhaps the first consideration should be of photographic *purpose* rather than of product variety. The next consideration should be an examination of the limitations and advantages of format within the framework of the purpose. Here we find a veritable mountain of marketing information designed to relieve the customer of his money as rapidly as possible without actually giving away very much. It would not be fair to say at this point that, in the general overall consideration, aesthetic appeal should not be given much attention. The oft-quoted argument that 'it is not the camera, but the person behind it, that counts', is misleading. The ergonomics of camera design, the way in which an instrument functions relative to the person using it, is just as important as the resolving quality of its lens. Further, the psychological considerations regarding ownership of a tool are invariably based on feel and appearance.

Consider the effort required to cut a log with a saw which does not feel right in your hand, has a blade that buckles at every stroke

The 35 mm format has been the mainstay of documentary photographers worldwide for decades. Modern lenses are capable of great resolving power and depth of field which is essential for this approach to subject matter. The sheer bulkiness of medium- and larger-format equipment inhibits the street photographer's rapid response to immediate situations which require quick thinking and execution.

The 'Zone' system of exposure and development enables the photographer to pre-visualise the printed result. Rather than use an averaging exposure method whereby all film is exposed for a given ISO and then processed accordingly, the zone system allows exposure to be made so that any one or a number of shades of grey may be obtained when development is adjusted to compensate. Ideally, the system is suitable for one-shot large-format work where several different exposures and development treatments can be given to each piece of film. With 35 mm cassettes it is only practical to select one option – that of development compensation. Here, detail in the shadows was more important than the highlights, but sufficient detail needed to be retained here. Tri-X, ISO 350, yellow filter, D-76 diluted 1 : 1.

and has 'foreign made' stamped all over it. The right camera for the right hands will go a long way toward producing the right results.

Format sharpness is relative. In practice, i.e. pictures taken in the field or studio as opposed to tests conducted within definite limitations, sharpness is only apparent and is always viewed subjectively. Light, selective focus, camera shake, flare, contrast, edge acutance, subject movement and end product quality are all contributory factors to sharpness. But, by being selective in the choice of format, the photographer has some control over the degree of apparent sharpness presented to the viewer.

A good-quality taking lens will be able to resolve at least 100 lines per mm, which is the measurement of its ability to render detail sharply. Modern lens coatings have made significant advances in recent years to the extent that even moderately priced 35 mm format optics are capable of good resolving power, and sometimes, if conditions are favourable, can produce results which might be considered outstanding. As a general rule of thumb, however, better-quality optics tend to be more expensive and, if consistently sharp results are expected, a larger investment must be made.

The human eye is upwards of 15 times more powerful than even the best lenses, so even when a near-perfect optic is used in conjunction with the finest-grained film, results obtained under average outdoor conditions may not be perfect.

Lenses designed for small-format use, as in 35 mm format, are generally computed to have greater resolving powers than those designed for larger formats. This is because smaller-format negatives generally have to undergo significantly greater magnification in the enlarger to achieve larger print sizes. The 4 × 5 in negative needs only to be magnified twice to make a standard 10 × 8 in print, whereas the 35 mm negative needs an 8 × magnification. For this reason, and contrary to popular photographic folklore, larger-format lenses are generally not sharper than smaller-format lenses, and using them with adaptors on smaller-format cameras will not normally produce sharper results.

Another factor to be taken into account today is the method by which lenses are tested. MTF (Modulation transfer function) tests are optical and electronic methods of testing a lens without using a camera or film. An electronic collimator measures image contrast at 'x' cycles per mm resolution of one sample. In practice, 'x' is a nominal figure equal to the finest detail discernible by the human eye for a given print size held at normal viewing distance. The results of such tests can be expressed in terms of a percentage figure where the maximum is 100 per cent, or in terms of lines per mm where the range covered is 0–100. MTF tests have been accepted by both reviewers and manufacturers as the new standard by which the majority of modern lenses are compared. The system can only be viewed as a very rough guide to the possible quality of an optic, since in practical field tests using film and paper a number of important variables must be taken into consideration. The final arbiter of whether a lens is any good or not will be its ability to produce a crisp and well-defined image under a variety of lighting and exposure conditions.

Next, we need to consider the resolving capability of film. Panchromatic emulsions for general-purpose photography are capable of resolving between 50 and 200 lines per mm. Films with a thinner emulsion base and slower ISO rating have a higher minimum figure, that of 150–200 lines per minute. Compared with the glass plates of years gone by, modern film is sharper on a format-for-format basis, but old plates were capable of immense clarity of detail and quality of tonal range which is often difficult to match when making use of modern smaller formats.

I know that many 35 mm users will want to argue that they can produce black-and-white prints of a quality equal to and perhaps even better than some larger formats. I have used the same argument myself, particularly in the early years of my career when it was necessary to be able to prove, not only to

myself, but to others, that really excellent results were possible using the smaller format. It took me some time to realise that, whilst quality could be coaxed out of the 35 mm negative given certain conditions, it was in fact much easier to achieve that same level by using a larger format. Going larger still, there was no denying that no matter how badly one treated a 5 × 4 in negative, the end result was in many ways far superior in terms of apparent sharpness and tonal range than anything I could produce using the smaller format. Once that was clarified, I knew that there would be certain assignments which could only be shot on a larger format – if quality was an end-product requirement. Other assignments, such as news, sports, fly-on-the-wall, and many other subjects, could only be photographed well by exploiting the operational versatility of the miniature. By establishing clearly the limitations of each particular format I was able to begin exploring the medium in a way I had never imagined possible. That realisation

opened up a whole new book of ideas and experiments which have so far barely gotten past the introductory stage.

In considering format, the darkroom photographer must also endeavour to match the quality of taking equipment with that used to make the print. As already discussed in Chapter 3, only the finest optics should be used for print-making. The type of enlarger illumination, whether it be low-voltage halogen, cold cathode, diffuser or condenser, will have a direct bearing on how the negative image is rendered on paper.

To sum up, these are the major points to consider in establishing format size:

1) Photographic purpose.
2) Own personality.
3) Ergonomics of equipment design.
4) Optical quality.
5) Own knowledge of medium.
6) Processing facilities.

Items 3 and 4 may be considered equally in

In this situation, it is unlikely that the subtle balance of colours and general ambience in this tannery would benefit from shooting on black-and-white stock rated normally. Some increase in contrast and tighter composition would be necessary to give a similar effect. Ektachrome 200. Available light.

In the darkroom I decided to run several tests on this film. The first followed the normal procedure of increasing the first development for push processing techniques (see p. 89). The results were far too contrasty and still underdeveloped. Next, I developed a strip of about six frames in HC110 diluted 1 : 9 for 40 minutes, washed and fixed the film as I would have done if it were black-and-white. The resulting negatives were still a trifle thin, so I gave the next batch another 10 minutes, which seemed to do the trick. I then made up a weak solution of potassium ferricyanide bleach and dunked the film until virtually all trace of the black and white image had disappeared. A thorough clearing wash followed this step before redevelopment in a freshly-made stock of old C-22 colour-negative developer. I left the film in this brew for something like 20 minutes until development appeared to have stopped.

assessing small and medium formats. Better-quality camera systems are known to have first-class optics throughout a lens range and in this case there may be very little to choose between the quality of one marque and another; there may, however, be numerous design and operating differences, and in that case only those differences will warrant consideration. Large-format cameras of the monorail and flat-bed field type can usually be fitted quite easily with a vast range of optics not necessarily supplied by the camera maker, and in this case more research may be necessary to establish which are the most suitable optics.

The professional photographer who hopes to satisfy the demands of innumerable clients will be equipped with a small arsenal of equipment of varying format size, though I hasten to add that there are exceptions to this general rule; in photojournalism, for example, 35 mm has long been considered the most versatile and practical tool for the task. In the field of amateur photography, cost invariably governs both quality and variety of equipment. A fairly small proportion will be using large format (4 × 5 in or

over); the fact that the roll film market is expanding again after a dull and relatively static period is an indicator of the returning popularity of the medium format; 35 mm, however, outstrips all other formats. Much of what follows is of particular relevance to the medium and 35 mm user, although there is no reason why the large-format user may not apply similar controls.

THE ZONE SYSTEM

Since the beginnings of photography, a variety of methods have been perfected which are primarily designed to give the photographer more control of exposure, development and print-making – EDP for short. One of the most accurate and also the most complicated to comprehend fully is the *zone system* developed originally by an American photographer, the late Ansel Adams (1902–1984), in conjunction with colleagues of the F64 group of photographers founded in California in the 1930s.

The F64 group became known throughought the photographic and art world not only for their interpretations of the wonders of nature, but for the clarity, tonal range and presentation values of their prints. Adams himself spent years developing EDP techniques based on the zone system, to such an extent that finally his prints were given the kind of acclaim normally reserved for painted works of art, and also, when put up for auction, they began to command the kind of exceptional prices one might expect for a work of art.

Adams wrote several books devoted to the explanation of light in photographic terms, and the first, *Exposure Record* (1945), is essentially a description of the zone system of exposure which he and another F64 group photographer, Fred Archer, developed from the results of tests conducted by the Western Electric Instrument Company a few years earlier.

Rather than follow the normal pretexts of photography whereby a particular grade of paper is chosen to match the contrast range of a negative produced quite arbitrarily through normal development and averaging exposure techniques, the zone system allows the photographer to pre-visualise the final print, to select fairly accurately a particular contrast and to visualise the gradation of tonal values of a subject from 0 to 10, where 0 is the richest area of black on the final print and shows no detail, and 10 is the purest white equivalent to paper base. In between are eight zones of varying shades of grey of which one, No.5, is always estimated to be equivalent to the tone of an 18 per cent Kodak grey card. By measuring the brightness range of the parts of the subject required for printing, it is possible by shifting exposure one full stop in either direction to render tones exactly as required, and then by compensating during development to produce a negative whose contrast exactly matches a pre-selected grade of paper.

Adams' techniques were particularly applied to the use of one-shot cameras, i.e. large-format instruments capable of exposing one plate or piece of cut film at a time. As the reader will have already realised, such procedures are extremely difficult to follow when using any type of roll or miniature film. In addition, the physical size of miniature film precludes making full advantage of tonal gradation due to excessive magnification of the negative.

ASSESSING EXPOSURE

Brightness range has already been discussed in Chapter 4 in some detail. In adapting the zone system to roll and miniature photography, the reader should be prepared to make a deeper investigation of the metering capability of his/her camera. The vast majority of small-format single lens reflex cameras use a through-the-lens (TTL) measuring device based on a full-frame assessment or centre-weighted. The latter type is more common, having maximum sensitivity in a central 60 per cent area of the frame and gradually decreasing as it reaches the corners.

Both TTL types are not practically suitable for adaption to the zone system of exposure measurement which is based primarily on calculating the brightness range of the subject — sometimes referred to as subject brightness range, or SBR. Remember, it is the luminescence of each of the respective tones which make up the subject that you are trying to record; averaging reflective light meters cannot accurately measure such subtle differences when they are used normally from the subject to camera distance. What you need is a meter with a very narrow angle of acceptance — a spot meter — which allows you to measure accurately each of the identifiable tonal differences.

In most cases where a small-format camera with integral metering is used, the normal practice of 'needle matching' or selecting a shutter speed/f stop to balance whichever priority mode is used, or utilising a programmed exposure, will be relied upon. All of these readings and automatic exposures rely on one small piece of user-input information, the setting of normal ISO film speeds, assuming that in most cases normal development will be given for each respective film exposed.

Each film may have up to 72 frames exposed on different subjects, and perhaps all

Sufficient texture and detail in the brick and woodwork was required only for recognition. Exposure was adjusted for the highlights of the face and given half a stop less than indicated. The film, Tri-X, was given an extra 10 per cent development and the negative printed on a grade 3 bromide.

demanding different exposures for changing levels of brightness. When the whole film is developed, each negative may have a different contrast as well as wildly different gradations of tone. To make acceptable prints, it may be necessary to spend considerable darkroom time matching the paper to negative in a series of tests before a final print can be produced.

It would be much easier at the outset to visualise, as Ansel Adams and his colleagues did, how the subject would best be rendered

Here are two examples of pre-visualisation exposed under two entirely different lighting situations. In the left-hand shot the light came from a single yellow filtered spot some 40 ft away on a balcony. I used Tri-X rated at 650, a Nikkor 105 mm lens wide open at f2.5 and moved in close. Exposure was 1/60th second and the film developed in concentrate D-76 for 10 minutes. In the second picture the light came from a large window on a wintry morning. The camera was tripod-mounted which I used to give me an exposure reading of the highlight only areas. The film (Tri-X) was then developed in dilute D-76 and a print made on a grade 3 paper which was burned-in slightly around the figure to eliminate the cluttered background.

and on what grade of paper. Exposure for the gradation of tones and development for contrast is the key. How can this work unless the film is cut and each individual frame processed separately?

The normal procedure in assessing exposure is based on the measurements indicated for the brightest and darkest parts of the subject – the average of the two being taken as a general reading for the whole scene. The drawback with this procedure is that the resulting print is deficient in both shadow detail and highlight detail when measurements are taken in bright, contrasty light; in even, diffused light, prints lack a pure black and base white. Result? A print of even, mud-grey tones.

To overcome this deficiency some photographers bracket their exposures a half to one full stop or more either side of the so-called 'normal' exposure, in the hope that one or more negatives will have sufficient gradation and contrast. This hit-and-miss approach *may* produce the odd negative from time to time from which an excellent print can be made. However, the system is full of bugs and offers no guarantee of success at all.

In most instances, the photographer will be aiming to produce effect, rather than a pure record. The resulting print is a tonal interpretation of that part of the scene which moved him/her to make the exposure in the first instance. Using roll and miniature formats, some latitude in EDP is desirable if the end result is to come anywhere near our expectations, and Table 1 may be useful in helping to determine certain tonal values, contrast and negative density.

The figures are based on techniques which I have used for a number of years to obtain predictable results from the following types of lighting situations.

1) Bright, contrasty, deep shadow, little cloud.
2) Bright, haze, sun and cloud.
3) Bright, diffuse light.
4) Overcast or dull.
5) Available light.

Over-exposure or under-exposure systems geared to percentage increase/reduction developing techniques allow the photographer more control at the print stage. Normal metered readings are used in most instances where the light is even or diffused, except

Table 1: EXPOSURE COMPENSATION DEVELOPMENT

Times are given for a working solution and tank temperature of 20°C (68°F). Films = Ilford HP5 rated at 400 ISO (slight variations for Kodak Tri-X at same rating). Stock solution of HC110 diluted to a working strength of 1 part stock developer to 9 parts of water.

Exposure	Development time in minutes % of development increase/decrease							
	0%	10%	15%	20%	25%	30%	35%	
−3 stops							9.78	⎫
−2.5 stops						9.4		⎪
−2 stops					9.06			⎪
−1.5 stops				8.9				⎬ Increase
−1 stop			8.34					⎪
−0.5 stop		7.97						⎭
Normal	7.25							
+0.5 stop		6.5						⎫
+1 stop			6.16					⎪
+1.5 stops				5.8				⎪
+2 stops					5.4			⎬ Decrease
+2.5 stops						5.08		⎪
+3 stops							4.7	⎭

© Jonathan Eastland

where more, or less, emphasis is desired at the main point of interest. In bright, very contrasty conditions which would normally render shadow areas in the 0 to II zone of blackness, and lighter areas as zones equivalent to VII, IX or X, some further adjustment may be necessary to control the extent of the brightness range. In this case, pick out the zones which are of most importance and work on the assumption that only 7 zones including deep black and brilliant white are available. Most medium- and slower-speed emulsions can cope with these situations easily. With high-speed film it is necessary to increase the contrast range. This can be done by lowering film speed and decreasing development. Use the table to make accurate adjustments.

CAMERA METER ZONE TECHNIQUE

Unlike the professional whose work frequently demands one or more rolls of film to be exposed on one subject, the amateur has usually to be more economic in the use of film. This restriction does make it difficult for the miniature or roll format user to take full advantage of the zone system.

There are, however, a variety of simplified versions which when properly manipulated are capable of producing excellent results. These rely to a large extent on the discipline of the operator and sophistication of equipment to hand. That is not to say that if you do not own the latest, most outrageous multi-function-all-flashing-silicon-chip SLR that the various methods described cannot be implemented.

Most modern electronic 35mm cameras incorporate a centre-weighted average light metering system which is coupled to a microprocessor. When the photographer activates the meter, either by depressing the shutter button or by turning some other switch, a numerical assessment of what the exposure for the subject should be is flashed through light-emitting diodes onto, or to one side of, the viewfinder screen. By selecting one of several metering modes, the photographer can: either let the camera set shutter speed and aperture (as in programmed mode); let the camera select shutter speed only when the aperture is fixed – or vice versa – (shutter/aperture priority); or take complete manual control. The current trend in camera design is more and more towards full automation with only a patronising nod in the direction of the purist; the exceptions in this minefield of optical manufacture are the makers of top-line professional equipment – Nikon, Olympus, Canon and Leica. The first two make models which are purely mechanical, Canon F-1 (New) continues to function even when the battery dies, and Leica of course have the M series rangefinder cameras. While many of the rest have a manual option, in as much as the shutter speed can be selected by the user, these cameras rely heavily on electronics. Once the power fades, there is no back-up.

Both systems have their obvious advantages. There is probably some misconstrued evidence in the purist camp which encourages the belief that mechanical cameras are less likely to break down as frequently as their electronic brothers; the opposing view is that electronic cameras are more reliable and more accurate when it comes to exposure evaluation.

What you believe is governed largely by usage. In my view, both types have practical advantages. From a purely sentimental viewpoint, I don't doubt I shall always prefer the 'feel' of a manual camera because that is the kind of instrument that I trained with and have mostly used over two decades of professional photography. Somehow, the knowledge that someone, somewhere, took great pains to put all those tiny nuts, bolts and ball bearings together is a comfort. I understand magnetism but a circuit board film just doesn't stimulate my photographic ego!

A combination of the two essential characteristics is something else; on the one hand, the reliable nut and bolt, and on the other the accurate silicon chip. The Olympus OM3 is the result of this marriage. It is a superb tool and, as far as I can see, probably the only contemporary 35 mm SLR currently available which employs a metering system which can be exploited by those interested in the zone system.

The OM3's meter is essentially a spot meter measuring 2 per cent of the total picture area. The same meter is used in the OM4. In the OM3, however, the spot operates in tandem with a centre-weighted averaging system made possible by incorporating what the makers call a Silicon Blue Cell in the electronic mechanism. The image transfer mirror is only half mirrored in the central section; this allows some light to pass through the mirror where it is directed by a fresnel sub-mirror past a series of three focusing lenses to the Silicon Blue Cell light sensor. This is aimed in the direction of the film plane and, in the normal centre-weighted metering mode, part of this cell is activated to provide an average light reading. As soon as the spot meter is activated, readings are given for the 2 per cent central area of the subject.

The OM3 has a sophisticated CPU – central processing unit – with an integral RAM (random access memory) allowing up to eight spot-metered evaluations to be computed simultaneously or selected individually. Pretty impressive stuff. From a zone user's point of view, the more interesting

These three prints clearly show the colours of the various grades of paper (2, 3 and 4 Agfa Record Rapid) used. The film was exposed in shaded summer daylight at an EI of 320 and developed in HC110 as per Table 1. I wanted a negative full of detail in shadow and highlight to print without dodging or burning on a fairly contrasty paper to give good blacks and whites as well as plenty of middle tones. Because the exposure and development were matched as closely as possible in advance to the requirement, neither print on the softer grades of paper is suitable for snappy reproduction.

aspect is probably not so much the sophistication of the SBC/CPU circuitry, but the way in which the Olympus designers have transferred the visual information for the photographer to use.

My initial reaction to the liquid crystal viewfinder display was actually one of despair. I regret to say that the sales brochures really do not prepare one for the shock. I figured that the reason for my reaction was simple: disbelief that so much could be got into such a small area. At first, that was enough to throw me off. One other factor of course was that when you have been weaned on one particular brand of milk and stuck with it for many years, a change to a different brand takes a little getting used to.

On further inspection and with time, one began to ask why no one had thought about viewfinder displays in a like manner before. Because the Olympus presents such a large and clear subject image to the viewer, this seems to me to be the predominant factor. The information relating to exposure is contained in a strip in the lower margin of the viewfinder and, once I had mastered what it was telling me, I hardly noticed that it was there. Other viewing systems present the information in a much more random fashion making more demands on the user to expend effort to locate that information, and thus detracting the eye unnecessarily from the subject matter.

The manual mode liquid crystal display in

both the OM3 and 4 is also set out in such a way that it facilitates a set-up whereby 9 of the 10 zones previously described can be visualised in step form on the LCD. If zones 1–9 are used, the central marker is taken as zone 5, which would be translated as a medium grey patch. The markers either side of the central marker are used as shown below.

OM3 ZONE SYSTEM LIQUID
CRYSTAL DISPLAY

IX VIII VII VI V IV III II I
 :   :   :   : : :   : : :
 +   *   *   > I <   * * —

The markers at either side of the central marker indicate tonal values corresponding to the Roman numerals. The display allows a rapid comparison of tonal values and enables the photographer to set spot readings at pre-determined tonal print values.

DEVELOPER CHARACTERISTICS

The best developer for your film is not necessarily the one recommended by the film manufacturer, even though that film may have undergone exhaustive laboratory and practical tests. Because conditions outside the laboratory vary so much with equipment used for measuring liquid quantities, in mixing dry powder chemicals and temperature controls, and in handling techniques, the recommendations normally accompanying film are given as a user-guide only. In practice, in the home or professional darkroom, recommended developers are often found to be lacking when more critical results are desired.

With few exceptions, most film developers currently available may be used in conjunction with almost any type of film. Except for one or two formulae designed especially to enhance characteristics of slow and some medium-speed emulsions, and some others which have been formulated to take advantage of the characteristics of higher emulsion speeds, nearly all developers will give different effects when used to develop the same film type. Some reduce contrast, boost shadow detail, enhance edge acutance, produce fine or coarser granular structure and so on. Others will have the opposite effect.

In selecting a developer, the following points are worthy of consideration:

1) Effect on contrast.
2) Effect on grain structure.
3) Ability to enhance shadow detail, control highlights.
4) Economy of development time.
5) Economy in use.
6) Powder or liquid mix to stock solution.
7) Storage life.

The trade names in Table 2 are commonly available through most photo-dealers and, if not available off-the-shelf, can be ordered from the manufacturer. They can be used with most panchromatic film except where indicated by an asterisk (*). Development times given are for normal film speed ratings. Times may have to be varied according to local conditions and these can only be successfully established after tests.

Development times for a particular contrast, suitable for printing through a condenser or diffused enlarger system, must also be taken into consideration when conducting first tests with these times. You may be surprised to find that some figures will vary quite dramatically. Some readers may also be surprised to find that their favourite 'soup' is not listed in this section, although it may be in the following one. The reason for this is fairly straightforward.

Processing roll film is a fairly tedious occupation at the best of times. It will not be made any easier, particularly for the novice, if it is felt that the whole list must be experimented with before any kind of standard developer can be adopted. By all means do try them all, but I would not advise trying to attack the list in one hit; aside from the fact that having to mix all those dry powder developers into stock solutions is a long-winded affair, it would be better initially to select one type and work with this until you

Table 2: DEVELOPMENT TIMES (IN MINUTES)

Developer Dilution in brackets, e.g. (1 : 'X' water)	Film Type								
	1	2	3	4	5	6	7	8	9
Aculux (1 : 9)	9	9	9.5	6	9	7.5	5.5	5.5	6
Acuspecial (1 : 29)	*	*	*	13	14	18	12	12	15
Acutol (1 : 10)	*	*	*	7	6	7	5	*	*
Acutol (1 : 15)	*	*	*	*	*	*	*	7.5	9
Atomal (n/d)	10	11	10	8	12	9	6	9	7
D-76 (1 : 1)	10	17	13	7.5	14	9	7	12	10
ID-11 (1 : 1)	10	17	13	7.5	14	9	7	12	10
HC-110 (B, 1 : 7)	7.75	6	7	6	9	5	4.5	5.5	4.5
Microdol-X (n/d)	11	13	13	7.5	14	8.5	8	10	8
Perceptol (1 : 1)	18	21	16	11	16	11	8.5	14	15
Rodinal (1 : 25)	8	6	7	8	5	4	6	4	6
Unitol (1 : 9)	10	10	10	*	*	*	*	*	*
Unitol (1 : 14)	*	*	*	11	8	5.5	5	8.5	6

n/d = undiluted, stock solution.
* = not recommended, or not applicable at this dilution, see next line.
Film types
1) Tri-X; 2) HP5; 3) Agfapan 400; 4) Plus-X; 5) FP4; 6) Agfapan 100; 7) Panatomic-X;
8) Pan-F; 9) Agfapan 25.

can get a feel for its temperament and the results it will produce.

Nearly all photographers interested in their craft eventually manage to find the time, either through necessity or pleasure, to try out the many different types of developer available. Some I know have gone through just about every available off-the-shelf product only to revert to formulae long age discarded by the packaging industry. Using developer and discovering which is the most suitable for your purpose is a little like wearing in new shoes; at the end of the day one is either glad to be rid of them or comfortable in the knowledge that until they wear out there is no reason to buy another pair.

Because different formulae produce varying developed results, a notebook for recording characteristics, times, temperatures and agitation sequences will be useful for future reference for the occasions when you feel that certain exposures should be given different treatment. This darkroom notebook is also useful for other reasons which I will come to soon. While researching my own notes for this book I came across some interesting entries. First, I discovered that, over a period of some 18 years, two types of developer were given fairly constant entries: D-76

and HC-110, both manufactured by Kodak. One is available in powder form, the other comes in a thick, syrupy liquid form which is further diluted to make the stock solution. Scattered through the notes and requisition pads are entries for other types, and it is fairly apparent that when these supplies were exhausted I seemed to have automatically returned to old favourites. I recall that, at one time, Agfa introduced a product called Studional Liquid which in order to work effectively over long periods with high throughput needs a replenisher. I was given a sample by the Agfa rep one day but it was not used immediately. Several months later I decided to push through some of the then new Agfapan 400 I had also been asked to try out. The results were, as one might expect, superb.

With a little adjustment, both Kodak and Ilford emulsions were quite happy in this brew; it produced crisp, fine-grained negatives that printed well on Agfa's papers. Unfortunately, I could not get the same results on other paper stock, whereas the contrast range of negatives developed in D-76 or HC-110 could be printed on almost any make of paper. In recent years, I have stuck rigidly to HC-110. It is a great all-rounder which can be diluted to virtually any strength within the boundaries recommended. In the day-to-day operations of a news and feature agency this is a great asset because it allows total flexibility in the running of a fairly busy darkroom.

When there is a rush on to produce negatives and prints by midday from a morning assignment, film can be loaded, processed and dried in 15–20 minutes. Rush prints are made in a dry-to-dry stabilisation processor, captioned and delivered to the customer or train station within an hour. Damp film can, when necessary, be ready for use in the enlarger in a few minutes. If there is more time to coax the very best quality that this developer can deliver, the stock solution is diluted further and time adjusted for film type and contrast required. When very short development periods are called for, agitation sequences have to be adjusted to counter

the possibility of streaking. Here, again, too vigorous agitation can also cause perforation streaking; this is caused by the wave action pattern of developer rushing back and forth through perforations in the film and is manifested typically in an uneven development sequence on the horizontal frame edge of the film. With roll-film, the phenomenon does not exist because there are no perforations, but unevenness is sometimes apparent when nylon spools are used. The slightly thicker groove mouldings, being of different shape to stainless spools, set up other wave patterns which can cause problems. When development times of less than 5 minutes are used regularly, it will pay to pre-soak the film in a water bath, which, as already described, helps to dislodge air bubbles and swells the gelatin sufficiently to allow more effective development.

The type of tank used and quantity of and dilution of solution in which the film is immersed is another factor which will affect the gamma (contrast) gradient. On average, contrast tends to be higher when small tanks are used with a solution of less dilution. Deep tanks, i.e. those that accept a full length of 36 exposure film folded and weighted in the centre, require slightly longer development times to achieve the same contrast rating.

PUSH PROCESSING

As we have already seen, film speed in ISO terms is established by the manufacturer after extensive laboratory tests calculated from the amount of light required to give a density of 0.1 above the base fog level: the point at which non-image-forming silver is changed in character during development and begins to show traces of having received exposure from a point source light.

In practical photographic terms, there is really no such thing as a change of film speed. Once that speed has been established, it is there for good, no matter what

The colours of black-and-white. Compare this with the colour picture on p. 59. Here we have three ships of more or less identical colour. As a straight record, the flat lighting does little to portray the interest value which primarily revolves around the colour and shape which sparked off the photographer's interest. Given time, different vantage points and different light, this black-and-white record might have been turned into a picture.

developer one might use, and in fact most developers used as directed for type 'x' film will not change the film speed for all practical purposes. As we have just seen, contrast and actual negative density can be changed, but that is not the same thing as speed.

If the film speed is fixed by the manufacturer, how does the photographer determine a new speed and how is that defined for the purpose of development?

Let us say that you were using a 100 ISO film in the camera and the subject required an exposure of one full stop more than was indicated by your light meter. If you expose the film at the metered reading, your film will be under-exposed by one stop. The new effective ISO is defined as *Exposure Index*. It is a variable which the photographer can change at will depending on lighting conditions at the time of exposure. So the under-exposed 100 ISO becomes EI200. If you were to reduce exposure by two full stops, the EI becomes EI400. In effect, what you are doing by utilising this method of exposure is no different from the basic theory applied to the zone system where each step of the 1–10 zones is equivalent to a brightness twice as bright as the previous zone.

Exposure Index is constantly changed in practice. Because different panchromatic emulsions are more or less sensitive to certain colours of light when you change from one subject, say out of doors, to one indoors lit by tungsten light, there is a significant shift which affects the ability of the film to record certain details. Emulsions which are more sensitive at the blue end of the spectrum may have difficulty in recording subjects under certain lighting conditions like tungsten if no allowance is given. It was not that long ago that some manufacturers specified two ISO speeds for their film – one for daylight and one for available, or tungsten, light.

Another variable factor has to do with colour filtration. Whenever a coloured filter is used with black-and-white film, the effective EI is changed by a factor corresponding to the particular filter in use.

Push processing techniques are widely used by many photographers, and in every-day practice EI is hardly ever referred to as a means of measurement. Working photographers simply say. 'This film was rated at . . . 200, 400, 650, 800 or 3200' and so on. What they mean is that a new ISO speed was applied to the film, set on the camera ISO indexer or hand-held meter. The whole film is then exposed at this new rating and processed as if it had been given that rating by the manufacturer in a developer known to give acceptable results at the new speed rating.

Suppose you had inadvertently exposed your 100 ISO film at EI 200. If this were developed for the standard time in a standard developer for that film at its given 100 ISO rating, the resulting negatives would be thin, if not translucent. In order to build up the deposits of silver halides on the areas of film which have been exposed, more development time is needed to obtain a printable negative. However, push processing, or forced development, also has one or two undesirable side-effects.

In a scene of low average brightness such as a floodlit football match or street scene, where the bulk of the picture area is comprised of say 85 per cent shadow and 15 per cent highlights ranging in strength from fairly dim to excessively bright, forced development of the exposed parts of the image simply adds more and more silver. In the 85 per cent shadow area, even the parts of the scene which have received some exposure may not have had enough. The result is usually very much one of compromise. Contrast of the resulting negative, if not chemically fogged, may be so high that no matter what grade of paper is selected for printing the overall effect will be one of 'soot and whitewash'. There is loss of detail, definition is impaired, grain clumping takes place and unless the resulting effect is deliberately planned ahead, most prints from push-processed negatives leave a lot to be desired in the way of quality.

Low-contrast subjects are much better suited to this technique. There are many everyday scenes which can benefit from a slight effective increase in film speed. Many press photographers, for example, often rate

HP5 and Tri-X at EI650, for much of their general day-to-day work, particularly where light levels are fairly low and diffused: street scenes, crowds, accidents, sports and so on. Aside from the fact that the contrast of faster emulsions is improved slightly for newsprint reproduction, the higher effective film speed also allows the photographer a higher shutter speed to help counteract camera shake, and smaller apertures to increase depth of field. Any advantage that can be gained in this department can sometimes mean the difference between obtaining a usable picture or losing it completely.

There is one other school of thought which argues that forced development can and often does produce negatives which, because of their opacity, i.e. density of silver deposit, are quite unsuitable for printing on condenser source enlargers. Most diffuser source enlargers (colour head and cold cathode) are better suited to the more dense, more contrasty negative, a phenomenon produced by over-development. If you use only condenser types, as I do, you will soon begin to appreciate that there is a fine art to the production of any negative, whether it be one produced through normal developing methods or by the push-process technique. I switched from the diffuser type many years ago simply because I found that higher-contrast negatives gave me prints that were altogether too soggy. Now someone I know is going to tell me that you cannot tell the difference between a print from the same negative produced using either type of light source. Whatever the truth of the matter, the choice of light source is often as much the result of subjective feelings toward the characteristics of the print as any technical or practical consideration.

CHROMAGENIC FILM

Chromagenic black-and-white emulsions such as Ilford XP1 400 and Agfapan Vario XL (ISO 125–1600) cannot be developed in conventional silver image chemistry. Standard colour negative processes such as C-41, AP 70 and other compatible formulae are used. These are available to the home user or

professional; stock solutions are available in liquid form in fairly small quantities. If you are already processing your own colour-negative material using C-41 or the Agfa AP70, black-and-white chromagenic film does not require any change in sequence or chemistry.

Using Agfacolor process F in daylight-loading tanks, Table 4 shows the developing sequence for Agfa Vario XL.

The advantages of this type of film in low light photography are its excellent speed-to-grain relationship, enormous exposure latitude, fine grain and superb definition. It performs best in the mid 200–800 ISO range. If fine grain is the main criterion, black-and-white chromagenic film is best exposed at ISO 125. If high emulsion speed is essential, as is often required at indoor sports events, it should be exposed at ISO 1600. If faster emulsion speeds are required, it would be preferable to use a conventional panchromatic high speed emulsion such as Kodak's 2475 Recording. Chromagenic emulsions do not respond well to forced development and, in the majority of low light subject situations,

Table 3: TIMES FOR FORCED DEVELOPMENT

Film		Developer make and time in minutes @ 20°C (68°F)	
Standard ISO	New ISO		
Agfapan 400	800	Tetenal Emofin	2 × 2.5 }[†]
Agfapan 400	1600	Tetenal Emofin	2 × 3 }
Agfapan 400	1250	Acuspeed (1 : 7)	12
Agfapan 400	800	Promicrol (1 : 1)	15
Fuji Neopan 400	800	D-76	12
Fuji Neopan 400	1200	D-76	15
Fuji Neopan 400	1600	D-76	20
Ilford HP5 400	650	Microphen (n/d)	8
Ilford HP5 400	800	Microphen (n/d)	8.5
Ilford HP5 400	1200	Microphen (n/d)	9
Ilford HP5 400	1600	Microphen (n/d)	10
Ilford HP5 400	3200	Microphen (n/d)	15
Ilford HP5 400	6400	Microphen (n/d)	20
Ilford HP5 400	1600	Acuspeed (1 : 7)	9
Ilford HP5 400	800	Promicrol (1 : 1)	15
Kodak Tri-X 400	800	Tetenal Emofin	2 × 2.5 }[†]
Kodak Tri-X 400	1600	Tetenal Emofin	2 × 3 }
Kodak Tri-X 400	1600	Acuspeed (1 : 7)	9
Kodak Tri-X 400	1600	Promicrol (1 : 1)	14
Kodak 2475 Recording	1000	HC110 (1 : 32)	9[+]
Kodak 2475 Recording	1600	HC110 (1 : 32)	15[*]
Kodak 2475 Recording	4000	HC110 (1 : 32)	22.5

[†] = normal contrast; [+] = average subject brightness; [*] = low subject brightness.

Table 4: AGFA VARIO XL DEVELOPING SEQUENCE

Bath Sequence	Time (minutes)	Temperature (°C)	Time (minutes)	Temperature (°C)
Developer	7.5*	30±1	3.25**	38±0.5
Bleach-fix	11	30±1	8	38±1
Wash	4	30±5	3	38±3
Final bath	1	30±5	0.6	38±3

uprating above the recommended speed is not normally necessary.

It is probable that, in the not-too-distant future, silver image granular structure such as is used in conventional film manufacture will be replaced by the current technology of 'T' grain structure now used in most colour-negative emulsions of the HR and VR type. Conventional silver halides are crystalline in structure, similar in shape to snowflakes but so small (1/10,000 in) that their shape is un-identifiable to normal unaided eyesight. The problem with conventional structures is that, in order to increase film speed, the grain size has to be increased, which makes it more noticeable to the print observer as both film speed and magnification increases. 'T' grain structures are more uniform in size and dis-tribution over the light-sensitive film layer and are closely interlocked, unlike conven-tional halides which are deposited in a more random pattern. This new technology is al-ready used in black-and-white X-ray emul-sions and will shortly be introduced into other black-and-white emulsions.

With the gradual improvement of glass types used in lens construction (SD types – low dispersion) and their more general availability in lower cost independent lenses, optics with improved resolution capability will become the norm. When used in con-junction with current film technology, max-imum use of the optical potential is lost. The new technology black-and-white films, when they become available, will redress the balance somewhat.

7
Black-and-White Print Making

It is ironic in a peculiar sort of way that since the very earliest days of photography, way back in the mid-1800s, practitioners, pundits and critics of the craft have mostly concentrated their energies in the direction of inventing, improving or slating the medium of colour. From the earliest days of commercial photography, practitioners hired colouring artists to hand-tint the portrait photograph; a skill as much in demand in some circles today as it was then. The inventor sought ways to delineate the colours of nature onto a single photographic plate and has been improving it since about 1907, when the Autochrome process became the first practicable method. Critics of course have been harping on about the lack of suitable colour emulsions for years. I wonder sometimes if perhaps they are not the same ones who have also, for years, aimed their misinformed knowledge of both the medium and the craft in the general direction of the student. Why then, when even the most prolific manufacturer of film only produces a mere 5 per cent, is there such a following for the evocative appeal of black-and-white photography?

The question is rhetorical. I use it and the preceding paragraph to illustrate the delusion of modern photography. What if the simultaneous inventors of the medium had struck gold at the outset and had been able to give us colour photography from the first day? Are there any grounds for believing that the scientists of photography would have struggled so gamefully to bring us black-and-white? Somehow I doubt it.

It is unfortunate perhaps that the term black-and-white is so inappropriate. We tend to use it in a slovenly manner and without a great deal of thought. In recent years, the word monochrome has become yet another fashionable adjective used to describe what is essentially not black-and-white photography but continuous and variable tone, from almost white through a variety of grey tones to a near black. Black-and-white prints are frequently not black-and-white but have some colour which is manifested through the ingredients of the paper, or, as is often the case, added in a further processing step after the developed image has been fixed.

The really stupid thing about black-and-white photography is that most of us do not view the world in continuous and variable tones of grey. The real world is coloured, and somehow a black-and-white reproduction of slices of it is not enough to satisfy our appetite for more realism; hence, reproductions in books and magazines which use continuous and variable tone are often tinted with a colour overlay. Magenta is commonly used because it adds more depth to black, makes the in-between tones and highlights appear brighter, and thus makes it easier for the brain to associate tone with shapes and shapes with detail. Sepia tints, or reddish-brown tints, are sometimes added to CVT (continuous and variable tone) prints to evoke nostalgic emotions; the mind recognises instantly that older prints are often faded, tinged with yellow or brown. Colour washes added by hand are common. Why? Why is it that, for some, black-and-white prints can only be improved when colour is added? Are they hoping that, through some miracle of what is now fairly ancient technology, the print will evoke that same feeling one associates in confronting the exquisite and original work of a painter? A canvas heavy-laden with the rich pigments of oil, or a board thick with gouache?

Let us get a few things straight. The photographic print is not, never will be,

In the two contrasting examples of the use of two differing types of light it will be appreciated that the picture on p. 94 would have made an ideal subject for black-and-white photography. Contrast and texture of the subject are ideally suited to the medium, and would have worked well on a black-and-white print. To obtain the most dramatic effect, a yellow or orange filter should be used with a fine-grained, contrasty film like FP4 and the exposure compensated to take into account the texture visible in the highlight areas. Rate the film normally (ISO 125) and expose for the mid-tones only. A marginal reduction in development time (say 2–5 per cent) would prevent the highlights from blocking and provide adequate texture within them for printing on a high contrast paper.

In the right-hand picture it is the colour of the light (sky) which prompted the picture to be taken. There is no texture and no great variety of tonal value. In a black-and-white print, the whole essence of the idea would be lost. A long exposure on Fujichrome 50 changed the colour of the sky from a near orangey-purple to the contrasting blue and orange seen here.

never could be and never should be assimilated in any way, shape or form with the works of artists or other practitioners using a different medium to express their emotions or interpret images of the real world. A print is a print, a two-dimensional image of some thing, some person or what-have-you reproduced by way of employing various mechanical devices. A photograph may be labelled 'work of art'; photographs and photography may use the traditional values of art and its own historical background in forming and reproducing the image, but the result of the silver image process should never be claimed to have the quality of art. I know I am going to plunge suddenly into very deep water here, but I am prepared to take that risk on the grounds that it took a long time to discover, quite accidentally, that photography and art are poles apart. And I forgive the reviewer who once said of the front cover of one of my books that it looked like an 'oil painting'! Such are the misconceptions of life. Photography is a medium; making a decent print is a craft.

As everything we do in photography is in

some way, large or small, related to colour (even the safelights are coloured), in order to convert the image to CVT the photographer in the field must begin to think and see the image in a series of mono tones. This thought process must be unbroken as it continues through the negative development stage and on to the enlargement process.

What we are mainly concerned with from this point onward, through to the final print wash and the drying, is quality. Black-and-white printing in most professional jobbing darkrooms is a hit-and-miss affair primarily aimed at offering the customer a degree of adequacy, and when you know what 'ordinary' quality is possible using a little common sense and basic knowledge, why settle for less? With a little care and attention to the basic process of exposure, development, stop, fix, wash and dry, using commonly available materials, even the novice can make great prints.

A little later in this chapter, various paper and paper developers will be listed and discussed, but for the time being let us assume that stocks of any 'regular' type resin-coated paper in grade 2, 'regular' print developer, stop and fixer are available.

TEST-PRINTING

First select a negative for printing that looks normal, i.e. one with good tonal gradation, clearly identifiable regions of translucency (black in the print) and reasonably dense areas of silver (light in the print). Select a negative in which the subject matter is bold – portraits, buildings, cars or objects, rather than vague landscapes or vast areas of wilderness.

Turn on the enlarger and remove the negative carrier. Adjust the printing easel to the paper size in use, but for maximum effect in conducting a test of this type the larger the paper size the better. 10 × 8 in is a useful size for evaluation in ordinary white light.

Inspect the negative to be enlarged under the light of the enlarger by holding it away from the body in a horizontal position, emulsion-side-down to the baseboard. Remove any traces of dust by gently brushing

the surface with a squirrel-hair brush. If there are traces of wash water deposit, finger marks or other foreign matter, one of the following procedures can be used to clean the surface.

Take an empty glassine negative bag or six-strip glassine leaf and lay it on the easel. Place the dirty negative emulsion-side-down on the bag and, while holding it in place with the tips of two fingers on top and bottom perforations, or edges, wipe the surface gently in one direction with one of the following:

a) a moistened well-washed white cotton handkerchief;
b) the soft side of a fine chamois leather;
c) a well-washed white cotton handkerchief dipped in proprietary film cleaner;
d) carbon tetrachloride;
e) the softest underpart of a finger moistened on the tongue.

Always stroke the negative rather than grind it; when all traces of foreign matter are removed, polish the negative surface using a clean part of the same cloth or the finger.

Lift the negative off the glassine bag, turn it over and while holding it obliquely against the enlarger light inspect the emulsion surface. DO NOT rub or stroke this surface with anything other than a squirrel-hair brush. A compressed-air blower may be used. Most dust particles, even stubborn ones, can be removed using a brush. Scratches on the glossy protective base can sometimes be filled in by lightly rubbing them with the softest part of a finger which has been stroked against the side of the nose. The grease from the skin acts as a gap filler to scatter light passing through the scratch, thus making it less noticeable in the final print. Finally, once you are satisfied that the negative is as clean as it is ever likely to be, carefully hold one edge between thumb and forefinger of one hand and flick the other edge sharply with the nail of the index finger of the other. This is a practised technique which relieves the negative of any stored or accumulated static electricity, which if allowed to remain will attract more dust as soon as the negative is positioned in the enlarger. Tapping the edge of the negative sharply against the easel will have the same effect. Now position the negative in the carrier and adjust the magnification and fine focus until the 10 × 8 in area is covered with exactly the portion of negative to be printed. It is important at this stage to ensure that image-cropping and picture-sizing is carried out as if the print were to be the final archive copy. Its success will depend on accurate exposure and development and any assessment made on the basis of a shoddy test will only tend to extend time spent in the darkroom.

The next step is to take the base of an empty paper box (10 × 8 in) and carefully cut off the raised parts until you have a piece of flat, matt black card. It must be black on both sides. Daler card purchased from an art shop which is blacked on both sides is quite suitable and has the advantage of being cut to any desired shape. Without paper in the easel, turn off the safelight closest to the enlarger and run a short, say 5-second, exposure. This will give you some idea of how the enlarged image looks when you stand slightly back from it. It is a good idea to repeat this procedure as many times as you feel inclined, even if it makes you feel like a lemon. The idea is that, by concentrating on the 5-second exposure, the negative image, its density and contrast values will form more clearly in your mind. After a while, and after you have successfully made many prints without too many failures, you will begin to recognise instinctively how certain negative images can be improved, either by holding back parts of the image (giving less exposure) or burning-in (giving more exposure). Do not worry too much about that now, though, there is more on these techniques later. What I want you to do for the moment is to learn to use your mind as if it were a camera, exposing the images in slow motion so they actually print on the mind. You may find that other safelights are still too bright and reduce your ability to concentrate. If that is the case, turn them off. In time, you will be able to leave most of them on.

Now reset the enlarger timer to say 3 seconds. Adjust the lens aperture two stops down. If you are using an f4 lens, stop it down to f8. If the enlarged image looks too dark, i.e. virtually indiscernible, open up one full stop to f5.6. With the timer off, insert a sheet of paper into the easel. Lay the black card over the image at right angles to it leaving a 1-inch (2.5-cm) gap at the right-hand side. Each time you make a 3-second exposure, the gap will be increased by a further inch (2.5 cm) until you have completed 10 steps across the paper, or 8 steps if the image is vertical (portrait style) rather than horizontal (landscape). Now begin the exposure sequence. Take your time. Move the card, *after* each exposure is complete, to the new position.

When this test exposure is finished, return the sheet of paper to a *safe* box. You can use an empty paper box for this purpose. Then take another sheet of unexposed paper, fold it diagonally and cut along the fold. Insert one half into the easel and position as if it were a whole sheet. Do not forget to return the unexposed half to the paper box. Now lay the black card along the diagonal edge of the paper, leaving a $\frac{1}{2}$-inch (13-mm) gap. Begin the exposure sequence again using the same time as above. Move the card the same distance at the end of each exposure until the whole half-sheet has been exposed.

Return this exposed paper to the safe. Now move to the wet bench area and check that all three solutions, developer, stop and fix are of even temperature. This should be one of a range of temperatures recommended by the manufacturer. 21 °C (70 °F) is a useful working temperature. Note the maximum development time, and if you have a darkroom wall clock above the wet bench set this time on it. If not, use a watch or conventional darkroom timer. Take the exposed full 10 × 8 in sheet and place in the developer tray face down, simultaneously drawing it through the solution, and quickly turn it emulsion-side-up. Start the clock immediately. Agitate the dish evenly by lifting each corner alternately. Keep an eye on the time; 15 seconds before time is up, take hold of one corner of the paper, begin lifting and drain for 10 seconds. Swiftly transfer to the stop bath for half a minute and then into the fix. Agitate vigorously for the first 15 seconds and then gently keep the print on the move for a further minute.

Repeat the same procedure with the second half-sheet of paper. When the fix time is up, lift and drain, and transfer to the wash. Resin-coated paper only needs a minute at most in running water, so you should be able to remove these test strips to a white light area very quickly. While you are waiting for the wash to complete, check that all unexposed paper is carefully repacked and sealed. You should always make a habit of doing this *before* turning on any white light. It will save a lot of frayed tempers in the long term.

ANALYSIS

Although it is not absolutely necessary to dry the prints before viewing, if you have never made a test print before, make the effort to dry these two off before laying them face-up on a convenient display area. Use a rubber-blade squeegee to remove the surplus water after draining, and then hang the prints in an airing cupboard using two plastic pegs on a piece of line, if you do not own a print dryer. Hang each print from a corner. Properly squeegeed prints will dry in a few minutes. RC papers curl when air-dried, but distort when overdried. If placed on a cold surface after the normal drying time has elapsed, the paper will gradually assume its normal flat state.

The test strips should show clearly delineated steps of exposure increases in strips. The top one, the one you started the exposure sequence with, will be almost black throughout its entire range of tones. There may be some highlight detail just visible. It will be fairly obvious that neither this nor the next step will be close to the ideal exposure required. As you proceed down the steps, the ones closest to the middle of the 10 × 8 in sheet will show a marked improvement in tonal values. Select the one which is about

Here colour is the key to the picture. Try to imagine this in black-and-white.

midway and then each one up and down the scale either side of it. You will notice that parts of the print in all three strips will look just right, and other parts may look a fraction heavy or a shade too light.

Make a mental note of the exposure times of each of the three steps, which, if you used 3 seconds to start with, will be that figure multiplied by the step number calculated from the first step, i.e. Step 5 × 3 seconds = 15 seconds.

Now take the half-sheet which was exposed diagonally. Find the same exposure value strips as the three selected on the full frame print. Look carefully at the highlights and the shadows and compare one with the other. You should, by now, be able to make fairly accurate subjective decisions with regard to the way in which each separate tone is manifested. It is up to you to decide whether detail in the shadow area is important and if so in what direction. Will the overall effect be better if the shadow detail is eliminated, particularly near the print threshold, or better if more detail is visible? If the answer to the latter is yes, look again and see if there is enough detail to print and whether this shows on the test steps at the minimum

exposure end of the scale. Next, look at the highlight end. If the negative has been properly exposed, i.e. if you made the exposure having previously judged the tonal value required for the highlight areas, definite areas of bright white should be visible within the upper end of the tonal range.

If the negative exposure was based on a TTL average of the scene, the chances are that tones in the highlight region will appear to run together in the test strips selected for inspection. In the strips where maximum print exposure has been given, the light areas at the very top of the brightness range may be quite clearly delineated, even if they appear to be more grainy and less sharp than other darker areas. More subjective application is needed here to help decide which parts of the negative are important to print with more or less exposure. Taking the three basic exposure times for each selected step in the areas required will tell you exactly how much more or less exposure must be given for those areas.

Now look at the mid-tones. Are all of these satisfactory? Is detail clearly visible in this, the main part of the picture? Is there any area here which could be improved by more or less exposure? A useful accessory in establishing which parts of a print need further manipulation is a yellow chinagraph pencil. The areas concerned are ringed or marked more carefully so they can be identified on the test print when new prints are being exposed. Write the exposure times of relevant steps on the back of the print with a felt-tip.

To assess how much more, or less, exposure will be necessary, first calculate from the test print the basic exposure required for the mid-tones of the print. Remember that you will be developing all prints from now on by time and temperature, until the day comes when you can actually assess what is emerging under the developer. Note the areas of the print where further work is to be carried out. That means make a physical note on paper and include the additional time:

main exposure ± difference of the required
step tone

or time reduction.

PRINTING METHOD

At this point, we are not concerned with

paper contrast, brightness range or colour when processed and dried. Colour of CVT papers is frequently described by the ability of that paper to produce 'neutral', 'warm' or 'cold' tones.

The main requirement is to produce an acceptable print, a print in which the subject matter is presented with sufficient impact. This aim is defined as follows:

a) the subject matter is clearly defined and identifiable;
b) the print gradation flows from rich black to white paper base with clear delineation of mid-tones (if any);
c) the subjective intention is clear;
d) the presentation is faultless.

We are not interested in showing prints which:

a) are clearly over-exposed and under-developed;
b) appear as a collection of mud-coloured tones: no whites, no black and nothing much in between;
c) are speckled with foreign matter appearing as irregular white dots, hairlines etc.,

Singer Felice Taylor. Nikon F, 105 mm, Tri-X rated at ISO 650 and processed in D-76 full strength for 8 minutes. Available stage light. Printed on a grade 4 paper and burned in around the edges.

Table 5: PAPER GRADES AND THEIR CHARACTERISTICS

Paper grade	Negative characteristic					
	very thin	thin	normal	dense	very dense	match with
0 = very soft					*	very contrasty
1 = soft				*		contrasty
2 = normal			*			normal
3 = hard		*				soft
4 = extremely hard	*					very soft

Grade	Paper characteristic
0 = very soft	Produces softly-graded grey-looking prints.
1 = soft	Produces well-graded prints from normal negatives but paper characteristic varies with maker.
2 = normal	Good tonal range from normal contrast negatives, but some grade 2 papers are equal to other grade 3.
3 = hard	Produces contrastier image. More snap to blacks and whites, slight merging of in-between tones.
4 = extremely hard	Soot and whitewash from normal negatives. Good blacks and whites, fewer in-between tones. For 'thin' negatives where subject warrants.

which have collected on the negative or in the negative carrier.

Part of the key to success relies on the following:

a) the ability to recognise a good negative, i.e. one that contains all the requirements of exposure and development previously discussed;

b) the ability to assess correct print exposure at a glance, to within half a second;

c) the ability to match paper contrast grade to negative on a subjective basis without regard to technical accuracy, i.e. the finished print can be visualised, EXCEPT when the print is required for reproduction by a process known to produce a result equal to the desired print effect − in this case, the print becomes part of an ongoing process and must be exposed and developed accordingly;

d) a disciplined approach to print-making − each stage should be carried out methodically until it becomes second nature.

Notice that, in (*b*) above, I have made a point of not making any reference to mechanical or electronic exposure aids in printing. You will learn more, more rapidly, by taking the trouble to make a test strip as already described. Some readers may find this approach contradictory. After all, quite a large proportion of funds invested in camera equipment covers the cost of expensive in-camera or hand-held light meters with which to measure negative exposures accurately. Why do without similar equipment in the darkroom?

Print exposure meters of any kind, provided they can be relied upon to work accurately, are very useful and I would certainly not recommend that you be without one. However, until you have learned to print without one, there is very little a print exposure meter can teach you. They are invaluable time-saving aids when many negatives of different contrast have to be printed quickly, but as most meters of this type are either linked electrically to the enlarger, or give a numerical read-out which is then transferred to the main timer, my experience is that they are practically useless as teaching aids. I would even go so far as to say that, in the wrong hands, information assessed by such meters can be positively misleading.

Assessment of exposure time for the print is based on three factors:

a) the average negative contrast;
b) the degree of enlarger magnification of the negative to baseboard image;
c) the 'f' stop required on the enlarger lens.

Ideal exposure can range from 1 to 30 seconds. When a negative requires a full minute or more to produce a fully developed print image, beware. Exposures of more than this time are perfectly possible, of course, especially when floor-thrown magnifications are being used to make a much larger than normal print. But if we take 10 × 8 in as being a nominal average size, the exposure for a 'normally graded' negative will be relatively short.

For purely practical assessment, it will be obvious that a 'thin' negative, i.e. one that is less dense, will require less exposure time than the one which appears to be darker or more dense. However, a negative which appears to have larger areas of translucency may not necessarily be 'thin'. Closer

Simple burning-in techniques involve the use of hands or a piece of black card in which a small oval-shaped hole has been cut. In the first picture a straight print with no burning or dodging produced a fairly flat result lacking depth. In the second a hand used to burn-in the large areas of sea and sky has produced a much more acceptable result. Burning and dodging techniques also employ the use of matt acetate sheet, lipstick and chinagraph pencils to achieve the desired effect. Control using hands, fingers and black card cut-outs is very effective for most work and not difficult to master.

inspection may reveal parts of the negative which have been correctly exposed and which will, given the right treatment, print perfectly on a normal grade of paper.

See if you have two negatives in which the subject matter has been rendered correctly. One should be a general scene with a good range of tones, the other should have very few tones.

Compare both negatives on a light box or suitable illuminated source. Look closely at the lightest highlight areas under a magnifying glass. (If you do not possess an inspection glass, remove the 50 mm standard lens from your camera, hold the rear element close to the eye and the front element almost touching the negative.) Make a mental note of the apparent density of the highlight areas in both negatives. If they look similar – an accurate check is difficult without the aid of a densitometer – then both will print acceptably on the same grade of paper.

If, however, the apparently thin negative is obviously less black in its highlight areas (less silver deposit), this is going to print as a darker shade of grey, given the same

exposure and same grade of paper as the other negative. Because of under-exposure in the camera, or too little development, or both, the negative has insufficient contrast range to print correctly on a normal grade of paper. Paper contrast, therefore, will have to be increased to allow for the contrast reduction in the negative.

Several things happen when paper contrast is lifted to higher than normal, but first Table 5 shows a range of paper grades and in addition matching types of negatives which can normally be made to print on them.

In general practice, selection of the correct paper type and grade, and attention to accurate exposure and development technique, will allow the photographer a great deal of latitude in making acceptable prints. As you will see from the summary chart, some paper manufacturers make grades of paper which, although numerically equal to other makes, actually produce a different result. If, as I do, you are prepared to experiment with different makes, you will find after a process of elimination which are most suitable for your

In this picture, both burning and dodging techniques were used to even the overall density of the main image while retaining some recognisable detail in the background. The middle and lower right-hand side of the print were shaded during exposure and slightly more exposure than normal was given to the upper left portion to reduce the flare effect.

4) If there is any doubt, use a normal grade of paper and make a test print as already described.

5) Density and contrast are NOT the same. Over-exposure and normal development, and over-development and normal exposure, can both produce negatives which *look* dense. The former may be less contrasty than the latter.

6) As a general rule, thin negatives of normal contrast will print well on normal to hard grades of paper. Thin negatives which lack contrast print better on hard or extra-hard grades. Dense negatives of normal contrast print well on softer papers, but dense negatives that lack contrast will print better on normal to hard grades.

7) A negative which is excessively thin or excessively dense may not print acceptably on any grade of paper. Chemical manipulation using an intensifying or reducing formula may be necessary before the negative will produce an adequate print. I make a habit of dumping negatives which fall into either of these two categories. They are invariably the result of sloppy workmanship and attention to detail in exposure, and are frankly not worth the effort. Exceptions to that rule of course are earth-shattering news events where only one negative exists.

The sub-heading to this section on printing included the word METHOD. Everything that you do in the darkroom must follow clear-cut routines. For example, you will find little mention in this following sequence of print tongs. These instruments are rather like miniaturised old-fashioned laundry tongs that Grandmother used when she was boiling the clothes in a cauldron. Tongs are useful if:

a) you are used to using them;
b) you are allergic to the chemical compounds used in photographic solutions;
c) you don't like getting your hands wet.

(*a*) and (*b*) are good reasons for using tongs. (*c*) is not.

My darkroom is arranged so that, during and at the end of each develop, stop and fix

style of photography and certain specific requirements, i.e. for newsprint, magazine or book reproduction.

Before attempting to make a first-time, first-class print from the test negative, here is a short re-cap on several points discussed so far.

1) Before mixing any chemical solutions for developing and fixing the print, assess the contrast, sharpness and density of the negative.

2) Use the paper characteristic summary to select a grade of paper on which the negative will give the desired result.

3) Remember: if the negative lacks contrast, choose a harder grade of paper; if the negative appears too contrasty, choose a normal-soft range of paper.

To establish just how much burning and shading would be required for the final picture, I first made a 'thin' print on Ilfospeed grade 3 (top left). This enabled me to see clearly any detail in shadow areas which might need to be retained in the final print. Next (top right) I made a print with more or less correct highlights. I used the exposure for this as my guide for the final print. Shading and dodging were carried out with fingers and hands in steps, completing one side and then top and bottom of the print (bottom left). Finally, I chose a grade 4 to give better whites against the darker areas and shaded more under the horse and behind the rider's head to bring them out of the picture (bottom right).

sequence, I can reach over and give my hands a thorough swill in fresh running water. Clean dry towels are kept handy at all times, and provided a meticulous and disciplined approach to this part of the operation is applied prints will not be marked and you will be unlikely to end up with badly stained fingers. The alternative is to wear surgical gloves, but you will still have to rinse your hands in between and after each stage.

BURNING-IN OR HOLDING-BACK

There is one more thing before we actually get down to making the print. During the analysis of the test prints, I mentioned that parts of the negative may require more or less exposure than the main part. This is called burning-in or holding-back. There are a variety of methods by which this exposure technique is carried out, and these include the use of specially made 'dodging' tools, shapes of black card stuck on the ends of lengths of piano wire or translucent plastic strips; holes cut or torn in squares of black card, identi-shapes which correspond to that part of the negative to be held back during printing, and so on. All of these items you can make yourself from sheets of black paper used to inter-leaf cut film, double-sided black card, empty paper boxes; just about any gash item that comes to hand which is inherently black or which can be blacked with matt black paint.

Except on very odd occasions, most of my own burning-in and holding-back is done

This fire scene was shot with a 200 mm Nikkor lens on Tri-X through a medium yellow-orange filter, and developed in dilute D-76. The print was made on a grade 3 paper and required some careful burning in the smoke areas to achieve the right effect. Because of the shape of the subject this was quite easily done using the hand in a scooping and circular manner.

tive that will obviously be over-exposed. You must keep the hand on the move at all times, but you can count out the number of seconds in units of a thousand as you go. With practice, you will become quite adept at this technique, being able to tell more or less instinctively when the time is up.

Burning-in can also be done with the hands by allowing extra light to pass through a couple of fingers while the rest of the hand blanks off the negative area which has already received enough exposure. Using thumb and forefinger to make a small hole for light to pass through is another method which, when practised efficiently, can help to improve a print very quickly without having to revert to other, more complicated methods.

PRINTING

Well, now that you have established more or less what the main exposure for the first print will be, make a note of the areas to be given more or less exposure. Load the negative back into the enlarger, open the lens diaphragm and switch on ready to focus.

Switch off the closest safelight, or all of them if you feel more comfortable working with the enlarger light source only. Satisfy yourself that the composition on the easel is the most suitable for the subject. If not, readjust enlarger magnification and coarse focus.

If you are using a condenser source enlarger and glassless negative carrier, there is a fairly good chance that, during the course of the time it takes to focus accurately the negative image, the negative will buckle under the heat created in the lamphouse; this will be especially noticeable when no heat shield is used. If the enlarger is now turned off, the negative will assume its pre-focus shape as soon as the lamphouse begins to cool. This will happen quite rapidly, certainly within the space of time it will take for you to extract a sheet of paper from the box and fit it into the print easel. When you have made the exposure and the print is processed, it will appear to be out of focus.

You can get round this problem to a

with a square or rectangle of black paper or card, usually an interleaf from a box of cut film; the centre has a hole about $\frac{1}{4}$-inch (6 mm) in diameter cut, torn or punched. It helps sometimes if the hole is oval in shape with ragged, torn edges.

When I am not using this method, I use my hands and fingers for a little local and often very discreet holding-back, just a few seconds taken out of the main exposure to keep more detail in some shadow areas. This is not an unusual technique and is used by just about every newspaper printer with a degree of flair that would confound even the slickest magician.

Begin by trying just a few fingers. Imagine that you are holding a shallow plate and that you are scooping water out of a garden tub. That is the action you need to practise. Just allow the fingers or whole hand to come into the image area; as it does so, it is scooping away excess light reaching parts of the nega-

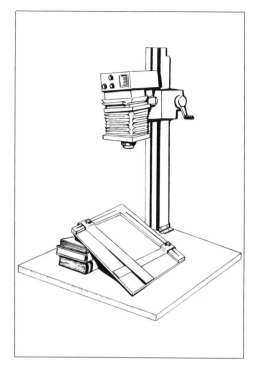

The most common cause of vertical distortion, particularly in architectural photography, is caused by fixed-axis lenses. Some correction can be effected using the time-proven method of raising the easel at one end on a pile of books. More control can be obtained from enlargers utilising a swinging head and negative carrier. Distortion in the accompanying photograph, however, was deliberately employed at the time of exposure.

certain extent by using the built-in enlarger safelight. Simply swing this in place in front of the lens while paper is extracted from the box and placed in the easel. Once ready to expose, turn off the focus switch, slide the safelight away from the light path and begin the exposure. If repeat prints are to be made at any time, simply check the focus before each sheet of paper is exposed. There is more about this in Chapter 9, where techniques in exposing and processing long print-runs are discussed.

To check the focus of any negative accurately a really good-quality grain image magnifier is essential, particularly if you are using medium- or larger-format negatives which are medium- or fine-grained. Do not rely on subject detail, although if you are using an adjustable glass carrier the edge of a negative is often a useful guide to sharpness.

Once you are certain that the easel image is sharp, swing the enlarger safelight into place, or switch the timer from focus to time. Now take a sheet of paper and place it in the easel. Set the time ready to start the exposure. Remember that this will form the main exposure for the print, but parts of the image

may need to be held back and/or burned in. Start the clock and simultaneously bring your hand scooping in to the area which needs less exposure. Do not worry about the rest of the image; it will not move while you are manipulating the exposure. Count, not too fast, '1000, 2000, 3000' and so on until you think that the shaded part has been obscured long enough. DO NOT jog the enlarger bench or touch the easel once the main exposure has begun. Now take a square of card with a hole rough cut or torn out of the centre. Hold this horizontally just below the enlarger lens with the hole in the card to one side of the image axis. Re-start the timer.

You will see the image on the card now. Carefully manoeuvre the hole towards the part to be burned-in. Simultaneously begin to move the card in eccentric circles. Now look for the part of the image being exposed on the paper. Move the card to areas of the negative which still require more exposure, making a mental note, if these areas fall on the edge of the frame, to give those parts a really good dose. It is absolutely essential to keep the card moving all the time the negative is being exposed.

Do not worry overmuch at this stage that the print may be over-exposed in these areas now being treated. Complete one full cycle of the re-exposure time (same as the main exposure). Because the card is continuously being moved about, these areas will in fact receive a lot less exposure than the overall exposure.

When you are satisfied that the print has received sufficient overall exposure to give the effect you want, return the exposed paper to a safe box. Switch on the darkroom safelight and check the temperatures of all chemicals and wash water. Developer temperature is not too critical, provided it is kept within a certain range: $20-24\,°C\ (68-75\,°F)$ is practical. When print developer temperatures are increased above or decreased below this range, the colour tone of the print will be affected. Cold developer works sluggishly, forcing extended development times and risking stains on the print, particularly if the solution has been standing around for any time. Keep the stop bath and the fixing solution within the same working temperature range.

Resin-coated papers are normally fully developed in about a minute and a half at $20\,°C$ $(68\,°F)$. Try to stick to the manufacturer's recommended times; if you extend them because the print is obviously not developed within that time frame, something is wrong.

Remove the exposed paper from the safe box and insert in the developer as already described in the section on making a test print. Swiftly pull it through the developer and turn emulsion-side-up. If you prefer, take the exposed paper by the middle of the longest side, hold one side of the tray an inch off the bench and place the opposite edge of the paper on the raised side of the tray. Lay the paper flat in the developer as the tray is smartly lowered. As soon as it is covered with solution, turn the print over, emulsion-side-down. Now start the timer and begin agitation. Every one has a sort of habitual agitation sequence, but if you are starting from scratch try to adopt the procedure of raising each corner of the tray in alternate rotation.

After 30 seconds have elapsed, turn the print emulsion-side-up, if it is not already. If your exposure was correct, the print image should be clearly visible and developing rapidly in the shadow areas. After one minute, the print may look as if it is going to over-develop. Allow the development time to complete, and then, 10 seconds before time is up, remove the print by a corner, drain and transfer to the stop bath. Give it a fairly rapid and vigorous rinse here for 30 seconds and then drain again and transfer to the fix. Give more vigorous agitation for the first 15 seconds and then rock the tray gently for a further minute. You will now be able to remove the print to the wash, rinse, drain and inspect it under white light.

Do not be disappointed when you inspect the print under ordinary room lighting if it is not quite right. However, if your original negative selection and subsequent test prints were fairly accurate, the print you are now inspecting should be very acceptable. If the main areas of the print look right, make a close inspection of the areas which you held back and burned in. This is invariably where further work will have to be done if you are a perfectionist and intend to get the print right. If you are reasonably satisfied that you have made progress, even if another print has to be made, you will have achieved a lot. Prepare to start the same procedure over again making absolutely certain as far as possible that you follow the same sequence as before. It cannot be over-emphasised that it is essential at this early stage to adopt a disciplined method whereby all future prints will be made using the same technique.

8
Other Black-and-White Techniques and Print Materials

If processing is the most tedious part of photography, then printing must rate as the most exciting occupation next to using the camera. In some cases, no doubt, it takes precedence over even that. 'That's a fine assumption to make,' I can hear the wailing from some quarters. And I do sympathise, to a certain extent, with those who for various reasons cannot seem to produce the nearly-perfect print.

The apprenticeship to print-making is often long and pock-marked with disasters. With the benefit of hindsight, I can look back on my own career and pinpoint exactly where those disasters took place. More to the point, I know now why they occurred: lack of knowledge. Lack of knowledge about materials and the application of same; concerning the technicalities of original exposure; concerning the chemical properties of certain materials and how they were likely to react to certain chemicals, to certain lighting techniques; and about many other things.

Ultimately, it is only by dint of application of all the knowledge that you gain that producing acceptable work becomes a little easier, though I still do not profess to know nearly as much as I would like. So make note of your mistakes, be patient and try to develop as much style in the darkroom as you do out in the field with your camera. It will come together in time.

So far, exposure and contrast have been discussed at length. The more technically minded may advise the photographer that printing papers must be accurately matched to negatives, and in fact I have even been told on more than one occasion that this is the only acceptable way to make a print. My methods make use of a modicum of knowledge regarding contrast and the levels to which print contrast can be manipulated

irrespective of the negative contrast.

The reasoning for this is quite simple: 99.9 per cent of my work is produced entirely for reproduction around the world in a variety of publications. Some publishers use widely different printing techniques, from hot lead letterpress of appalling quality, lithography and web offset processes, through to fine art gravure using etched copper plates. All of these reproduction processes take a different approach to the technique of *origination*, the method by which photographs are processed onto film or metal blocks for eventual transfer to the printing plate. The final reproduction is made with ink which is a very different medium to the one photographers use. In order to get the best possible reproduction using ink from a photograph, a number of other processes are necessary, and all of these have inherent characteristics which, if allowed, will distort the photographer's images. To combat this (not always successfully), certain tolerances must be incorporated into the print at the darkroom stage. For this reason, I doubt whether any of the thousands of prints kept on file in my picture library would ever qualify to be hung as exhibition prints.

A really good graphic arts technician will no doubt dispute my argument on the grounds that 'what is not in the original cannot be reproduced'. That assumes that if everything which should be in the photographic print is, it should be possible to reproduce it on paper using ink. It is possible to make very accurate reproductions of original prints, but only using the finest gravure process. Most ordinary lithographic processes are totally incompatible and are subject to an enormous range of potentially troublesome errors, not least of which is that, when the machine-minder goes for tea, there is an even

how far I can push a print exposure and nearly boil it in developer to get a rapid print. But it is as much the method by which these various techniques are utilised which helps to keep a degree of control over what is going on.

For example, I know that the print developer is way above the normally practicable temperature range. To get rich blacks and fully developed highlights in double-quick time, the paper is given a heavy exposure, dunked in the developer for a few seconds, and then whipped out into a basin full of cold water as soon as the blacks in the image begin to appear. This sudden dive in temperature slows down the development process but allows it to continue in the brighter areas. By the time I have finished swilling the print around, the image is nearly complete. Back into the developer for a final few seconds and then stop and fix normally.

If I make a marginal over-exposure and, instead of using an acid stop bath, use plain water, I can process up to a dozen or so 10×8 in prints of the same subject, simultaneously. Hot and cold water baths can also be used to manipulate the paper image using normal exposures, to help intensify highlight areas and reduce the development action in shadow areas. Keep a basin of each in fairly close proximity to the developer so that, whenever necessary, prints can be fished out of the developer and quickly dunked.

chance that ink levels will change, sometimes dramatically.

When (rather than if) there is time and I can spend a few uninterrupted hours in the darkroom alone, I find that enormous amounts of energy are expended in getting the print right.

How do I know when it is right? When it looks right. This is a totally subjective evaluation loosely tied to knowledge of acceptably printable contrast ranges and so on. The actual process of producing a print, however, is fairly meticulous, with each stage of the operation closely monitored to ensure that unnecessary wastage of paper and chemicals does not occur.

When there is very little time and prints have to be got out rapidly, I adopt a different approach. This is also based on a sound knowledge of material capability, knowing

Such methods are frequently frowned upon by more academic technicians, but I can assure you that these practices work when called for. One needs a degree of deftness and a little elementary experience to take full advantage, though I do not advocate use of the practice on a continuous basis. Try to make your exposures accurate in the beginning and utilise the time and temperature method to its fullest extent. Enhancement techniques such as those described are put into practice when: *a*) speed is of the essence; *b*) normal processing methods fail to produce the desired result.

There are, of course, other methods by which prints may be made. The traditional tray method is convenient if you have a large

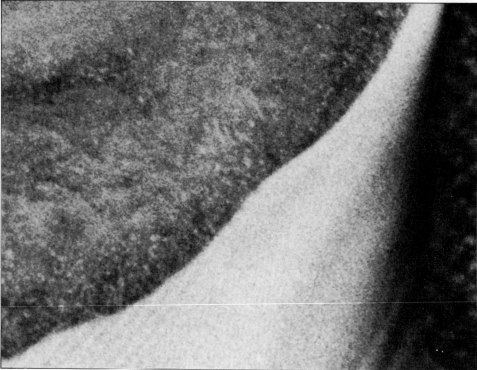

The effect of grain in fairly small reproductions and prints from 35 mm negatives is not easily seen by the unaided eye. Used large, or printed large, grain patterns become more noticeable, but any unpleasant side-effect may be just as easily overlooked by the viewer if the subject matter and compositional presentation is good enough. Different development techniques, particularly the method adopted for agitation, push processing and so on, whether large or small tank, will all have an effect on the resulting print. In this picture Tri-X was exposed on a bleak wintry day at 400 ISO and developed in diluted D-76 to give a fairly thin negative which printed well on grade 3. Grain structure is barely noticeable and quite acceptable in the original 12 × 10 inch print. Note enlarged section.

enough bench space and, despite the claims of the manufacturers of some automatic print processors, large quantities of prints can be tray-processed very rapidly and often more economically.

Just recently I have had the pleasure of using one of the relatively new *Nova Print Processors*. This is a simple plastic tank with integral water-jacket and thermostat to control the temperature of processing solutions. A unique paper clip allows the operator to agitate each print while avoiding the hands-on technique. The makers claim that it is possible to process up to thirty 10 × 8s in an hour, though I must admit that I have yet to prove that. Its greatest asset, however, has nothing to do with throughput, but lies in the tiny amount of space it occupies. Provided that print exposures are accurate and you have a tried and tested time and temperature method, the Nova is undoubtedly one of the most convenient print-processing methods available.

In addition, the tank can also be used for colour processing and in fact was primarily

This print was made from two-thirds of a 6 × 6 cm negative, shot on HP5 with Bronica EC and Planar standard lens. Developer was HC110. The right-hand picture shows an enlarged section in which it is apparent that grain structure is more fragmented and clumped than in the preceding illustration. This is equivalent to a 12 times enlargement of a 35 mm negative and proves beyond any reasonable doubt that 'apparent' sharpness is not only relative to the ratio of enlargement and format size. Developer type, method of application, resolution ability of exposing objective, filter quality, atmospheric conditions at time of exposure, light quality and choice of film, all play an important part in establishing absolute 'sharpness' – i.e. the point at which the recorded negative image visibly begins to deteriorate.

designed for that purpose. It is certainly economic in use and makes a lot less mess than conventional methods. A print-washer of similar construction can be used in tandem with the processing tank. The whole set-up utilises about the same amount of space as the area of a single 16 × 20 in tray, so anyone working under the stairs or in a loft/attic conversion where space is at a premium would certainly benefit from the Nova system. One other point in its favour is that mixed solutions tend to keep longer when not in use, provided the water-jacket temperature is maintained. Even a heavily concentrated developer mix left in a tray overnight begins to deteriorate quite rapidly when temperatures fall. With the Nova, I have been able to carry on processing after a gap of several hours without any noticeable deterioration in print quality.

Automatic print processors using the activator-stabilisation process have largely been superseded by a system which uses conventional replenishment developer and fix solutions in conjunction with some resin-coated materials. The early Agfa and Ilfoprint methods and machines are gradually being phased out, although at the time of writing paper, chemicals and machines were still available from Ilford, who had no immediate plans to discontinue the line.

For sheer convenience, though, and at the cost of some sacrifice in print quality, it cannot be beaten. From my miniature Ilfoprint machine, I can produce a damp dry print that is fully stabilised, from exposure to white light, in a matter of seconds. Exposure is fairly critical; there is not the latitude one has even when using resin-coated materials in tray-processing. The other main disadvantage is that prints are only partially fixed-stabilised. They do not like exposure to ultra-violet or very strong fluorescent or tungsten light, and if left lying around the workroom for a week or less soon begin to change colour. To maintain proper permanence, stabilisation prints should be fixed in the normal manner on exit from the machine, and then washed and dried. To me, that additional process somewhat negates the ad-

vantage of rapid machine processing where usually the only requirement is for a print of reasonable quality that can be used as a proof, placed on a wire transmission machine or handed to a client for more or less immediate reproduction. Once the art of exposure has been mastered, it is possible to make prints of very good quality; some of the illustrations used in this book are examples.

The professional with a large throughput of CVT – black-and-white – material will do well to consider alternative processors such as the Ilfospeed black-and-white model, the Metoform 5040, or those manufactured by Kreonite Ltd. There are many other manufacturers of auto print processors in the UK, Europe and in the USA, including some small units which are suitable for amateur usage. Ilford are currently working on development plans for a small benchtop processor of the Ilfospeed type for resin-coated materials and once this is available (possibly about the time of publication of this book) many darkrooms currently using conventional tray-processing for smaller print volumes could easily benefit. Until now, apart from the stabilisation processors, the choice of benchtop resin-coated machines has largely been out of reach of the amateur due to investment cost. Ilford's machine, a prototype of which was shown at Photokina in 1984, may well rectify that position.

Of the three mentioned above which are already available, I would say that certainly the most versatile is the METOFORM 5040 which is made by Meteor-Siegen in West Germany. This is an extremely sophisticated machine capable of processing all resin-coated black-and-white papers with a throughput of up to 120 10 × 8s an hour. In addition the machine can be used for colour negative and reversal print processing. As one might expect with all automated machinery of this nature, investment costs are high, but in the long term so too are the savings in time.

PAPERS

The resurgence of interest in black-and-white photography over the last decade has

This shows approximately half of a 10 × 8 print from the full frame of a 35 mm Tri-X negative exposed through a 24 mm Nikkor lens without filter. The film was processed in a Kreonite auto film processor for a rating of 800. In the enlarged section, grain structure and image disintegration is clearly seen, even though the recorded image remains sharp.

led to an unprecedented re-introduction and re-structuring of papers that were once considered obsolete by modern photographic standards. I suppose much of the interest in this medium stems from the fact that, as far as the amateur is concerned, black-and-white affords the user so much more control than colour photography (and is one reason why at least two thirds of this book is devoted to the former). In my humble opinion, it is the very lack of manipulative control as well as the materials used to render the image which makes colour photography so unexciting. It is of course perfectly possible to manipulate colour in colour photography, but the result is invariably a lack-lustre *effect* that is frequently inferior in both quality and depth to the effect which it is possible to achieve with black-and-white. This, of course, is aside from all the other factors which influence taste and the stirring of deep emotions. But more of that later.

Resin-coated (RC) papers as we know them were originally introduced by manufacturers for a variety of reasons, not least of which, one suspects, was the consideration of a bigger profit when all the other factors – handling convenience and speed of processing – were noted. As I am one of those lucky photographers who began a career at a time when the general availability of RC papers was not a threat to quality, it must be said that, on the whole, those two factors, handling convenience and super processing speeds, are about the only things that RC papers have to their advantage. The ability to produce a print of sophisticated tonal quality or even sharpness is not one of its strong points, so if your pleasure is exhibition quality do not even think about RC; conventional fibre-based papers are what you need.

RC paper is made up using a layer of paper which is coated both sides with a synthetic polymer – usually polyethylene. This forms the base onto which the emulsion is coated. As the base is virtually impervious to water and does not, like fibre-based papers, act like a sponge, development and fixing times are much faster. Washing and drying times are equally rapid, for the same reason, whereas to remove all traces of hypo from conventional papers lengthy wash times are necessary.

In making a choice as to which type of paper might be more suitable for general use, several factors need consideration.

1) The facilities available for washing and drying prints.
2) Fibre-based papers can be air-dried, but are better glazed using a ferrotype, highly polished stainless or chromed steel plate. The quality of a drum-glazed glossy-fibre print is far superior to any resin-coated paper. Motorised drum driers are no longer readily available; one can only hope that they will become so. Flat-bed heated driers can be used, but accurate thermostatic temperature control should be provided. Cheap models simply bake the print which shrinks the paper and distorts the tonal values of the image.
3) Fibre-based papers need large volumes of water for effective washing. This can be reduced, however, when a washing aid such as that manufactured by Paterson is used. Single weight papers need a minimum of 30 minutes and double weight at least double that time for non-aided washing to remove at least 90 per cent of chemicals retained in the paper base.
4) RC papers can be washed in a few minutes, squeegeed and air-dried or dried rapidly in a hot-air blower type machine (see Chapter 2).

PAPER TONE

CHLORO-BROMIDE

This is paper type using a mixture of silver salts of bromide and chloride to give an image tone from warm black to reddish brown, depending on length of exposure, type, length and dilution of developer. Fixing is more critical with these papers than with ordinary bromide. Rapid fixers with hardeners can be used, but the clearing time should not exceed that recommended by the maker – usually 5 minutes. If the time is greatly extended, the silver image is attacked and dissolves out of the paper. Exposure latitude is superb and development time can be as long as ten minutes in some developers. Paper speed is about a quarter to a half that of ordinary bromide.

BROMIDE

This gives a neutral to cold black tone which is only slightly affected by development type and technique. Fibre-based papers are capable of immensely superior quality to that of RC papers. Paper speed varies with the make, as does contrast. An interesting point here, though, is that one or two photographic magazines have made observations regarding different paper makes after conducting so-called 'tests', and in one I noted that two papers of a different but popular alternative label were given different results. On checking my own files I discovered that both papers were manufactured by one of the two packet trade names who told me that the 'other' was the same as their own, but re-packaged. Freeze-dried coffee is packed and sold the same way.

BLACK-AND-WHITE PRINTING PAPERS AND THEIR CHARACTERISTICS

Here then is a list of some of the best papers currently available. Prices vary and will be different from country to country.

AGFA PE PAPER

This is water-resistant resin-coated base for high-speed processing. There are two types, as follows. *Brovira-Speed* is a bromide paper which gives neutral to cold tones. It is available in five different grades. *Portriga-Speed* is a chloro-bromide paper which gives slightly warmer results. Four grades are available in standard sizes.

AGFA-BARYTA PAPER (fibre-based)

This has a baryta coating on a fibre base under the emulsion. It is not resin-coated. Three types are available as follows. *Brovira* and *Portriga* baryta papers exhibit the same characteristics as PE versions. *Record Rapid*, third in the range, is a chloro-bromide paper with variable tonal characteristics depending upon the processing method used. It is ideal for exhibition work.

Note: It is possible that chromagenic film negatives used with chloro-bromide papers may have the effect of reducing contrast due to the inherent brownish colour cast of the film. Light tones on the print may appear darker than when a normal silver image negative is used, thus creating the effect of more visible detail in those areas.

FORTE

This paper is manufactured in Hungary. *Fortespeed* is a resin-coated material with medium black and fairly average overall gradation. Three grades are available. *Forte Porturex Speed* is another resin-coated chloro-bromide paper with warmish tones. It is fairly slow in use. Three grades are available. *Forte Porturex Rapid* is a slow chloro-bromide with a light cream coloured base. It gives rich blacks and good overall tonality. One grade is available.

ILFORD

Ilford are noted worldwide for their excellent range of papers. *Ilfospeed* and *Ilfobrom* are two of my favourites for general press work. They are very tolerant of shoddy workmanship with good exposure latitude and handling qualities. Ilfospeed resin-coated paper is probably about the closest thing to perfection in a plastic-based paper. Proper drying ensures super flat prints with no curl tendency. The emulsion surface is a little soft and scratches quite easily. Both types are available in a variety of grades and surface finishes.

ILFORD GALERIE

This is a near-exhibition-quality fibre-based paper with neutral tones and a very white base. The tonal rendering is not to my liking but may suit some people. It is available in four grades and two surfaces (gloss or matt).

ILFORD MULTIGRADE II

This is a variable contrast paper – you dial in the filtration to vary the contrast – similar to Kodak's *Polycontrast*. It is great if you do not

Effect of exposure tends to be cumulative. Sensitivity of film emulsion decreases as exposure is increased; simultaneously, contrast is increased until a point is reached when detail in the negative, which would be normally visible in the subject with the unaided eye, becomes blocked by increased contrast and over-exposure of highlight areas. The first picture represents the scene as the human eye would see it, recognisable but lacking detail. 1/8th second @ f 5.6. The second picture: exposure of 4 seconds at f 5.6. In the third picture an exposure of one and a half minutes at the same f stop has effectively blocked out all detail. HP5, ISO 400, developed in HC110 for 6.5 minutes.

want the hassle of keeping several different grades in stock. It gives good blacks, but the white is a trifle off-white. Pearl or gloss finish are available. It needs time to get used to and to discover how the contrast of different parts of the image can be changed at will.

KENTMERE

BROMIDE

This is a good all-round paper with neutral image tone; but it is one of the papers in which a grade 2 is more contrasty, nearer a grade 3, than some other makes. Quite a number of prints in this book were made on varying grades of glossy Kentmere Bromide. The single weight dries well with a good glaze. The double weight is more troublesome and requires attention to detail.

KENTHENE

This was one of the first manufacturers to bring a polyethylene-coated paper onto the market, and in the early days of a decade ago it was not the best of the bunch. Today's version is fast, and normal grade 2 is closer to a 3. It has a nice finish when dried; and a neutral image tone.

KENTONA

This is not one of those coloured papers, but a chloro-bromide with a very pleasing range of tones. It has a good white base and a much slower speed than other Kentmere papers. There are two grades and two surfaces: gloss and stipple.

KODAK

Kodak's range includes the following: Kodak *Elite*; Kodak *Kodabrome IIRC*; Kodak *Polycontrast*; Kodak *Polyfiber*; Kodak *Polyprint*.

Once you get to know their respective characteristics compared with other makes, the chances are you will not want to shuffle about by chopping and changing. Kodak materials are consistent in quality with a paper finish that is unrivalled. Their RC paper is fast with plenty of punch, but *Elite* doesn't quite come up to expectations. Somehow one always expects more from the yellow box. Nevertheless, their papers are diffi-cult to fault; The tone is often described by some as 'neutral', but to my mind it's far more than that. Kodak papers have an intangible tone quality all their own which is possibly why, when using it, one takes a great deal more care over producing the print.

ORIENTAL SEAGULL

As its name implies, this is a product of the Far East – Japan to be exact. It is highly rated in America where it was imported long before it became available in Europe. It is a fibre-based paper with neutral tones and brilliant whites. It is suitable for exhibition-quality printing and is available in four grades in double weight gloss or stipple finish. The designation code is RP-F. RP-R stands for Resin Coated.

PAL

Pal Print and *Pal Brom* are both fibre-based papers, the former with a maximum black and slightly warm compared with some other makes. Pal Brom has a warmish base, too, and is much faster than the Print version. Brom is available in four grades and Print in three, single and double weight. Brom is available in gloss finish only and Print in gloss, matt, crystal and silk.

GUILBROM

This paper is made in Paris by the oldest makers of light-sensitive materials, R. Guillemont Boestflug et Cie who began manufacture in 1858. It has very good tonality with rich blacks and an extremely white base. It is a bit prickly to dry, and available in double weight in grades 2 and 3. The same company also manufactures Guilbrom for Zone VI Studios Inc., of Newfane in Vermont, USA, who market it under the trade name of *Brilliant*. Zone VI claim that 'Brilliant's technical specifications exceed those of any other paper. They make possible the more ethereal qualities that artists demand. Prints on Brilliant create an illusion of depth, substance, clarity and light.' As far as I have been able to establish from the English importers and Silverprint Ltd, who market the

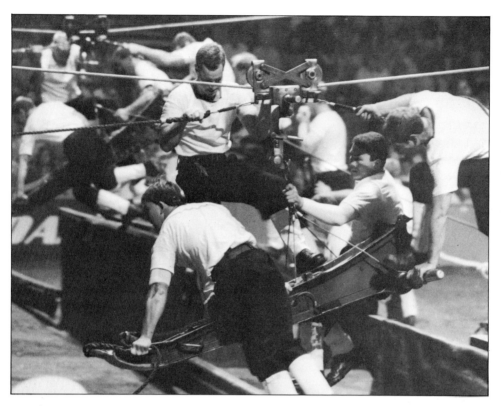

The advantages of chromagenic film in low-light level photography are its excellent speed: grain relationship, enormous exposure latitude, fine grain and superb definition. This picture was taken as part of a series on the famous 'Field Gun' event held annually in London. For the black-and-white I used Agfa's Vario Xl rated at 1600 and an f /2.8 180 mm Zuiko lens. Simultaneously, I was using a 300 mm lens on another body in which I thought I had put the same film stock. When I had finished shooting that roll, I discovered to my horror that the body had been accidentally loaded with a roll of Ektachrome 200.

paper, Brilliant and Guilbrom are one and the same paper.

PAPER DEVELOPERS AND OTHER CHEMICALS

Most of today's paper developers are products based on fairly ancient, tried and tested formulae. Until you have had a chance to try out some of the various types, it will be best to stick with those recommended by paper manufacturers. This will permit the standardising of print tones and development times necessary to establish a particular effect. Most universal paper developers such as Kodak's *DPC* or Ilford's *PQ Universal* can be used with virtually any make of resin-coated normal bromide paper and will provide acceptable results. If you want longer development times for more control, it is best to experiment with other types of developer; some of the powder-based types and some photo-mechanical types (those used for the processing of graphic arts film material) can be used to boost contrast or give a softer,

warmer tone. If you are making prints for reproduction in magazines and newspapers, general-purpose print developers that allow plenty of manipulation and which are noted for their longevity (*Suprol*) and aggressive action are probably best. The quality of reproduction in the vast majority of newspapers and magazines, and in great many books, is appalling, and in order for your prints to stand any chance of reasonable reproduction a fully toned, medium-to-high contrast print is desirable. Many working photographers complain of atrocious reproductions of their work, often without realising that the fault is often not with the publisher's printer, but with their own random approach to bromide print-making.

NORMATON ST18 DEVELOPER

This is a black-and-white print developer from Ornano of Milan. It is a neutral-tone high-capacity dish developer for fibre or RC papers. Dilution 1 + 9. It has a good working dish life. Development time: 2 minutes at

20 °C (68 °F). Shorter times and higher temperatures can be used with RC papers. Dilution between 1 + 5 and 1 + 14 gives contrast control without change in image colour.

EMBASPEED DEVELOPER

This is a PQ type rapid print developer from May and Baker. It has a rapid image appearance of around 6 seconds at dilution rate of 1 + 9. Its dish life is around 24 hours depending on throughput and circumstance. It is available in 1 and 5 litre concentrate. *Suprol* is available in 250 ml, 1, 5 and 25 litre liquid concentrate. 5 litres of concentrate is said to develop more than 2,800 prints of 18 × 24 cm in size. It has a fast image time with most papers and a long working life. It produces an image tone inherent in paper which I found a little soft with normal grades of Kentmere and Ilford resin-coated papers. It is ideal if you have huge quantities of prints to process. Suprol can also be used as a film-developer, producing fine grain and high acutance at high levels of dilution. The makers also market *Suprol A* which is thermally stabilised for use in tropical climates. *Embrol* is specially formulated for variable-contrast printing papers such as *Multigrade* and *Polycontrast*.

AGFA BLACK-AND-WHITE PAPER DEVELOPERS

These have an excellent shelf life, also suitable for other paper makes. The range includes *Neutol*, *Adaptol* and *Metinol*. Other makes of developer, however, do not appear to bring out the best of Agfa's paper qualities. In particular, Neutol and Record Rapid paper work well together. With other regular PQ type developers, the paper lost a lot of its snap and blacks were warmed.

UNIVERSAL (FX-26)

This developer dilutes 1 : 7 for prints and 1 : 19 for film. It is recommended as a beginner's developer, but do not expect exhibition-quality results, especially from film with high ISO ratings processed in this brew.

Acuprint (FX-17) is a general-purpose paper developer which will work with virtually anything. It produces good blacks, highlights and shadow detail. *Pro-Print* is similar to Acuprint but with cooler rendition of tones. All three products are by Paterson.

DEKTOL

Until the advent in Europe of Kodak's *Elite* printing papers, this developer was normally only available in the USA. It is a cold tone developer with excellent working properties and is particularly suitable for producing images of exhibition quality. It is available in liquid form. Kodak's *D-163* is a power-based general-purpose print-developer which must be properly dissolved in the correct order to make a liquid stock solution. Gives a neutral-warm image tone with Kodak and other make bromide papers. It is a pretty ancient formula and of a type being superseded because of its inconvenience. Liquid stock concentrates are easier to use. Kodak's range of chemicals is huge, particularly of developers for film and graphic arts use. Their professional handbook is a valuable asset for any working photographer.

FIX

Virtually any type of fixer solution is suitable for black-and-white papers. Prolonged fixing of prints (and/or negatives) in fixers containing ammonium thiosulphate to which a hardener has been added will cause 'pinholing' and eventual bleaching away of the image. RC papers are usually temporarily fixed in most rapid fix solutions in about 30 seconds; a minute and a half will fix them permanently, while 5 minutes is enough to fix fibre-based prints for archive permanence. Typical Trade names are *Hypam* (Ilford), *Amfix* (May & Baker), *Acufix* and *Pro-Fix* (Paterson). When using these concentrated solutions it is not wise to exceed the recommended times.

If space is available, the two-bath method of fixing is desirable. This extends the life of fixing solutions which would normally become rapidly exhausted when a single bath is used. Even the use of a stop bath does not prevent large quantities of alkali being carried over from the developer. The simplest way to test for exhaustion, apart from using chemical test strips, is to keep all the cut-off leaders from miniature film. Drop one into a tray of well-used fix from time to time and note how long it takes to clear. When the duration exceeds one minute before the first noticeable signs of clearing, the solution will already be well on the way to exhaustion. Using a replenisher system is more economic when large quantities of film and print materials are being processed.

Ordinary hypo can be made by dissolving 500 g of anhydrous sodium thiosulphate in approximately 5 litres of cold water to which is added 125 g of sodium metabisulphite. The salts are normally readily available from a pharmacist. Add the anhydrous salts slowly to the water, stirring all the time, until complete dissolution takes place. If the powder is added too quickly it will form a large lump that is difficult to break up. This formula makes a non-hardening acid fixing bath which is ideal for most amateur use. Most modern film and paper emulsions are now hardened considerably in manufacture; so there is no real need to use a hardener, which in any case slows down the actual clearing process. The above quantity is sufficient to fix twenty-five 10×8 in prints or ten 135 mm/120 format films.

Plain hypo exhausts quite rapidly and can be tested without resort to chemicals using the method described above. Give approximately double the clearing time for complete fixation, though this may never be enough in a solution which is nearly exhausted. Another way to test the strength can be carried out by adding one part of a 4 per cent solution of potassium iodide to 10 parts of used fix solution. If a yellow precipitate forms that cannot be dissolved on shaking, the fix solution will be overloaded with silver, preventing any further efficient clearing action. Fixing times for paper using hypo are between 5 and 10 minutes at temperatures of between 15 and 24 °C/(59 − 75 °F). Temperatures of fixing solutions which are higher than the latter figure are best avoided as considerable swelling of emulsion will take place with consequent risk of mechanical damage to the film or paper. Temperatures colder than 15 °C (24 °F) will slow the clearing time significantly. For best results, hypo concentrate should be about 35 − 40 per cent of the mixture. Higher concentrations will only increase the rapidity of the clearing time by fairly insignificant amounts.

WASHING

Fibre-based papers, popular for their superior image quality and longevity, have one big disadvantage. Paper retains processing chemicals requiring up to 30 minutes for single weight papers and double that for double weight to ensure the removal of 90 per cent of the chemicals. Paterson introduced a washing aid which reduces recommended washing times and improves image permanence. After fixing, prints are rinsed in water for 30 seconds and then aid-treated for 1 minute. Films are then washed for 5 minutes and prints of either weight for 20 minutes. Liquid concentrate is diluted $1 + 4$ with water and is reusable. 500 ml will treat twenty 35 mm or 120 size films and twenty-five 10×8 s or equivalent area. It is available in 1 litre concentrate.

9
Black-and-White Variable Contrast Printing

Variable-contrast printing papers have been with us on and off for a very long time. In 1940, the Ilford Company of Great Britain introduced the first variable-contrast paper called Multigrade. It was generally available in the post-war years until the early 1960s when for what appear to be purely economic reasons it was discontinued. What this means in plain language is that there was simply not enough demand for the product. But much research had been carried out, and when the same company took advantage of what were then relatively new polyethylene-coated papers being used in colour photography and introduced the *Ilfospeed* system in 1974, the reintroduction of a much improved variable-contrast paper four years later was just the next logical step up the ladder toward improving the lot of those who still had a need for black-and-white pictures. In its own way, Ilford has probably done more than any other company to maintain as well as create the 'new' interest in black-and-white photography; partly by producing products which have a 'convenience' handling factor as well as very high quality, and partly through their annual competitions for best photographer and best printer, both of which carry generous awards and produce a high volume of excellent-quality work. Such is the esteem which these awards carry that when Kodak re-introduced its range of black-and-white papers, the event was heralded by the simultaneous announcement of a competition with bigger prizes and which was no doubt designed to woo many of Ilford's loyalists.

All that aside, the new *Multigrade II* (Ilford) and Kodak's *Polycontrast* range of printing papers have become the mainstay of many professional photographers and small jobbing print houses who cannot or do not wish to carry vast stocks of conventional or RC papers. It has found favour with many amateur photographers for the same reasons and, in view of that, it will be worthwhile to discuss them further in this chapter.

In a nutshell, variable-contrast paper is just what the name implies; its contrast being variable by the introduction of filters of varying strength at the exposure stage. In practice, this means that paper from one box can be exposed and processed at any grade in the equivalent conventional range from 0 to 5. It also means that any one sheet of paper can have separate areas exposed by varying the amounts of exposure through individual or a combination of filters to produce differing grades of contrast in those separate areas.

For example, suppose you had a negative in which the foreground was a trifle thin and the background or skyline a little dense. Printing on a normal grade of paper would produce a print with blocked-up shadow detail in the foreground and possibly acceptable tonal values in the sky areas. Landscapes, seascapes and other photographs where large areas of light and shade predominate are often the ones which require some manipulation in the printing, either by dodging or by burning-in. Using variable-contrast paper, the same techniques can be used but to a lesser extent; much more local control is afforded by the use of filters which allow the printer to vary contrast of the paper in the areas which require it. So, you might print the forepart of the picture through a filter to produce a relatively hard grade and the sky through another filter to produce a softer contrast which will bring out the highlight detail in clouds and sky.

ILFORD'S MULTIGRADE SYSTEM
When Ilford introduced the new Multigrade

system, they also produced various sets of filters which could be used in a holder below the enlarger lens and larger filters which could be used in the filter draw of conventional machines. In the first Multigrade series of several decades past, the filters were yellow. In the *Multigrade I* series, a combination pack of yellow and magenta of different densities were supplied, with No.7 being upgraded just prior to the introduction of *Multigrade II* which now uses a combination of green and blue.

A little later in this chapter you will find tables for the various filter packs as well as conversions for the dial-in colour heads of some enlargers. I have included the now discontinued Multigrade I system as at this time there is still a reasonable supply of the material, also, as the paper will keep in good condition for at least two years when properly stored, there is every chance that many amateurs will still have plentiful stocks and the filter pack to match it.

Ilford's own P-400 and the newer P-500 enlarging heads are capable of producing a whole range of contrasts at the touch of a button, and are part of an integral Multigrade system which includes the enlarger head, voltage control box and exposure probe. Owners of enlargers with dial-in-filter systems used for colour printing have also found that it is a very simple matter to convert Ilford's specified filter values to correspond with variable values of the magenta, cyan and yellow.

The contrast range of Multigrade I can be extended slightly by combining filters 1 + 2 and 6 + 7, but exposure times will be abnormally extended. Depending on the enlarger

light source and lens in use, filters at the top end of the range (5, 6 and 7) also make it difficult to focus the image when negatives of near normal contrast are being printed. To avoid disappointment, focus the image on the baseboard without a filter and then insert the correct grade as soon as you are ready to print.

Multigrade II filters and paper have been specially designed to match the contrast range of Ilfospeed papers, and each whole filter number corresponds to the full grades of both Ilfobrom and Ilfospeed. The half grades will give contrasts mid-way between each whole grade of paper. Unlike the Multigrade I series which required a set of tedious exposure factors to be applied whenever a change of grade was made because the effective speed of the paper changed, Multigrade II does not inherit that problem.

Multigrade I filters can be used with the series II paper although contrast spacing will be uneven and the MK I calculator cannot be used to determine exposures. Instead, a practical trial is necessary to determine the correct exposure for the filter used. When changing to a new filter (of the old type) the old exposure time is multiplied by the new filter factor as shown in Table 7.

Photographers with Dichroic colour heads will find the dial-in filter facility extremely useful in making minute adjustments to print

Table 6: MULTIGRADE I CONTRAST RELATIONSHIP WITH CONVENTIONAL GRADES

Multigrade I	Equivalent to Ilfospeed grade
1	softer than Grade 0
2	harder than Grade 0
3	harder than Grade 1
4	harder than Grade 2
5	equal to Grade 3
6	softer than Grade 4
7	harder than Grade 4

Table 7: MULTIGRADE I FILTER FACTORS FOR USE WITH MULTIGRADE II PAPER

New filter	Old filter								
	white light	1	2	3	4	5	6	7(1)	7(2)
1	1.6	—	1.2	1.1	1.0	0.7	0.5	0.25	0.3
2	1.3	0.8	—	0.9	0.8	0.6	0.4	0.2	0.25
3	1.4	0.9	1.1	—	0.9	0.6	0.4	0.2	0.25
4	1.6	1.0	1.2	1.1	—	0.7	0.5	0.25	0.3
5	2.3	1.4	1.7	1.6	1.4	—	0.7	0.3	0.4
6	3.5	2.1	2.5	2.4	2.1	1.5	—	0.5	0.6
7(1)	6.5	4.0	4.9	4.6	4.0	3.0	1.9	—	—
7(2)	4.3	2.6	3.3	3.0	2.6	2.0	1.3	—	—

7(1) = first Mk I filter.
7(2) = later Mk I filter.
To find the new exposure for a new filter, take the old exposure, say it was 10 seconds using grade 4. New filter required = Grade 5, factor = 1.4. New exposure time = 10 seconds × 1.4 = 14 seconds.

Evocative appeal of black-and-white.

contrast. Ilford recommends using the filter values shown in Table 8 which correspond to the listed Kodak grades.

The advantage of using this system as opposed to a system which combines yellow and magenta to maintain a fixed paper speed is that the printing light is effectively brighter, necessitating lower exposure values, but paper speeds are changed as they are if you were using a regular Multigrade filter kit. In this case, paper speed from grades 0 to 3.5 remains the same, but the speed is halved using grades 4–5. Practical tests will definitely be required to establish correct contrast levels for individual colour heads as the filter characteristics frequently differ. Table 8 above is based on Kodak Colour Compensating Filter values.

Table 9 shows the filtrations required using two popular enlarger makes. The left-hand column lists Multigrade II filters which correspond with approximate values given under each enlarger.

Ilford's own enlarger heads can be adapted to fit a variety of instruments currently available, including some Durst models, Beseler, Omega, Leitz and De Vere. Once the head is set up and calibrated, electronics are used to determine accurate exposure irrespective of grade or magnification changes. Using manual Multigrade filters and Table 8 above,

Table 8: FILTER VALUES FOR MULTIGRADE II PAPER

Grade	Yellow	Magenta
0	80	0
0.5	55	0
1	30	0
1.5	15	0
2	0	0
2.5	0	25
3	0	40
3.5	0	65
4	0	100
4.5	0	150
5	0	200

tests will have to be made to establish the exact parameters of the material. As a rough guide, exposure increases are approximately 10 per cent per grade increase towards 7 from 2. The reduction in exposure for lower-contrast grades is insignificant.

OTHER VARIABLE-CONTRAST PAPERS

The discerning photographer/printer will be aware that, while Ilford's Multigrade II can be relied upon to meet most demands of general-purpose printing, there will often be a need for a variable-contrast (vc) paper which closely approximates to the qualities of conventional fibre-based products.

Kodak's range of VC papers offer a wide choice of finishes and paper type from polyethylene-coated to a heavy double weight variable-contrast fibre paper. The papers and their characteristics are listed below.

POLYCONTRAST II RC PAPER

This is available in two finishes, glossy and semi-matt. The paper is a medium weight

Table 9: FILTRATIONS USING DURST AND DE VERE ENLARGERS

Multigrade Mk II filter	Durst	Exposure factor	De Vere	Exposure factor
0	110Y	1.8	170Y	2.3
0.5	90Y	1.6	150Y	2.1
1	70Y	1.5	115Y	1.8
1.5	30Y	1.3	85Y	1.5
2	—	1.0	—	1.0
2.5	30M	1.3	20M	1.1
3	45M	1.4	70M	1.4
3.5	55M	1.5	90M	1.7
4	95M	2.0	120M	2.0
4.5	130M	2.3	200M	2.8
5	200M	—	—	—

'selective contrast' resin-coated developer incorporated type for dish or machine roller-transport processing, and is available in sheets and rolls. The paper is designed for exposure using normal tungsten enlarger lamps filtered to control contrast by adjusting blue and green light proportions. The makers say that other light sources may also be used, but sources such as Cold Cathode may need additional filtration to provide the full range of paper contrasts. Light source correction filters are needed in addition to the appropriate *Polycontrast II* filters and are as follows for the light sources indicated:

Final print quality depends on several factors, the prime one of which is an understanding of what a first-class print should look like. If you are wallowing in the mire of turgid greys, a visit to a black-and-white print exhibition will open your eyes to what is possible. Adopting a faultless negative exposure/ development combination is the first step. Next comes a thorough understanding of paper characteristics and how to make the perfect test strip using a methodical approach to exposure and development. Once these skills are acquired, and they are not difficult, high-quality prints are relatively easy to make.

In reproduction, this picture loses much of the original quality of print, which measured 15 × 12 in. The print is from virtually the whole of a 35 mm negative taken on a 28 mm lens using Tri-X developed in D-76 diluted 1:1. The original print was made on a Kentmere double-weight grade 3 bromide over 15 years ago, and, like many others contained in my picture library, has lost nothing in the ageing. Mechanical photo reproduction using normal lithographic and web-offset techniques cannot retain the quality of a really good original. For that quality to be retained in print, a gravure process using etched copper plates is the only suitable process.

Table 10: RECOMMENDED DILUTIONS AND TIMES USING DEKTOL

Paper	Dektol powder dilution	Dektol liquid dilution	Time (minutes) recommended	Latitude	Capacity (per litre) 10 × 8 s
Polyfiber and Polyprint RC	1+2		1.5	1–3	30
		1+9	1.5	1–3	30
Polycontrast RC	1+2		1.0	0.75–	30
		1+9	1.0	2.0	30

1) fluorescent lamps, cool white (4,500K), use CC or CP 40Y;

2) fluorescent lamps, white (6,500K), use CC or CP 70Y;

3) mercury vapour lamps, use *Wratten* gelatin filter No.6 + CC or CP 40Y.

The paper has an incorporated brightener and gives a warm-black image tone. It can be processed in activator/stabiliser machines as well as in machines using conventional chemicals. After processing in the former, the paper should be fixed and washed normally if longevity of image is required.

Table 10 details hand development times, latitude and capacity using Kodak's Dektol.

POLYPRINT RC PAPER

This is a medium-speed, medium-weight resin-coated, non-developer-incorporated paper designed mainly for dish processing. It is available in a gloss and semi-matt finish in sheet form. Rolls are available to special order in the semi-matt finish only. The same details regarding enlarger light sources as for Polycontrast II RC are applicable.

Enlargers with dial-in filtration can be used in the same way as for Ilford papers. Using a *Chromega* enlarger, the lowest contrast is reached at 35Y and the highest at 100M. Printing speed will vary with filtration, and practical tests will have to be made to establish paper speed and contrast combinations.

POLYFIBER PAPER

This is a heavy double weight selective-contrast paper available in a gloss and semi-matt finish. The former may be glazed in the traditional way using a drum glazing machine or ferrotype or chromed plates on a flat-bed drier. When naturally air-dried on muslin stretchers, both papers yield a high-quality finish suitable for exhibition and display purposes. Polyfiber has an incorporated brightener and dries with a neutral black image tone.

The paper is designed mainly for dish processing and has a very wide processing latitude. Kodak recommend toning the paper for extended image life.

Table 10 gives recommended dilutions and times in minutes for the above papers using Dektol powder and Dektol liquid developer.

Kodak variable/selective-contrast papers rely on the use of acetate or gelatin filters fitted below the enlarger lens or between the lens and light source. The filters are the same colour as Ilford's Multigrade II types, and filtration as given in the tables above using earlier yellow/magenta types can be utilised for Kodak VC materials. The Kodak Polycontrast II filter set for between the lens and light source is available in two sizes: 90 mm square or 150 mm square. Ilford's P500 enlarger head is also suitable for use with these Kodak materials.

Larger sheets of acetate filter material in grades 1, 1.5, 2, 2.5, 3, 3.5 and 4 are available from Eastman Kodak in Rochester, New York, in sizes from 10 × 8 in up to 12 × 48 in as well as in 12 in × 100 ft rolls. Kodak recently introduced these alternatives because of the growing demand from photographers to contact-print larger-format negatives.

The secret of success with variable-contrast papers, as with all other conventionally graded types, lies in the key areas of method of application and in the disciplined control of those applications. It has already been noted in the previous chapter that excessive heat, for example, used to dry resin-coated papers, creates a tendency for the paper to curl. Kodak advise that air temperatures should not exceed 88 °C (190 °F) for variable-contrast RC papers and that normal room temperatures should be used for the drying of Polyfiber papers – 'low drying temperature gives best dimensional stability and least curl'. It is interesting to note Kodak's concern with long-term conservation of print materials. At the end of each technical data sheet a recommendation is made to tone prints which are liable to be displayed or which may be subject to adverse storage conditions such as may induce rapid oxidation of the silver image.

Of great importance to the print connoisseur is the stability of image tone. In modern polyethylene-coated papers a degree of instability is inherent in the product. When RC prints are exposed to light for any length of time, the layer beneath the emulsion containing a white pigment of titanium dioxide releases an oxidant which encourages the fading of the silver image and which will ultimately cause a breakdown of the polymer base layer. Some manufacturers now add anti-oxidants, but the long-term effect is uncertain, and for that reason perhaps any prints which are required to be kept for long periods should be made on fibre/baryta base papers.

The only practical advantage in using RC paper would appear to be in its rapid processing characteristics. If storage of RC prints is essential for long-term re-use, as in photolibrary applications, control of relative humidity between 30 and 40 per cent and the avoidance of extreme fluctuations in storage temperatures should be avoided. I have noticed a significant physical change in RC material printed and processed more than a decade ago and which was stored unstamped and uncaptioned in cardboard light-tight boxes, compared with conventional fibre-based prints stored in the same way in the same place. Prints made on quality RC materials by well-known manufacturers have certainly fared better over long periods than those made on paper which is noticeably inferior in quality.

Most toning processes will prolong the life of a photograph; this is the reason why many photographs from the past have survived so well. Many of the prints produced by French photographer Eugene Atget during his thirty years as a pioneering photojournalist documenting the growing pains of Paris from the turn of this century were toned as a matter of course. Perhaps he knew, even though he never received the recognition he justly deserved for his work during his lifetime, that his prints would become collector's pieces. With today's toning concentrates readily available in liquid form, the practice is much simplified.

All toners tend to change the actual black and white (or CVT) as well as changing the overall colour of the print. Kodak's Selenium toner diluted 1:20 (20 parts of water) produces no significant tonal change in the print and is possibly the best answer for those looking to add a degree of protection against constant manhandling and fluctuations in atmospheric conditions.

VARIABLES IN ENLARGING USING VARIABLE CONTRAST MATERIALS

It is possible that, in some circumstances, contrast changes may occur in enlargement from small to large print sizes especially when condenser-only enlargers are employed.

With Multigrade II paper speed and contrast remains the same throughout the normal exposure range of 0–70 seconds. Thereafter, paper speed and contrast decreases. Disregard the halving of paper speed (doubling of exposure) of grades 4–5. In practice this means that the same grade selected for say a 5 × 7 in print will be the same for a bigger enlargement up to say 12 × 10 in, provided the exposure time does not exceed the maximum figure stated, i.e. 70 seconds. If the exposure time is exceeded it may be necessary to make a test strip using different filters to assess the new grade and exposure required.

As exposure is cumulative, any burning-in should be taken into consideration when making the print. Excessive burning will have the effect of lowering contrast in the areas worked on; therefore, if the cumulative exposure exceeds the maximum amount it may be prudent to select a higher (harder) filter grade to compensate before burning commences.

Compare the picture on p. 122 with these two prints made in a rush for newspaper reproduction. These are straight prints from the negatives with no dodging and no time for test strips. The negatives were made with an 80–200 mm Nikkor zoom lens on HP5 and processed in ID-11. Sharpness of the subject in the top picture is accurate, but not very flattering to Mrs Thatcher. In the other print slight pre-focus of the lens has resolved the main problem and in newsprint reproduction the softer image would be more flattering. However, both prints are of relatively soft gradation even though they are of the same grade as the picture on p. 122. There are no really deep blacks and the whites are muddy caused mainly by slight over-exposure of the print and 'pulling' from the developer before full development had taken place. This technique can often work well for the purpose stipulated above, provided the main subject image is fairly large and the negative contains a reasonable range of tones. It obviates the need for shading and burning when time is short.

RECIPROCITY FAILURE

Other causes of low contrast, or a shift in contrast from high to low in enlargement when magnification is increased, can be due to reciprocity failure and localised fogging. The latter is often the cause of darker patches or streaks evident on the paper after processing, and is the result of flare from the immediate enlarger surroundings as well as the possibility of safelight fog. Walls and benches close to the enlarger should be painted a dark colour, preferably with a matt finish which helps to absorb any reflected light. The area immediately behind the enlarger column should be painted matt black to a height of at least 18 in (45 cm) above the top of the enlarger column.

Other obvious sources of flare are the enlarger baseboard; even the masking easel, the white base of which will reflect some light back through RC and single weight fibre papers resulting in a slight loss of base brilliance. The enlarger itself can often cause problems. Chromed columns, shining safelight stalks, dirty rear lens elements and dirty condenser surfaces all contribute to lowering of the print quality.

Another frequent but often misunderstood source of irritation which I have found more noticeable with some variable-contrast RC materials is the ease with which slight accidental staining can occur during processing. Because these papers have rapid induction times, irregular development can take place during dish processing if correct agitation procedures are ignored.

Processing several sheets at a time can also cause problems; the nature of the material makes it difficult to interleave more than ten sheets easily in less than a 2-litre volume of working solution (10 × 8s in a 12 × 10 in dish), although Kodak's Polycontrast II RC and Polyprint RC are treated with a special back coating to facilitate multiple dish processing. When transferring to other solutions, however, staining will frequently occur if several sheets are transferred together. For best results, begin draining sheets singly when development time taken from the time of the first sheet immersion is complete. This should be no more than 10 seconds per print. When water is used instead of an acetic acid stop bath, continuous agitation of the print is necessary to remove residual developer before draining again and subsequent immersion in the fix. Here, best results are achieved when the print is given vigorous and constant agitation for the first 15 seconds. Thereafter, the paper may be allowed to settle while each consecutive print is given the same treatment.

INTERLEAVING AND MULTIPLE SHEET DEVELOPMENT IN DISHES

The following notes apply to dish processing techniques where a high throughput of paper is demanded in one session.

Where large quantities of prints are required from a single negative, processing discipline must be strictly observed if quality is to be maintained with the minimum wastage. For professionals and semi-professionals who may only have occasional demand for large print quantities, dish processing is actually more economic as well as faster than a bench-top processing machine. Only a roll head paper projection processor has the capacity to make life more agreeable, but such machines are a luxury in the small darkroom where print quantities are frequently less than 1000 a month.

1) Before paper exposure begins, make up large quantities of developer, stop bath and fixer solutions, preferably using a two-bath fixing system. If 10 × 8 in prints are required, use dishes capable of processing 12 × 10 in prints and make up a minimum of 2–3 litres of each solution. For example, using Kodak's DPC or Dektol, or Ilford PQ Universal print liquid developers, dilute 200 cc of concentrate developer with 1800 cc of water to make 2 litres of working solution. At 20 °C (68 °F) this will be enough to process up to sixty 10 × 8 in prints before signs of exhaustion become apparent.

Use a larger volume of stop bath or water. Use a larger volume of fixer, up to 4 litres if

Red windows, Paris. OM1, 180 mm wide open on Fujichrome 50 ISO. The camera was tripod-mounted for an exposure of 1 second. Slight reciprocity failure made the reds in the window artificially bright. This effect might have been lost using higher ISO film or by push processing.

tray capacity will allow. The wash tank should be filled with fresh, filtered running water. Bring all solutions to the correct working temperatures and have a basin of cold water handy, separate from the wash water.

2) When making exposures, allow for an increase in image density which may occur when several sheets of paper are stored for any length of time before processing. Density is also increased slightly during development when more than one sheet of paper is processed.

3) Expose each sheet of paper using the shortest possible, but convenient, time, and store, in a light-tight box or paper safe which should be sited out of the direct path of both enlarger and safelight beams. Unexposed paper is best stored ready for use in a heavyweight oversized black polythene bag so that the open end is long enough to flop over the paper when exposures are being made. I normally count out the number of sheets required for each negative and place them in a separate box or bag where they will be

conveniently situated for my free hand to keep up a rapid transfer rate to the enlarger without risk of fogging.

4) Once exposures are complete, and as soon as possible afterward, take up to ten sheets of exposed paper. Hold in the left hand (vice versa if you are left-handed) and fan out like a hand of cards emulsion side facing upward. Begin immersion in the developer by taking the bottom sheet of the fan and placing it face down in the tray, making sure that you push down on the centre of the paper. This action releases trapped air bubbles.

A timer should be started as soon as the first sheet enters the developer; this is difficult if you already have your hands full. If there is no wall clock already running, I use my watch to keep an eye on time. It is essential that you work to a time and temperature principle if you have already made a test print in this way.

Continue immersing all the sheets in rapid succession. As soon as the last is under the developer, bring the bottom one to the top of the pile so that it lays emulsion-side-

A sheet of 10 × 8 in paper cut diagonally in half and exposed in strips using a piece of black card. Start on the left with one half of the paper, then on the right with the lower half. Joined together, the two strips give an accurate assessment of the correct exposure for many areas of the print.

uppermost. Do this by lightly pulling on the edge of the paper with a fingertip until you catch the sheet with thumb and forefinger; flick the paper over in one easy movement so that it is face-up. Simultaneously, with the left hand on the bottom left corner of the tray, begin a gentle rocking motion.

Follow this procedure with each sheet of paper until the last is at the top of the pile. Now, once more take the bottom one – which was the first sheet immersed – and flick it to the top of the pile. Inspect the print visually for image density. Full development should be practically complete by the time this stage has been reached. I normally make my visual inspection whilst actually draining the print for transfer to the stop bath, which is invariably water.

Using the left hand, while draining the first print with the right, begin removing the remaining prints one by one from the bottom of the pile; drain and transfer to the stop bath where the right hand will take over agitation. It is imperative that you adopt the habit of keeping the right hand (or left) out of the developer from now on until fixation of all prints is complete. If you have never used this procedure before, you may find it slightly confusing dealing with a large number of prints which all appear to be rushing toward over-development very quickly. Try to work methodically from the outset; keep watching the clock, prepare to begin draining the first print immersed almost as soon as you have reached the end of the first interleaving cycle. From then on work as fast as experience will permit and don't worry about your prints being over-developed. The whole key to success in this procedure lies in the operator's ability to concentrate on the various manoeuvres required to move the prints from one tray to another with the least amount of fuss and bother.

When all prints are transferred to the stop bath, begin the same procedure to transfer to the fix. It will help if you keep the right (or left) hand hovering over the fixing bath continuously during the transfer operation, thus avoiding the risk of chemical contamination with other solutions. As soon as transfer to the fix is complete, begin interleaving the prints for not less than 30 seconds until each print has been successfully agitated for a minimum of 15 seconds. Resin-coated papers will be fixed ready to transfer to the wash in one minute.

For greater permanence, use a 5-minute double bath fix sequence, half the total time in each bath. Wash in running water for 5–10 minutes if no hypo clearing agent is used, squeegee and air-dry at temperatures up to 88 °C (190 °F).

Recommended wash times for RC papers vary with each manufacturer. The absolute minimum wash period should be one minute. However, it is highly likely that residual hypo and silver salts will remain in the print when such short times are used. These chemicals will combine to form yellow-brown silver sulphide, causing the print to fade and adopt that colour. Wash times for RC prints can be as long as 10 minutes in water of a temperature range of 13–18 °C (55–65 °F). Longer immersion will cause serious delamination of the paper base as well as a dulling of the synthetic gloss finish with consequent loss of image brightness due to the washing-out action of optical brighteners used in most of these papers.

Excessive washing of RC papers, especially in unfiltered water, can result in dried prints having a layer of scum on the gloss surface. This can sometimes be removed by using genuine turpentine applied to the print with a wad of soft cotton wool. Use a circular motion to clean the print which may require several passes to remove all traces of the scum. Polish the gloss surface using a well-washed, but clean, cotton handkerchief or lint-free cloth.

Strict control is necessary in both the fix and wash procedures of RC papers if longevity is desired. Very few prints made hastily because of the rapid handling characteristics of RC paper have outlived the usefulness of most of my bromide collection, some of which were made more than twelve years ago and are reproduced in this book.

Fibre-based papers need more time in the

fix, up to 10 minutes if the chemicals are relatively fresh, followed by 45–60 minutes in the wash. Constant interleaving is essential in all solutions to achieve even development, proper fixation and washing.

HANDLING PROCEDURES

All photographic chemicals in powder and liquid form must be handled with extreme care. Some people are not as sensitive as others to some chemicals, but others may show signs of allergy or dermatitis very soon after contact. In handling chemicals, whether powder or liquid, it is advisable to wear household rubber or surgical gloves if you are in any doubt as to the sensitivity of your skin. Some form of protective clothing should be worn by operators in the darkroom at all times. Information regarding product contents and precautions to be taken are normally available from the manufacturer.

10
Fundamentals of Colour Photography

There are essentially two distinct areas of colour in photography. These are amateur colour and professional colour. In the professional field of editorial and advertising colour photography, approximately 75 per cent of all work produced uses reversal (transparency) material as the base from which all other work is derived. In the field of general practitioning, i.e. portrait, wedding, industrial and commercial, the bulk of finished production is derived from the colour negative process; in the amateur field, prints from negatives are the main area of interest.

COLOUR PRINTS

There are obvious reasons for the latter case, the most important of which has to do with presentation. It is far easier for the average home processor to pass around a few prints for viewing under whatever available lighting exists, than it is to gather people in one place to watch a screened presentation of colour slides. As soon as the colour print is dry it can be easily viewed and analysed. To view a colour slide properly, one needs a light box and magnifying glass at the very least, but as that method is often totally impractical for more than one or two persons, a small screen and projector is the usual method adopted for viewing. Setting up the equipment takes a little time and frequently requires household furniture to be rearranged. Once the room lights are extinguished, the viewer is virtually compelled to watch whatever is being shown for as long as projectionists – usually the photographer – insist on. In this respect, photographers are often their own worst enemy when it comes to selecting material for others to view, a fact which is frequently more apparent in the process of slide editing than in selecting negatives worth printing.

Visually, however, the average colour print, whether home-produced or machine-made by professionals, invariably lacks in quality of tone, colour saturation and overall effect what an averagely well exposed colour slide of comparable subject matter is inherently endowed with. Professional slide presentations, even those which utilise duplicates, leave no doubt in the mind of audiences as to the brilliance and saturation of colour which it is possible to obtain using reversal materials. The reason why this is so is fairly easy to understand.

The colour print relies on a certain quality of reflected light to achieve any desired impact on the viewer. Viewed under the wrong light, colours will have the effect of changing from those intended, just in the same way as when a black-and-white print appears to change tone and image density when it is viewed under differing light sources. Properly exposed and processed reversal material is inherently more brilliant and apparently more highly saturated with pure colour even when the transmission light source is of low wattage or of the wrong colour (of white light), or both. A good colour print will look positively dull alongside an equivalent colour transparency projected to the same image size as the print using a normally powered projector. But, by the same token, hand-made prints using artificially brightened paper can look positively stunning. Numerous professional photographers engaged solely in exhibition work have proved beyond any reasonable doubt that colour negative, properly handled, can yield the kind of superior quality one might automatically expect from large-format reversal products.

REVERSAL MATERIALS

Until fairly recently, professional photographers intent on reproducing their colour work in published form as calendars, postcards, books, brochures, leaflets, and so on, have been obliged to use reversal materials. Reproductions from prints lacked definition as well as colour saturation; this was partly due to the quality of original film material available and partly due to the capability of instruments used for scanning and separating colours in the photo-mechanical process.

With the introduction of high quality 'T' grain and 'HR' (high resolution) negative materials and general improvement in instrumentation, quality reproduction using colour prints or original colour negatives is now possible. Slowly but surely there has been a noticeable move toward the acceptance by publishers and printers of print originals; there seems to be little doubt that, within a few years, colour-negative material will be widely used, particularly in newspaper and some magazine work where the quality of reproduction need only be maintained to a minimum acceptable standard.

Many years ago, I was involved in some pioneering efforts by a worldwide picture agency which had at that time decided to set up a colour department which would offer the more interesting of the world's news events as a regular weekly service to newspapers; a spin-off would be the production of 35 mm news 'stills' for television back-projection behind the newscaster's head, a technique which is very sophisticated and of which very few people are not now aware.

Several problems had to be overcome. It was commonly known that, in the duplication of original reversal material, much in the way of colour saturation and sharpness was lost, making the duplicate almost totally unsuitable for reproduction, particularly newsprint reproduction, where the emphasis would be on colour, and fairly poor-quality colour at that. Another problem was that, historically, many of the staff photographers of this agency had spent virtually the whole of their working lives living with black-and-white materials, a medium that, compared to

colour reversal material of that time, had enormous exposure latitude. Any competent darkroom printer could get a print 'a smudge', from a virtually transparent piece of film. The same kind of latitude was not possible with reversal materials and neither could the agency expect overnight miracles to be performed by its own photographers, or the many stringers it relied on worldwide to produce usable colour slides all of the time. Other factors which prevailed against the use of reversal materials included the agency's requirement to be able to produce black-and-white prints in a hurry from colour originals for telegraphic transmission. Using transparencies would have meant that an intermediate negative would have to be made and since processing the medium was an already long-winded process at that time, the argument for it was rapidly quashed.

Instead, the agency colour photo editor came up with a fairly novel idea. If colour-negative emulsion was used, several bridges could be crossed simultaneously. The material had (and still has) a wide exposure latitude, so if a photographer working under

A test strip easel, like this one from Paterson Products Ltd, is a useful gadget to have around the darkroom if you need to make larger test prints showing the whole of the negative area. Further stripping can be carried out within each hinged frame space to increase the variety of exposure.

combat conditions accidentally exposed film one or two stops over or, worse, underexposed it, results could be salvaged at the darkroom stage. Use of colour negative would permit simultaneous production of high-quality black-and-white prints without the need for an internegative.

Thirdly, by producing 10 × 8 in colour prints, the editor hit on the idea of making up a weekly story-board comprising the best colour stories from around the world. Each print was numbered and contact-mounted onto a large sheet of black card. A few hours before the despatch deadline, the whole board was whisked round the corner to a local studio where it was re-photographed onto a 10 × 8 in sheet of artificial light type Ektachrome. The results were stunning and ideally suited to newspaper and news magazine reproduction. Using this technique contrast was lifted marginally, but colour saturation got a real boost and, finally, picture editors received a dozen or so large-format transparencies instead of barely recognisable 35 mm duplicates. A spin-off benefit from adopting this system was that any number of 35 mm transparencies could be made using 'B' type reversal film by photographing individual pictures from the weekly 'World in Colour' series.

Some years later, when reversal colour printing became more popular following the introduction of the Cibachrome process, the agency reverted to reversal materials and a bench top duplicator for much of its television stills work. But even that was a fairly short-lived affair; when Kodak and Fuji began introducing improved colour-negative emulsions it was perhaps only natural that the agency should revert to using it on an almost exclusive basis. Today, it is probably fair to say that The Associated Press is the world's foremost news-media user of colour-negative emulsions; daily colour transmissions to their bureaux and customers around the world has been a key part of their operation for some years, running happily in tandem with black-and-white.

Considerable advances have also been made with colour reversal materials, notably in the E-6 processed chromes in the areas of definition, colour saturation and film speed. Particularly worthy of comment is the relatively new generation of E-6 processed Fujichrome film whose ISO 50 closely approximates to the qualities of Kodak's Kodachrome 25.

Professional photojournalists have relied on KR25 for years as being the only colour medium in the 35 mm format capable of excellent, and in particular sharp, reproduction. Fujichrome 50 has the advantage of being able to be user-processed and produces images which are almost as grain-free as the Kodak material, and in the larger formats has no real competitor. Additionally, the colour rendering in all of these Fujichrome materials is, in my opinion, more naturally balanced, capable of superb saturation and has fairly tolerant exposure latitudes.

CHOICE OF MEDIUM

Each medium has a specific use, produces or can be manipulated to produce a specific effect, and should be matched by the photographer to the subject and the ultimate requirement; purpose is a key word and should be given careful consideration in the application of the medium. For example, there is very little point in turning up at a wedding with your camera loaded with reversal material when it is known that the client's primary interest is in colour prints. It is perfectly possible to make prints from slides, using one of two techniques, but neither will yield a product using average processing conditions which is in any way comparable to the subtlety of colour or contrast range of a print made directly from an original colour negative.

For the amateur user, the professional GP and in some areas of professional editorial freelancing the colour negative process has definite advantages. These are mainly in the printing and processing stages, which to my mind allow greater freedom of manipulation of the medium using a single developer and bleach/fix process which can also be used to process chromagenic CVT materials.

Professional photographers shooting colour for editorial reproduction rarely use colour-negative emulsions for originating the work, although more and more use is made of it today than ever before, especially for news work where colour prints are required for wire transmission. The top reproduction is from a colour print made from a 5 × 4 internegative of the original Kodachrome 25 transparency, and the bottom one is from a Cibachrome Print made by the reversal print process direct from the transparency. The latter is more contrasty and loses all of the shadow detail available in the original. The top print is softer and more accurate in terms of colour rendition of the original, but less evocative because of the lower contrast inherent in colour-negative materials.

Key West. Kodachrome 25, Nikon F, 200 mm Nikkor. If you want to retain the brilliance of real colours, use fine-grained emulsions known for good rendition and richness. Correct exposure is essential. If in doubt, slight under-exposure with reversal materials and over-exposure with colour-negative will help save the day.

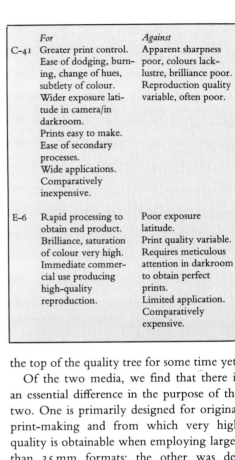

	For	*Against*
C-41	Greater print control. Ease of dodging, burning, change of hues, subtlety of colour. Wider exposure latitude in camera/in darkroom. Prints easy to make. Ease of secondary processes. Wide applications. Comparatively inexpensive.	Apparent sharpness poor, colours lack-lustre, brilliance poor. Reproduction quality variable, often poor.
E-6	Rapid processing to obtain end product. Brilliance, saturation of colour very high. Immediate commercial use producing high-quality reproduction.	Poor exposure latitude. Print quality variable. Requires meticulous attention in darkroom to obtain perfect prints. Limited application. Comparatively expensive.

However, and with particular regard to the editorial field, it must be remembered that whereas the immediately processed colour reversal film can be ready for use as soon as it has dried, colour negative generally requires further treatment to obtain a print film transparency, although, as we have already seen, there are some organisations willing to accept the colour negative for immediate use. Further, it is my opinion that, while the quality of negative emulsions has been improved enormously of late, results from 35 mm formats leave little doubt that reversal originals such as those employing Kodachrome 25 or Fujichrome 50 will remain at the top of the quality tree for some time yet.

Of the two media, we find that there is an essential difference in the purpose of the two. One is primarily designed for original print-making and from which very high quality is obtainable when employing larger than 35 mm formats; the other was designed primarily to meet the very strict requirements of colour reproduction using machine/ink processes. As such, it is hard to beat no matter what the format, and the larger the format the more impressive the quality.

As with all products which need improvement because of user demand, colour-negative emulsions are continually being worked upon in the race by manufacturers to provide the ultimate emulsion suitable for a variety of tasks, and for that, perhaps, we shall always be indebted to the boffins at Kodak who through work on the disc-camera format managed to find a new grain structure which gave noticeable improvements in effective ISO speeds, colour saturation, definition and contrast.

As colour reproduction from negative materials becomes more and more acceptable, it is likely that the popularity of reversal materials will decline except in the highly specialised photographic fields such as science and medicine, and in fine art book and calendar publication. One hopes that, by then, colour-negative emulsions will have been improved yet again so that they may be more widely acceptable to the printing and publishing industry.

To sum up, the photographer should decide at an early stage what the main requirement from the medium is likely to be.

COLOUR-NEGATIVE EMULSIONS

Photographers who use reversal materials tend to standardise on one or two makes and types of film for the bulk of their work just in the same way that they rely on one make and type of black-and-white emulsion. Experience, traditional values and to a large extent market demands, especially with reversal films, largely dictate what will be used on a regular basis.

Modern colour-negative emulsions come into a different category. At the time of writing, I have spent the best part of a year using Fuji negative materials because I feel the material has a slightly better edge definition than most others and I like the colour rendering. However, the choice of material available off-the-shelf is very wide, and for the benefit of those still undecided, or those anxious to know at a glance what, other than their regular brand, is available, a general list is given in Table 11.

The observant reader will notice that I have not included the huge additional array of 'own brand' materials which are sold over-the-counter and through the mail. The fact is that most of these brands are manufactured by some of the better-known regular film producers or by independent factories. Some of the latter claim to market high-resolution colour-negative materials based on the new film grain technology. Considering the results obtained from some of these emulsions, it is more likely that some manufacturers are using out-dated formulae discarded by regular producers. The films may be attractively packaged and accompanied by exaggerated claims concerning

Table 11: COLOUR-NEGATIVE EMULSIONS

Make and name		ISO	Format	Type
Agfa	XRS100	100	35, 120, sheet	Pro
Agfa	XR100	100	35, 120, 110, 126, rapid	Amateur
Agfa	N100SP	100	120, 5 × 4 in	Pro
Agfa	XRS200	200	35, 120, sheet	Pro
Agfa	XR200	200	35, 120, 110, disc	Amateur
Agfa	XRS400	400	35, 120, 5 × 4 in	Pro
Agfa	XR400	400	35, 120, 110	Amateur
Agfa	XRS1000	1000	35, 120	Pro
Fuji	HR100	100	35, 120, 126, 110	Amateur
Fuji	HR200	200	35, 110, disc	Amateur
Fuji	NSP160	160	35, 1/220, 46 mm, 70 mm, 35 mm bulk, sheet	Pro
Fuji	NLP160	160	120, sheet	Tungsten
Fuji	HR400	400	35, 120, 110	Amateur
Fuji	HR1600	1600	35	Amateur
Ilford	HR100	100	35, 126, 110	Amateur
Ilford	HR200	200	35, 110, disc	Amateur
Ilford	HR400	400	35, 110	Amateur
Kodak	VR100	100	35, 120	Amateur
Kodak	VR200	200	35, 120, 620, 110, 127	Amateur
Kodak	VPSIII	160	35, 1/220, 46 mm, 70 mm, 35 mm bulk sheet	Pro
Kodak	VPLII	100	120, sheet	Tungsten
Kodak	VCSII	100	120-high contrast	Pro
Kodak	VR400	400	35, 120, 110	Amateur
Kodak	VR1000	1000	35	Amateur
Konica	SR100	100	35, 120, 110, 126	Amateur
Konica	SR200	200	35, 110, disc	Amateur
Konica	SR100Pro	100	120	Pro
Konica	SR400	400	35, 120, 110	Amateur
Konica	SR1600	1600	35	Amateur
3M	XR100	100	35, 126, 110	Amateur
3M	XR200	200	35, disc	Amateur
3M	HR100	100	35, 120	Pro
3M	XR400	400	35	Amateur

sharpness, colour saturation and so on. If you want consistently good results, use tried and tested materials that have the guarantee backings of well-known producers.

The ISO ratings listed are those given by the respective manufacturers and as far as I can establish are reasonably accurate when allowances are made for inaccurate hand-held, or in-camera, meter readings. Some older-type high-speed emulsions were notable for their bleached highlights and black, black shadows, but there appear to have been improvements, some only marginal, in this area. Use the higher speed ratings for overcast conditions and indoor available light for better results. The 200 ISO emulsions in larger than disc format are mainly the result of technology gained when that small format developed. The difference between 100 ISO

Photocolor chemistry comes packed in convenient liquid concentrate packs in a variety of sizes.

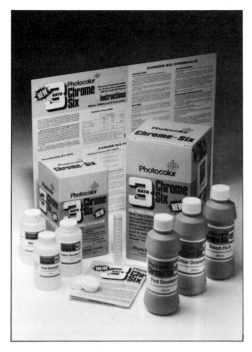

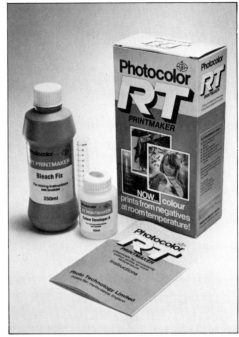

emulsions and 200 is barely perceptible in machine-processed and printed results, particularly on satin or lustre finishes. The 200 ISO emulsions do have less exposure latitude, however; they tend to react in much the same way as reversal materials giving negatives that are either spot on or underexposed; I frequently tend to over-expose colour-negative emulsions by about half to one full stop depending on the subject and subject contrast range, and some photographers I know who use this material often set their camera ISO indexer to 150 or even 100. Over-exposure does not seem to affect the results dramatically and, if anything,

slightly improves contrast and colour balance between the highlights and shadows in some high-contrast subjects.

In processing, colour-negative emulsions also react in a similar way to black-and-white emulsions. They can, with care, be 'push processed' to give an effective increase in film speed but at the risk of dramatically increased contrast. Cutting development reduces contrast, as well as colour saturation, but as there are no alternative contrast grades of paper available for such techniques, the practice seems a trifle irrelevant; better to use the correct film speed for the task and make sure your meter is functioning properly.

11
Colour-Negative Processing and Print Making

A decade ago, processing procedures for colour-negative emulsions, or for that matter reversal materials, were time-consuming and fairly involved, requiring elaborate mixing techniques and constant attention to things like temperature, proper agitation and chemical transfer techniques. Only the most enthusiastic of amateurs were prepared to get involved in a procedure that could take up to two hours in preparation and processing. Apart from studios equipped with the necessary machinery, most professionals who only had occasional use for the material preferred to use a laboratory.

That has all changed. With the advent of new emulsion technology, colour processing has been modified to the extent where it is now no more difficult than the techniques required for black-and-white work. Chemicals are readily available off-the-shelf in kits or by larger quantities from most photographic retailers. As these are in liquid form, no messy powder mixing is involved; just add water at the correct temperature, load the film into a tank, start the clock and begin processing.

In many ways, colour-negative development is actually easier than black-and-white; the reasons for this are partly psychological and have to do with the exposure and contrast latitude of the emulsion materials available.

Whereas with black-and-white one tends to be more manipulative because of its enormous exposure and development latitude which is linked to the printing stage by a whole range of differently graded papers, making a range of different results possible, one tends to regard colour materials from a different standpoint.

In the first place, there is not the great latitude of exposure available which can be easily controlled in processing, and secondly contrast graded paper is neither available nor necessary in dealing with the problems of colour.

Because it is the overall effect of colour rather than graded mono-tones which is of primary importance, the photographer is reliant to a large extent on the manufactured properties of colour emulsions and how they will best interpret the colours of each subject photographed. To change colour, to change subtle hues, to place emphasis on a chosen colour known to be inherent in one film type, the photograper relies on a knowledge of the range of colours available in standard emulsions. Any further manipulation away from the norm can only be achieved by complex development procedures and mechanical manipulations in print processing; i.e. Posterisation, Sabattier effect, mechanical toning, silk screen printing and so on.

Understanding colour theories is one thing. Understanding and being able to use the various mechanical and chemical processes to achieve an effect which no longer relies on the inherent properties of standard colour-negative (or reversal) emulsions, is another. It is not the purpose of this book to elaborate or experiment with these effects and if that is the aim of the photographer I would refer the reader to a superb book on the subject: *Creative Darkroom Techniques*, 3rd Edition, revised. The book is published by the Consumer/Professional & Finishing Markets division of the Eastman Kodak Company, Rochester, New York.

This section of the book is intended primarily to give instruction in the basic processes necessary to get one started on the road to understanding modern colour processing techniques; and to show how it is possible for the amateur enthusiast to achieve very pro-

Granularity in colour varies immensely. For 35 mm work, superb detail can be obtained with Kodachrome 25. Virtually grain-free prints can be obtained from this material using the Cibachrome print process.

fessional results using the simplest of equipment.

If you do not already possess a developing tank or automated machinery, refer to Chapter 2. To develop colour-negative film (and E-6 reversal types) and prints, a film-processing tank of the larger size in stainless steel or black plastic is the only requirement. Both Paterson and Durst make a range of tanks ideally suited to the task. For my own colour processing I use the same stainless steel tanks and spirals as for black-and-white work. Two large polythene measuring jugs capable of holding at least 1 litre each are necessary, together with two large plastic buckets of 5-litre capacity. A thermometer and timer are the only other equipment requirements for the film processing stage.

CHEMICALS

A vast range of chemicals in the form of kits or in concentrated liquid form for higher throughput of film and paper is now available at moderate cost. As nearly all of these chemicals are manufactured to similar formulae, they nearly all produce the same kind of results, though one or two give slightly improved colour saturation. Which type is best is largely a matter of personal choice after several different makes have been experimented with, to discover which:

a) are easier to use;
b) can be used for both film developing and printing;
c) give the best acceptable result;
d) are economical in practice.

Apart from those illustrations reproduced in this volume which were supplied by manufacturers, and some colour illustrations processed by professional laboratories, all of the colour in this and the following section on printing and reversal processing was developed and printed using chemicals supplied by Photo Technology Ltd and Paterson, as follows.

Photocolor II and Paterson 2NA

chemistry was used for the C-41 colour-negative process. Both can also be used for developing black-and-white chromagenic film, Ilford's XP1 and Agfa's Vario XL (recently discontinued).

Photocolor RT printmaker chemistry was used for making colour prints from negatives.

Photocolor Chrome Six was used for all E-6 process compatible reversal materials.

Photochrome R was used to make some colour prints from slides.

PROCESSING METHOD

Although the number of steps required to develop a colour negative film have been dramatically reduced, it is worth noting here that accurate temperature controls of chemistry are important if consistent results are to be obtained. Processing temperatures are high (38 °C, 100 °F). Unless a thermostatically controlled water bath is available, the operator must revert to more basic means. Use one of the 5-litre plastic buckets, or a basin, to stand mixed chemicals in. The water-jacket temperature should be kept at approximately 1 °C (1.8 °F) above the working temperature. If you have access to mixer taps on the kitchen sink or in a bathroom, use rubber hose to run a constant supply of water at the right temperature through the water bath.

Contamination of chemicals must be controlled to avoid film staining. An easy way to mark measuring vessels or separate containers, if you use them, is with a red felt-tip marker. The ink will wipe off when lighter fluid is applied with a cotton wad. Alternatively, you could use large self-adhesive labels which are marked and stuck on each container before they are filled. I prefer this method as the lettering is more obvious, especially after time and constant washing-out has taken its toll.

Paterson 2NA chemistry is suitable for all C-41 emulsions producing negatives with rich colour saturation, bright whites and rich browns and blacks. It may also be used for the development of colour prints, but I prefer the Photocolor RT chemistry for this as it allows a wider working temperature range. Photocolor II uses a print additive concentrate with the developer which seems in practice to produce more saturated print colours. Its main advantage, however, is that it is equally suitable for a wide range of applications from dish and hand to rotary machine processing and is available in replenisher format. This is very useful if one has a high throughput.

1) Load the film to be processed into the tank in total darkness. Make sure that all darkroom equipment lights, such as tiny light-emitting diodes on some timers are either extinguished or obscured from the loading path; otherwise you may just end up with a fogging veil over parts of the film. Follow the same instructions for spiral/spool loading as in Chapter 5. Close the tank and switch on the main lights.

2) Adjust the temperature of the chemistry water-jacket to 1 °C (1.8 °F) above that required according to the manufacturer's processing instructions. Mix sufficient quantities of the Developer and Bleach–Fix as directed in the 2NA instruction leaflet. Place the chemistry containers in the water-jacket and check their temperatures frequently. To avoid any possible risk of contamination, two graded thermometers should be used, one for each solution. I always use a pre-wet bath before development commences, so into the water-jacket also will go a container of filtered water. You may decide not to employ the water rinse between the developer and bleach-fix (blix) stage, in which case adequate supplies of conventional stop bath as used in black-and-white work may be used. Fill a container with the right quantity and place this too in the water-jacket.

When using the higher temperature of 38 °C a relatively short development time of 3 minutes is all that is required, and when such short times are used consistent agitation is important.

3) As soon as the chemistry has reached the correct working temperature, begin processing. Carefully pour in the pre-wet bath and invert the tank slowly, then turn it back to a standing position. Give the tank a gentle tap on the bench to remove any air bubbles and allow it to stand for 15 seconds. Now pour this away. Do not worry about the slight discolouration of the water; it is just dyes used in the film make-up and will not affect development.

4) Immediately pour in the developer, a mixture of what used to be called the 'first' developer and 'colour' developer. Start the clock running simultaneously and watch agitation times carefully. Bang the tank on the bench top (or sink) to remove air bubbles and agitate fairly vigorously for the first 15 seconds. Invert the tank twice at every 15-second period following this throughout the duration of the development time. Approximately 10 seconds before time is up, begin to pour the chemicals back into their container. Do not worry too much if you exceed the stated development time by a few seconds. If the film was exposed at the manufacturer's recommended ISO speed, there is a good chance that some darker shadow areas will be a trifle under-exposed. A little extra development will do no harm. When processing colour-negative emulsions, I tend to follow the same kind of procedures that I use with all of my black-and-white development techniques, including the omission of the last agitation stage, in the belief that edge acutance is slightly enhanced by allowing the film to stand in perfectly still developer for a while. If I omit the habit of beginning the changeover 10 seconds before the end, this more than makes up for the loss of agitation.

5) As soon as the tank is emptied of developer, pour in the water rinse or stop bath and agitate for a further half-minute. Discard a water rinse. The stop bath can be returned to its container for further use.

6) Now pour in the bleach fix (blix). Agitate for the first half-minute and then, if you wish, allow the tank to stand. Agitation is not so critical at this stage, although it is good practice to invert the tank every minute or so. When time is up, pour the blix back into its container. You may now remove the tank to facilitate washing of the film. For

Paterson Auto Colortherm processor rigged for colour negative/reversal film processing (top) and for colour negative/reversal print processing (bottom).

Reproduction from colour-negative stock using prints using modern scanning technology can be every bit as good as that from reversal material, provided colours are well saturated. Detail in the shadow areas here has been burned-in to emphasise the orange tube and blue sky.

weighted clip and allow all surplus water to drain off before turning on the heat. Two or three minutes is normally sufficient. DO NOT overheat in drying. A constant supply of warmish air is all that is required. If you are drying the film on a line in an open space, try to prevent the main access door to the room being constantly opened and shut. This simply stirs up the atmosphere and deposits all kinds of nasty foreign matter onto the emulsion as it dries. To speed up the drying process, allow the film to drain for at least five minutes, and then begin applying heat with a hair drier set to the lowest setting. Start on the non-emulsion side at the top of the film with the nozzle of the drier about 4–5 in (10–13 cm) from the film surface. Work steadily downward until you reach the bottom and then go back to the top. After five minutes, begin working in the same fashion on the emulsion side. As the film begins to dry it will curl inward (emulsion out) first, and then assume its normal shape.

The 2NA chemistry may be re-used for further processing with some adjustment to the developer and blix times which you will find in the instructions. In processing chromagenic black-and-white emulsions, exactly the same procedures are followed in conjunction with the longer development and blix times necessary. These are also given in the instructions.

There is no good reason why, if manufacturer's instructions are followed to the letter, and if your original exposures are reasonably accurate, you should not be able to achieve success at your first colour-negative developing attempt. It really is very easy. The fault chart in Table 12 will give you some indication of how to remedy any faults that may occur. Apart from under-exposure in the camera, the most likely and frequent cause of problems is contamination. Do watch out for this, particularly when checking temperatures before processing begins.

Similar procedures are followed using Photocolor II chemistry with slight variations for times given in Table 13.

best results, use filtered water of between 32 and 38 °C (90–100 °F). At least two changes of water are required every minute for four minutes.

7) When the wash cycle is complete, refill a measuring jug with a litre of water to which is added a few drops of wetting agent. Paterson Anti-Static, Kodak Photo-Flo or a drop or two of domestic washing-up liquid will make the water more miscible with the film emulsion, allowing it to drain evenly and rapidly without risk of drying marks.

The processed film will have a slightly milky appearance which gradually disappears as drying takes place. If you use a drying cabinet, hang the film with a

Table 12: COLOUR NEGATIVE FAULTS

Negative problem	Likely cause
Lack contrast and density	Film under-developed; temperature too low; incorrect development time.
Too dense, too contrasty	Film over-developed; temperature too high; incorrect development time.
Dense brownish unexposed-areas of film	Blix contamination of developer.
Density low, contrast normal	Film under-exposed in camera.
Density high, contrast normal	Film over-exposed in camera.

Table 13: PHOTOCOLOR II CHEMISTRY PROCEDURE

Stage	Time (minutes)	Temperature
Preheat tank	1	2 °C (3.6 °F) above process temperature
Development	3.25	38 °C (100 °F)
Stop bath/rinse	0.5	38 °C (100 °F)
Bleach-fix	4.0	35–40 °C (95–104 °F)
Wash	5.0	30–35 °C (86–95 °F)

Note: times increase as the temperature decreases. The full range is given in the comprehensive instructions with the kit.

FORCED DEVELOPMENT FOR COLOUR-NEGATIVE EMULSIONS

Unlike conventional black-and-white panchromatic emulsions, emulsions using the C-41 process do not much like being under-exposed and then pushed in development. It can be successfully done, however, but any gains in an increased contrast level are not equalled by equivalent gains in colour saturation. In normal outdoor situations where lighting is even and bright and colours are well defined, forced processing of a film under-exposed by two stops will produce a result, though not altogether satisfactory in my view. Under available light conditions, the result may be pleasing depending on the type of light available with a general rendering of brighter colours in more subtle hues.

One or two stops is about the maximum which it is possible to push this emulsion type. In general, films with a higher ISO speed give better results than slow or medium-speed emulsions, and it is recommended that films with an ISO speed of less than 400 be given an effective increase of only one stop. 400 ISO emulsions can be successfully up-rated to an EI1600. If you know in advance that you are likely to require the extra speed afforded by faster films, results will be better using an emulsion with a higher manufactured rating.

Using Photocolor II chemistry, increase development by 50 per cent at 38 °C (100 °F) to achieve printable negatives. Base fog level, negative contrast and grain 'clumping' will be increased, which may necessitate longer printing exposures.

Photocolor II can also be used to process chromagenic film in the same way as Paterson 2NA. Follow the same procedure as for colour negative emulsions but use a development time of 4 minutes at 38 °C (100 °F) as a trial time. This can be adjusted to personal taste up to half a minute either way, and best results will be achieved from film which has been consistently exposed at the same effective EI speed. Both Ilford's XP1 and Agfa's Vario XL may be given up to 50 per cent more development for an effective increase in film speed, though contrast and grain will also increase. Use clean water in place of a stop bath for the rinse sequence between developer and blix. Ensure that bleach-fixing is not less than the recommended 6 minutes at any working temperature. Incomplete fixation will result in higher contrast and coarser grain due to the residual silver image.

PRINT MAKING FROM COLOUR NEGATIVES

Now that you have successfully processed your first colour negative film you will want to start making prints from the best negatives. One of the great advantages of being able to print your own work is that you can be more selective in the choice of negatives and choice of colour balance as well as the size of the print. Sending work to a Development and Printing house invariably results in a shoebox full of prints that are hardly ever looked at, and there is no guarantee that developed film will not be returned scratch-free once it has travelled in haste through the machinery used in some of these establishments.

The first essential to grasp is that colour printing is no more difficult than film processing. The actual time from exposure to completion of a fixed print is approximately 15 minutes, and that includes a few sips from the coffee cup while-you-wait. It is great fun and in some ways less complex than black-and-white printing. The stumbling block for amateurs has always been colour filtration and the correction of various imbalances in print colours or casts. With modern dial-in dichroic head filtration and better papers, filtration is not the mind-boggling problem it was a few years ago, and no doubt as time passes it will become easier.

For this section, I used Photocolor II chemistry, a Durst Colortrainer chart, my own vintage MPP enlargers and a set of Kodak Colour Printing filters which are inserted in various combinations into the filter drawer between the light source and negative. This method takes a little longer when adjustments to filtration become necessary, but is one which I have been happy with for a number of years. It also allows me to retain the use of the double condenser light source in preference to the semi-diffused systems of many modern enlargers, some of which are fitted with filter materials which do not conform exactly to Kodak standards.

There is a variety of methods by which the colour print can be developed and fixed. Dish, tank, rotary tank, roller processor and the Kodak Ektaflex system allow a broad choice. For the occasional print, a dish or standard large size tank capable of developing up to $8 \times 35\,mm$ films is perfectly suitable. Rotary drums and roller processors only become necessary when large outputs on a regular basis are envisaged. I used the Nova darkroom tank for the production of some of the prints reproduced here. Greatest convenience, however, is afforded by the humble dish. Depending on dish capacity virtually any size of print and test print, or combinations, can be processed rapidly without the need to dry out a tank after each separate print has been made. A degree of consistency in colour balance between different test strips is easier to control; temperature of the chemistry is easier to maintain using a secondary larger dish with a water bath.

The Kodak Ektaflex process is completely different in make-up and application and relies on a lamination process and special equipment for the production of prints from negatives, and positives as well as the production of display transparencies. The process is described at the end of this section.

If you are already well equipped with dishes and tanks for black-and-white processing, no other equipment will be needed apart from a set of colour correction filters, if these are not already a feature of your enlarger. Gelatin filters come in a variety of sizes and are available as *Colour Compensating* (CC) or *Colour Printing* (CP) from Kodak. Colour compensating filters are used in a holder between the negative and enlarger baseboard. If you have a filter drawer below the lamphouse, use of the CP type will not affect the printed image sharpness. Another very useful item that occupies no more space than a strip of negatives is a colour control patch of the type used in graphic arts work and by professional studio photographers for checking colour balance on test shots. Its use will be explained a little later.

COLOUR FILTRATION

Most of the confusion for beginners in colour photography seems to stem from the fact that the correction of colour casts in prints relies upon the 'subtractive' principles of colour synthesis.

When the three primary colours, red, green and blue are mixed together in equal proportions and viewed by transmitted light, the mixed colours produce a white

light. This is known as the 'additive' principle of colour theory. Early colour photography was based on this thinking but required complex tri-pack plates which were mechanically criss-crossed with printed filters in the primary colours. Subject matter was exposed three times, once through red, green and blue filters, but could only be used in conjunction with still-life subjects. Newton had discovered much earlier that when white light passed through a prism it effectively split into seven separate colours. If one or more of these colours were blocked, the remaining colours combined to form a new colour when re-transmitted through a converging lens. This new colour was complimentary to the blocked colour.

Many technicians and photo-scientists worked for years in an endeavour to produce a colour process suitable for general use which required only a single exposure through the camera lens. One-shot colour cameras simultaneously split the colour image through primary colour filters to produce three separate black-and-white plates, each one of a comparable density to the value of the filter through which it was exposed. To view the result, three similar primary filters were used through which to expose the plates onto paper. And so it went on until two Kodak technicians called Leopold Godowsky and Leopold Mannes invented Kodachrome film in 1935.

This material used the subtractive principles of colour photography which had first been investigated by de Hauron as far back as 1862. The primary colours as we know them would be more accurately described as the 'additive' primary colours which when projected onto a screen in equal proportions not only give white light where those portions overlap, but other colours where only two of the primaries overlap.

These other colours are the complimentary colours or 'subtractive' primaries each transmitting two thirds of the spectrum. Each one of these colours represents white light minus one of the three 'additive'

Use of filters when exposing film will help to eliminate unwanted casts and effects caused by atmospheric conditions. The left-hand picture was exposed without any filter. The right-hand one employed a UV absorption filter which improves red tones and reduces the overall blue cast.

primaries. For example, yellow (red and green primary), is *white* light without blue; magenta, formed primarily by the mixing of blue and red, is *white* light without green, and cyan (green and blue primary) is *white* light without red.

Filters which transmit the subtractive primary colours each transmit two thirds of the spectrum; in other words, only two thirds of the colours forming white light. Any two filters combined together transmit one of the additive primary colours while absorbing the rest. When two additive primary filters are combined total absorption of the complimentary colour takes place. The Mannes and Godowsky invention used these subtractive principles for the production of amateur cine film and, a year later, for 35 mm still photography. All additive processes became redundant from that time on, with the exception of the Dufay process, later used as a basis for the exploration of instant photography by Dr Edwin Land and his later successful introduction of Polacolor (see Chapter 14).

The confusion between reality, i.e. what we see and think of as real colours, and photographic colour, which is a synthetic mixture of unreal colours able to produce those real colours, is undoubtedly the cause of many an unsatisfactory print. In black-and-white photography, contrast between a variety of similar tones causes no such problem; the brain sorts tone and contrast into shape and form and gives it meaning. In colour, this simple process of rationalisation no longer works; the introduction of colour suddenly inhibits and confuses the process of assimilation, although, in due course, the brain is able to fit the jig-saw together and recognise the image.

In producing a colour print from a colour negative (coloured prints are also obtainable from black-and-white negatives), the photographer is first of all faced with the problem of how to recognise the complimentary colours – the subtractive primary colours of the negative image – in terms of real colour. Once a test print is made, any imbalance in real colour, any apparent real colour cast, can only be altered by changing the subtractive primary colours using similarly coloured filters of differing density.

The problems created by this kind of confusion would appear at first hand fairly easy to remedy. Instead of thinking of colour as it is, think of it only in terms of subtractive primaries which when combined in varying strengths will produce the real colours of the world. This approach might work well if all colour photography were based on the negative to produce positives. Well, think about it. It is. Even the humble transparency begins life as a negative and then through chemical fogging is reversed to form a positive. If you were to process a colour reversal film first in black-and-white developer, fix it, and then by using a ferric bleaching process re-halogenise and develop normally as a colour negative, the result would be a highly saturated negative of complimentary colours. In duplicating a transparency, the same principles of filtration are applied as with a negative.

12
Colour Printing

Few figurative examples exist which in my view adequately show how one may easily remember how white light is divided into the complimentary colours of the additive primary colours, red, green and blue. If anything, a colour chart showing exactly how the complimentary or subtractive colours are obtained tends to add to the confusion, and how this can be so is easily understood if we look at Table 14 which identifies the colours in relation to each other.

COLOUR PRINTING FILTERS

For the benefit of those who do not have a dial-in filter facility (colour mixing head), or who prefer to control filtration by manual means, Table 15 lists the Kodak Colour Printing filters and their various denominations. Filters used in some colour mixing heads may not give the same balancing effect as the Kodak materials listed, and practical tests will have to be completed before a true assessment of their values can be established.

The Kodak CP filters are available in 5 in (125 mm), 6 in (150 mm), 12 in (300 mm) square sizes and 8 × 10 in (200 × 250 mm) size.

Kodak colour compensating filters are also available but in a much wider variety and for many different applications. They were originally designed for colour printing for use in front of the lens. However, no more than three should be used at any one time. Their greatest practical use is in photographic origination, where colour balance of the subject matter is changed during exposure. They can also be used for black-and-white photography to make subtle changes in tonal values and are useful for correcting casts when duplicating transparencies using tungsten and electronic flash light sources. A full description of the uses and values of CC filters can be found in any current edition of the Kodak Photographic Catalog.

Each filter allows its own colour to pass, but filters out the remaining colours by subtraction. When two filters are used in correct proportions, the primary colours red, green and blue are obtained. If all three filters are used, the combination forms varying degrees of grey through to black, so in colour printing only two of these filters are used at any time in varying values to subtract or add colour to the print, except when for reasons of convenience it is easier to add a value of a different colour when the colour shift required is minute. You will see how this works as we go along.

Modern colour emulsions of both negative and papers are far more stable than they used to be and invariably need only fairly small adjustments in filtration once the basic filter pack values for a particular batch of paper have been established. On the back of a

Table 14: SUBTRACTIVE AND ADDITIVE PRIMARY COLOURS

Subtractive primary colours	Additive primary colours	
	Mixed from	Omitted
Cyan	blue + green	red
Magenta	red + blue	green
Yellow	red + green	blue

Table 15: KODAK COLOUR PRINTING FILTERS FOR USE IN ENLARGER LIGHT SOURCE

Cyan	Magenta	Yellow
CP05C	CP05M	CP05Y
CP10C	CP10M	CP10Y
CP20C	CP20M	CP20Y
CP40C	CP40M	CP40Y
+ Ultraviolet absorber CP2B		

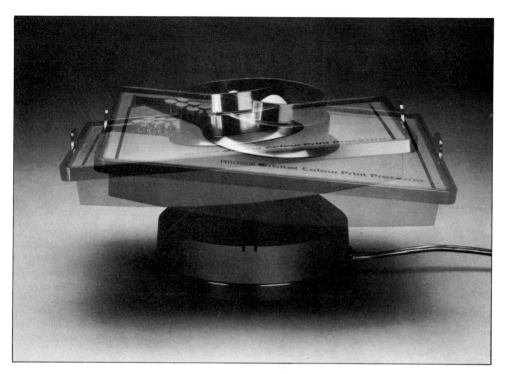

The Paterson Orbital colour print processor using a unique agitation method is ideal for print-making and uses very little liquid. (Photo courtesy of Paterson Products Ltd.)

packet of paper you will find an emulsion batch number, much the same as you find on a box of film. Underneath this figure is another set of figures which may read 'filter correction −20Y'. This means that the standard filter pack for that type of paper needs a filtration adjustment of −CP20Y before printing commences. Using a well-exposed and fairly contrasty negative, test prints using this filter pack should produce a first print of almost acceptable colour balance. If there is a dramatic shift in colour away from what you feel is right, first look to causes other than the basic filter pack.

Make sure that the ultra-violet absorbing filter, CP2B, is in place in the filter drawer. Check that the negative you are attempting to print has no obvious cast to it other than those normally associated with colour negatives. Check the temperature and freshness of working chemicals. Ensure as far as possible that the developer has not been contaminated by the blix. Is the correct safelight in use? Are all light-emitting diodes around the enlarger extinguished or covered?

If all of these items are found to be in order, then you can begin adjusting the basic

filter pack. First of all, check that this pack was made up from the correct values as advised in the paper manufacturer's instructions. Check that you have correctly adjusted the pack with the value given on the reverse label of the paper packet.

As with test exposures in black-and-white printing, colour printing requires the same dedicated effort to establish the basic parameters within which work will be done. As I have already mentioned, the filters in enlarger mixing heads will vary in value and type, so, if you have one of these, you must first of all establish their accuracy in relation to Kodak values. Ideally, test strips from negatives exposed of a well-lit subject which incorporate a. Kodak Colour Control patch are most suitable.

Process the film in the normal way using chemistry described in the previous chapter. Select a negative for printing. This will provide test prints which you can then match visually under normal daylight or a 40-watt cool white fluorescent tube against the original Kodak Color Patch. Adjust the filter pack to correct for casts which are not compatible with the original colours in the con-

These two pictures make use of one colour which has been effectively isolated and emphasised by the use of neutral colours in the background. A print from any of these may need substantial correction to keep the surrounding colours neutral.

trol patch. When a print of the closest acceptable match to the control patch is available, make a note of the filter pack values, exposure time and development used and compare this with the values given by the paper manufacturer for a basic filter pack using Kodak values.

The difference between the two sets of figures is noted and used as the standard bias for your enlarger whenever a new batch of paper, or batch from a different manufacturer, is used. If the new values are more or less than those established for your instrument, simply add or subtract the amount of bias from each filter required to form the basic filter pack.

Colour analysers and other measuring instruments can be purchased which will assist the photographer in making acceptable colour prints. However, all of these instruments will need to be calibrated for individual darkrooms and the conditions which exist; paper type and speed, light source type, filter type and chemistry must all be taken into consideration. Only when calibration has been accurately established for one printing session can there be any guarantee of success, which is why, if you aim to learn the basics of colour printing, the manual approach using individual filters will teach you more, a lot faster, than any gadget.

CORRECTING COLOUR CASTS

Exactly how filters behave in printing will soon begin to be understood once several test strips have been made. Think of each filter in terms of the colour that it absorbs, rather than the colour it will transmit:

> *Magenta* absorbs *green.*
> *Cyan*   absorbs *red.*
> *Yellow* absorbs *blue.*

In attempting to reduce a particular colour cast, *increase* the value of that same filter colour, or filter combination required to give that colour. Remember, the colour of the filter will subtract the same colour from the print; the higher the filter value, or combination of values, the less of that colour appears in the final print.

Alternatively, you may *reduce* the amount of filtration of filters of the complimentary colour.

In practice, a print with an overall magenta cast will benefit by an *increase* in the magenta filter value of the pack. If the increase is too much, the complimentary of that colour will be visible in the print, i.e. green. To remove it, increase yellow and cyan together, or *reduce* magenta.

Most modern papers and emulsions are balanced for correction using only two of the three subtractive primaries, *yellow + magenta.* *Cyan* is more often used in printing positives from colour transparencies, about which there is more later. Whenever possible, it will pay dividends to control filtration using only the *yellow + magenta* by adding or subtracting various values from the standard filter pack as and when required. On the odd occasions that *cyan* must be added or subtracted, values of the other two, *magenta + yellow* must be reduced. If they are already at zero or close to it, further reduction will not be possible, in which case correction

of the cast is achieved by a combination of filters which gives the same colour as that which it is required to remove.

For example, the print colour cast is *green.* Magenta cannot be reduced further because it is already at zero or at least a very low value. Combine yellow and cyan (=*green*) and increase in value until the cast is removed.

Table 16 identifies the various colour casts and shows how to correct them. Note that it is a simple matter to cross-reference both the 'subtractive' primaries and the 'additive' primaries so that, in order to facilitate the addition of colours, we only need reverse the procedure. Table 16 is for use when printing from colour negatives.

Use Table 17 when printing positives from colour slides.

Reading the theory behind colour practice is essential if you are a complete novice. However, one can often read too much too fast. A mountain of information seems to have been swallowed, but very little actually comprehended, which is why I have assumed from the outset of this chapter that you will want to begin printing as soon as possible. There is always the risk of course that a mountain of wasted paper will accumulate in the process of discovery. The possibility that this mountain might be marginally reduced in size as a result of reading the theory first is fairly

Table 16: CORRECTING COLOUR CASTS ON COLOUR NEGATIVES

Colour cast	Increase	Reduce
Red	magenta + yellow	cyan
Green	cyan + yellow	magenta
Blue	cyan + magenta	yellow
Cyan	cyan	magenta + yellow
Magenta	magenta	cyan + yellow
Yellow	yellow	cyan + magenta

Table 17: CORRECTING COLOUR CASTS ON COLOUR SLIDES

Colour cast	Reduce	Increase
Red	magenta + yellow	cyan
Green	cyan + yellow	magenta
Blue	cyan + magenta	yellow
Cyan	cyan	magenta + yellow
Magenta	magenta	cyan + yellow
Yellow	yellow	cyan + magenta

small, especially if confusion reigns supreme.

THE DURST COLORTRAINER

Start printing as soon as you are able. I used Photocolor II and Photocolor RT printmaker for most of the prints reproduced here, in combination with one of the best manual gadgets to be produced since colour chemistry became available in a two-shot liquid format; the Durst Colortrainer is about the size of a Scrabble board and divided into squares corresponding to both sets of primary colours in varying densities and strengths. In addition there are 18 squares of varying density from white through to black.

The Colortrainer serves several purposes, and even for those who know, or are supposed to know, it is a simple but effective teaching aid as well as a reminder that even the most experienced minds are fallible.

A collection of coloured chips whose hue and density matches the coloured and black-and-white squares on the board are scattered at random on a suitable desk or bench top. The colour student is then invited to try and match each and every one of the 72 coloured chips to its relevant square; the 18 black-and-white chips and white strip are also matched. When you think you have accomplished this task successfully, transparent trays are laid over the board's coloured squares and the procedure repeated by laying the chips in order in the trays. The trays have lids. When the task is completed, the lids are affixed and the trays turned over to reveal a picture. This elementary jig-saw is easily recognised and one can soon see where the blunders in matching the squares have been made!

When I first unpacked the kit, I had the uneasy feeling that someone might be trying to pull my leg. None of the colours, except perhaps the brightest ones, could be considered as a near match for the sort of colours that one experiences in photography. This was my first mistake, because on pulling out a random colour print from the files I soon discovered that one could easily match any colour and colour density in the print very

easily using the chips. On the reverse of the chip, the filter values required to remove the cast, or colour, are printed and these correspond to the values given on the board.

Rather than make another blunder, I read the simple instructions and spent another hour testing my skills at judging colour. In the past, assessing the colour balance of a print and trying to correct any casts that might be visible had always been done by overlaying the various filters on the print, or by viewing the print through the filter. Using a solid colour actually makes this task easier because the colours seen in a print are viewed by reflected light, not by transmitted light. The chips were beginning to make a lot of sense.

To make full use of the Colortrainer, the student is advised to photograph the board in its entirety using diffuse daylight or suitably controlled flashlight on the first few frames of a colour-negative film. After development, the best of these negatives is selected and four trial test prints made using varied exposures combined with a standard filter pack. From the dried prints, the best level of density and contrast is selected and the 0.70 grey density square on the print cut out. This is then matched with an equivalent square amongst the 18 density squares on the board, from which a new exposure is then calculated using a factoring table provided with the kit.

The new exposure is designed to give the correct density level for a standard print – NOT the correct colour. This is achieved by matching the cut-out density square with the nearest colour tone elsewhere on the board. If you are certain the colour match is correct, use the filter modification value to adjust your enlarger pack with. You can make a note of these adjustments in your notebook or on the very comprehensive and specially provided trainer work sheets.

You should now have the correct exposure and correct filter pack to give you a starting point for making any other prints provided you use the same film type, chemistry and light source. To my mind, this process makes the usual ring-around system of prints totally redundant. Use the standardised filter pack to make a trial exposure of the next negative, say a portrait shot. Using a subject in which skin tones are a major feature will soon establish whether you are making any progress.

Keep all the colour prints you make and write on the back of each one with a felt-tip pen the filter pack, exposure, f-stop, development + temperature and chemistry used, as soon as you have decided that the print is a dud. When you have made an acceptable print, write the same information used to make that print also on the back of the dud. You will soon begin to collect an assortment of prints with useful filter information written down, so should the time come when a repeat print is required, say a year later, that information will prove invaluable. Any slight shifts in colour balance can soon be corrected using the Colortrainer.

THE RING-AROUND PRINT SYSTEM

This is a system devised for both colour-negative and colour-slide printing techniques which is designed to show at a glance how the most likely cause of trouble in terms of exposure and colour filtration can be corrected. From a colour negative (or slide) known to be of correct exposure, colour saturation and density, a variety of prints are made; at least 9 and as many as 17 can be required for a full set. Included is one print which to all intents and purposes is accurate in terms of colour rendition, exposure and density. The other prints in the series are variations of exposure, plus or minus one full stop and plus or minus varying degrees of colour balance using the three additive and subtractive primaries. For good measure, several prints exhibit strong casts using each one of these colours. In my experience, this kind of system only has any value if it is possible to make the prints large enough for further comparative purposes. In other words, anything less than a 10 × 8 is virtually useless. So to begin with, some considerable investment is required for materials and

chemistry. Furthermore, these prints will become the standard against which all other work is compared and adjusted. If, instead of using a real subject photographed under variable lighting conditions, a standard colour chart were to be photographed instead, some sense of a ring-around might be made possible. This is in fact what Durst have done with their Colortrainer, and it seems to me that the investment necessary to purchase this kit far outweighs the time and cost of materials involved in trying to make your own.

CHEMISTRY

The Photocolor II processing instructions are very explicit. Liquids are available in a standard pack size of 1500 ml and a Professional outfit which will make 6 litres of chemistry. The contents comprise colour developer concentrate, bleach-fix concentrate, and print additive in the case of the 1500 ml size. The larger volumes are available as separate items, and include colour developer for negatives and prints, colour developer replenisher, colour developer for negatives only (no print additive) and two-part concentrates to make the Universal bleach-fix. A photo-stabiliser for films is also available.

As all the concentrates are in liquid form, little difficulty is experienced in mixing solutions to the right dilutions. Use polythene or glassware containers, not clear plastics as some grades are easily damaged by agents in the chemicals. Photocolor II chemicals have excellent keeping properties and when used in diluted form with increased times can be used to process large quantities of paper. The chemistry is ideally suited to processing Photocolor RC, Agfacolor type 5, 6 + 7 and Kodak Ektacolor 74 + 78 colour printing papers. At high temperatures (38 °C, 100 °F) development time varies between 1 minute 15 seconds and 1 minute 55 seconds. The lowest recommended temperature (25 °C, 77 °F) requires development times of between 6 and 9 minutes depending on the paper type used. These figures should not be confused with the time and tempera-

The effect of a large area of red here is largely subdued by the equally large area of contrasting blue. If these parts are isolated so that only the darker tree trunk and parts of the red container remain, you will see how saturation of the red area is apparently increased.

ture range for Photocolor RT Printmaker chemistry which has a far wider temperature processing range with an ideal working temperature of 20 °C (68 °F). Photocolor II chemistry is designed for use under stricter darkroom controls, but is in fact just as easy to use as RT provided you have the means to keep a high level of working solution temperature and can measure it fairly accurately.

In practice, I found very little difference in the result produced by either chemistry. The advantage of Phot II is that at 38 °C (100 °F) development and blix times are very short, which is great if you happen to be in a hurry. One litre of RT print developer will process about thirty 10 × 8s and one litre of Photocolor II approximately forty similar-sized prints when development time is gradually increased after the first five prints have been developed.

PRINTS FROM SLIDES

Nearly all of the foregoing information is applicable to making positive prints from slides. However, you must remember that this is a reversal process and, therefore, all filter corrections are reversed (see Table 17). Processing is carried out in the same way as print-making from colour negatives, using different print reversal chemistry. For the production of prints from slides in this book, various methods were used, including Cibachrome and Photocolor Chrome R.

Both produce different results, but for the home-worker intent on producing a record of slides in print form and the occasional larger print which may be required for wall-hanging or a gift Chrome R is to be recommended. Cibachrome has less temperature latitude and requires a fairly expert touch to obtain the superb results which this process is capable of giving.

It is suggested that, in the first instance, Chrome R is used while some knowledge is gained in the handling characteristics of reversal print materials. Although filter corrections can become progressively minimised, finding the right exposure balance to produce a print without the burned-out highlights and dense shadows characteristic of the reversal print can take a little time.

Chrome R chemistry is intended for use with Kodak Ektachrome R14 and 22 papers in conjunction with slides exposed on any type of reversal film. It is available in 600 ml and 5 litre outfits, and comprises First Developer concentrate, Colour Developer solutions A, B and C, and Bleach-Fix solutions A and B. The process may be used at any temperature in the range from 20 to 40 °C (68 to 104 °F) but the preferred working temperature is 30 °C (86 °F) which keeps times to within a reasonable and manageable level when using a static water bath to maintain working solution temperatures. 600 ml will process about ten 10 × 8 in prints using a drum. I used my stainless black-and-white developing tank when developing prints on a one-off basis, and this seemed perfectly satisfactory. Dish-processing is quite feasible but complete darkness is required for the first developer and first wash stage. Using Photo Technology Indicol stop bath in a 2 per cent solution after first development permits room lighting to be turned on, and the remainder of the process through colour development and blix can be carried out under the same light. I found it quite easy to use a combination of stainless tank and three dishes for much of this process which made life marginally more convenient.

Use the tank for the first development which, once the paper has been loaded in total darkness, can be continued under room lighting. A few seconds before the end of the first development time, turn out the room lights, remove tank lid and carefully remove the print as soon as the timer rings. Transfer immediately to the stop bath dish and agitate the print fairly vigorously for about 15 seconds. Turn on the room lights and continue the colour development, then rinse and then blix. Blix temperature is not critical and can be carried out at whatever the ambient room temperature is. Temperatures should not however be allowed to fall below 20 °C (68 °F). Using this method, there is an advantage to be gained if more than one print is to be made and you want to get on with the second one. Maintain a fairly low colour developer temperature (say 21 °C) which permits a 10 minute 15 second development time. While this is going on with intermittent agitation, a second exposed print can be tank-loaded and developed before the first print needs to be transferred to the blix. From 33 to 40 °C, first development times range from 2 minutes to 1 minute. That gives you a clear 8 minutes for changeovers, lights out, rinses and so on.

Ektachrome 22 paper gives a somewhat softer gradation in contrast than some other types of RC reversal colour paper. It is available in both glossy (F) and smooth lustre (N) finish. It should be remembered, however, as with black-and-white printing, that most problems encountered in producing satisfactory prints from slides will be met when endeavouring to print scenes of high contrast, i.e. when the brightness range of a slide is far in excess of the acceptable brightness range of the paper. Adequate results can be obtained by choosing slides which tend toward a lower than normal contrast range. Some sacrifice in tonal rendition will have to be made where large areas of highlight and large areas of deep shadow detail are present in the slide. It is much better to select a picture in which one or the other, but not both, of these areas may be sacrificed.

It is possible to reduce the first development, much in the same way as one might when processing transparency films, to 'pull' the contrast level down, but some compensation for this procedure must be given in the exposure. Initially, try an increase in exposure of one stop and reduce the first development time by 30 per cent. A series of stepped exposures should be made to establish the correct density level and new development time. Remember that in reversal printing an *increase* in exposure will produce a lighter print; *decrease* exposure for a darker print; put like this, it is fairly easy to remember: INCREASE LIGHT, DECREASE DARK.

COLOUR BALANCE

Reversal prints hardly ever need the same amounts of filtration required in making prints from negatives. Nearly all films have a slight colour bias, but if slides are first of all inspected closely using a Lupe over a decent light box using cool white fluorescents, any major bias can usually be detected.

To start with, make your test strip exposures using zero filtration. Slides of scenes shot under adverse conditions, i.e. at sunset and sunrise, or in hot and very cold climates, may show an overall cast if no correction filter was used at the time of exposure. It is often difficult to assess what, if any, cast might be present in early morning or sunset pictures, such is man's fickle taste for the romantic! However, early evening shots during twilight which have necessitated longish exposures may show decided colour imbalance due to reciprocity failure. When desirable, this can easily be corrected in printing the slide. Quite often, especially in the northern hemisphere, I find that reversal material

exposed at this time of day for more than a second or two produces a result which is actually better than the original scene.

When filtration is required, it is unlikely to be much more than in units of 05 to 15. Transparencies which have faded with time or taken on a cast through chemical change of the dye couplers may need considerably more filtration. There are no standard filter pack settings for these occasions for obvious reasons. As with colour negative printing, the final result is always very much in keeping with personal taste. Use Table 17 as a guide to correction.

COLOUR REVERSAL PROCESSING

Photocolor Chrome Six which I used for much of the transparency origination and duplication in this section is available in kit and larger quantities of concentrate to make 600 ml, 1200 ml and 5 litres of working strength solution. It is similar in function and application to the Chrome R chemistry just described for reversal print-making. Each kit contains a first developer, colour developer A + B solutions and parts A + B of the blix. Working temperature is best at about 38 °C (100 °F) but it can be used with progressively longer and shorter developing times from 20 to 45 °C (68–113 °F).

Lower temperatures will give processed slides a slight yellow tint, while higher ones tend to yield a blue cast. In practice, I found that a working temperature of between 34 and 35 °C (93–95 °F) gives results with a very faint warm bias. The reds and oranges are noticeably enhanced. Where these colours predominate in the picture, the overall effect is quite pleasing, and where blues predominate any enhanced red values tend to take the coldness out of the scene. Some tests may be necessary to establish a colour bias preference. This is well worth doing if you have the time. Why?

When I am exposing film outside during the colder winter months I usually endeavour to employ an 81C pale amber filter with daylight-balanced emulsions. This takes

Reversal processing for the amateur is a relatively simple operation requiring only three chemical baths. Photocolor Chrome Six is provided in liquid concentrate packs, is very easy to mix and use over a wide temperature range. Temperature control is critical and times specified must be rigidly adhered to or modified as development proceeds.

out much of the cold-colour effect which is usually evident in transparencies exposed in the northern hemisphere. A Skylight 1B filter will absorb much of the ultra-violet but, even though it does have a slight warming effect on flesh tones and some other subjects taken in close proximity, those wide open scenes still seem to suffer. If you had previously conducted several tests using say, Fujichrome 100, processed at varying temperatures, the noted record would give a very good indication of how colour balance could be shifted during processing to give a more pleasing result. The same thing applies to scenes of sunsets. Many of these are predominantly red or orange in color, but where high pressure weather patterns exist locally, upper regions of the sky may still be blue, or purple. Such subtle differences in hues are often difficult to expose predictably. Using a combination of on-camera filter technique and subtle shifts in processing temperature can often make life less tedious.

In reversal processing, the key to success in obtaining a correct level of apparently well-exposed images lies with the first developer. It is important to maintain the chemistry to within at least plus or minus 1 °C (1.8 °F) but less if possible – and to adhere rigidly to timing. In practice, there are several points to check before you even start exposing reversal film, especially if you have an in-camera TTL (though the lens) metering system.

The ISO indexing ring which on most cameras is fitted with TTL metering is designed to give exposures which will produce an averagely acceptable result. I do not recall an occasion when I have ever been able to use one of these meters and rely on the film manufacturer's rated ISO and my camera meter being in agreement as to exactly what the right speed is. When you purchase a new camera, always run a film through it and make exposures using a range of ISO settings. Keep a note of the frame numbers, exposures used and ISO settings so that you can check as soon as the film is processed whether your TTL meter is graded up or down from the actual indicated speed.

Nine times out of ten, one can be fairly certain that camera meters set to the manufactured film ISO will produce transparencies that are over-exposed by between half and one stop. Shaded details look fine, but highlight areas will invariably have that washed-out appearance, lacking contrast, colour intensity and brilliance. However, the camera manufacturer may well argue the point that the film maker is to blame, having rated the film at a slightly slower speed than it should be. All types of reversal film tend to vary in this respect, which is why it is well worth investing time, a little money and effort into finding the 'right' emulsion. The fact that I now use a lot of Fujichrome (and Fujicolor) has nothing to do with it. Before their later emulsions were heard of, apart from KRII and 25, I used Kodak Ektachrome, particularly in the roll film format. I have never liked the stuff, although I must admit that exposures were always spot on when I used the film roll instruction sheet. A friend who spends much of his time travelling in sunnier climes, in search of pictures for holiday brochures, wouldn't change it for the world; so don't just take my word for granted. Go out and experiment until you have found an emulsion that satisfies all of your needs.

Once you have fully investigated emulsions and matched the chosen one with an easy-to-use chemistry like Chrome Six, you will soon begin to understand just how flexible reversal materials can be. By pulling back the time on the first development, varying degrees of under-exposure are obtained; by giving extra time, an effective increase in film speed is gained and it is quite surprising just how far some reversal emulsions can be pushed.

Mixing, handling, appearance and capacity of solutions are well covered in the manufacturer's instructions of Chrome Six. If you follow the step-by-step guide carefully, there is no real reason why any competent darkroom worker should not be able to produce a set of superbly processed transparencies at the first attempt. You will need a large basin for the water-jacket if your darkroom is not equipped with a rotary processor with built-in water-jacket. But, other than that, a normal cylindrical film developing tank in stainless or plastic, thermometer(s) – more than one to avoid contamination of chemicals – and a clock are all the equipment you will need to begin with.

PUSH-PULL REVERSAL PROCESSING

Professional newspaper, freelance and agency photographers have been force-developing reversal colour emulsions for years – a habit largely induced by the lack of effective filmspeed for low light level photography. Modern emulsions are available in a variety of ISO values with some very high manufactured emulsion speeds; Kodak Ektachrome P800/1600 Professional film is a fine-grained transparency film with excellent colour rendition and colour balance adjusted for forced processing. It gives best results rated at the box speed, but can be pulled back to EI400 or pushed up to EI3200. 3M's 1000 daylight-balanced (5500K) transparency film gives good colour rendering under low light conditions also, where most lower ISO rated materials give an imbalance toward lower colour frequencies. Up-rating lower speed materials to a point where it is still necessary to use relatively long exposures – over one second – usually results in some interesting colours caused by reciprocity failure. High speed emulsions do not have this problem.

It would make a lot of sense to use such high-speed emulsions where light conditions warrant it. Sports photographers equipped with fast telephoto lenses of the dinner plate variety (f2.8 or faster) will find that not having to up-rate 200 or 400 ISO emulsions is a valuable asset. As there now seems to be an ISO value available off-the-shelf to cater for almost every demand, it seems only reasonable to ask why one would ever want to resort to push processing.

Well, there are still many photographers who enjoy manipulating the characteristics of some colour reversal films. Depending on how the technique is applied, and on what

type of emulsion, a variety of effects can be obtained: increased grain, increased colour saturation, increased contrast and others are all possible. For example, Ektachrome 400 (daylight) is usually only pushed to EI800. Beyond this, weird things begin to happen, with colours going haywire. Try exposing a roll under fairly low light conditions at EI3200, an effective increase of 8 stops.

Nearly all push processing is a matter of experiment until the right results are produced. Keeping notes of new times and any changes in temperature and chemistry make-up will be useful for future occasions.

Begin by carrying out a clip-test. Load a few frames of a fully exposed roll into the tank and, using the same temperatures as you would for standard development, increase the first development by 50 per cent to give an effective increase in film speed of one stop. Progressive increases in exposure values will not necessarily mean that the increased time of the first development should follow in exact increments. For example, an 8-stop increase in film speed should theoretically require a a 400 per cent increase in first development time. So if the normal first development time was 4 minutes, the new time will be 16 minutes. However, increased first development on this basis does not produce a sufficient increase in density levels, resulting in processed transparencies with a somewhat muddy appearance. Some adjustment is necessary to get the latent image held in the shadows properly developed. How much extra time is given will largely depend upon the subject matter and whether this was predominantly in shadow with few bright highlights or whether it was evenly lit with few shadow areas. Start by adding 25 per cent to the newly calculated time. In addition, to help build up the maximum density (black), dilute the mixed colour developer with water at the rate of 1 + 2 and increase the colour development time by approx 135 per cent. The original transparency of the stoker (see p.166) was shot some years ago before the very high speed emulsions became available. I had made several attempts to shoot this picture by using the light from the furnace only, using Ektachrome-X, the old version of Ektachrome 64.

Using exposures of between 1/15 and 1/30 second on a 28 mm lens wide open at f2.8, the first results of forced processing were hopeless. I had a picture, but no detail existed in the shadow areas or in the face, which was precisely where I wanted maximum detail. I went back to the scene several times over a period of few days. After gradually increasing the first development on consecutive occasions by employing calculated figures, I finally decided to double my original estimations, on the grounds that nothing more could be lost. The E-3 process at that time required a first development of 10 minutes at 24 °C (75 °F). I had already pushed that time way beyond what might have been considered reasonable limits – 30 minutes – with no effect. In exasperation, I put the last roll of exposed film in the tank and went for tea – for an hour!

I gave a good healthy re-exposure to a photoflood and then three times the normal colour development. Out of 36 exposures, I salvaged half a dozen that were more or less perfect. Later I tried to work out what the effective speed of the film was, having pushed it beyond what I would have normally considered an acceptable level. As there were no accurate figures to go on, other than a rough estimation of exposure value from my Weston light meter with which I had taken a fairly close reading of the furnace,

I could only hazard an approximate guess, taking into consideration development time and the brightness range of the subject matter from highlight to deepest (black) shadow. At the furnace door, the Weston had given an EV of 6.5 which approximated my 1/15 second at f2.8 exposure. Light from the furnace onto the stoker's visage was EV 1 or less, though it could not be accurately measured because of the intense heat at the final close proximity to which I enouraged the man to go. So, on the basis of that alone, the film was up-rated at least 8 stops, and if the development time is considered, allowing for a large percentage of time to develop the latent shadow image, the effective EI is close to 650.

Most reversal emulsions requiring E-6 chemistry for development can, when exposed under certain inclement weather or lighting conditions, be made to produce marginally better results if a small increase in film speed is assumed from the outset. A one-stop increase in speed when exposing under overcast, dull conditions, with consequent increase in first development time, will produce slightly contrastier transparencies with improved colour rendition. Best results are obtained by using medium-speed films of between 100 and 200 ISO. When conditions deteriorate so much that practically useful exposures can no longer be employed, better results will be obtained using a higher-speed film.

13
Duplication of Colour Transparencies

The photographer wishing to duplicate slides for projection, or display, reproduction and occasional audio-visual usage, can employ numerous methods, the most common and popular of which is a slide-copying attachment which fits onto the standard lens of the camera. The latter is then attached to the camera via a set of focusing bellows or extension rings. A flashgun or tungsten light is used as the light source behind the flashed opal screen of the duplicating accessory. Special duplicating units like the Bowens Illumitran are also used. When this equipment is not available, the only alternative may be a north-facing window, a roll of adhesive tape, a sheet of tracing paper and camera with macro lens; not a very efficient or practical answer to the problem.

The enlarger is the answer. Some, like the Kaiser models, have optional attachments which allow the head to be inverted and used as a projection box. The copying camera is mounted on the column and, with a set of bellows attached, can be used in much the same way as a professional duplicating unit.

Using duplicating or tungsten-balanced sheet film is a slower but better answer. It gives the technician more control and once the process is mastered will produce duplicate transparencies that are every bit as good as the original.

The biggest problem in duplicating from originals is that the contrast range in the duplicate is invariably much increased when no panchromatic mask is employed. Making the mask is not difficult, but in my view is not always necessary, particularly if the end result is to be used for reproduction and the format size of the dupe remains the same as the original.

Kodak Ektachrome Slide Duplicating Film 5071 is recommended for use in duping 35 mm originals. It is a specially formulated emulsion with low-contrast characteristics. The film is designed for use with Argaphoto or Photopearl lamps of 3200k. The emulsion speed is low, effective ISO 6. This film is now available in 36-exposure cassettes and the filtration details are marked on the side. If you plan to use a zoom-type copier with electronic flash, use Kodak's SO-366 which is balanced for daylight or electronic flash.

Kodak Ektachrome Duplicating Film 6121 can be used for same size or enlarged duplicate transparencies; it has excellent colour reproduction characteristics and does not require originals to be masked. Both film types are designed to be used with tungsten light sources and are processed in E-6 chemistry.

To make duplicates from any size original up to 16 × 20 in use Ektachrome 6121. I normally use the 5 × 4 in format, as most of my laboratory equipment is designed to handle that size. Two strips of three transparency originals will cover the format with a little to spare at top and bottom edge. I use a standard clear glass foam-backed contact printer which is positioned under the enlarger light beam so that the whole 10 × 8 in area of the print frame is covered.

When you have selected the transparencies for duplication, carefully tape them together in the 2 × 3 in format. Use a light box and thin strips of transparent sticky tape (Scotch) to make the joins. Ensure the tape does not overrun the frame edge of the picture. In the darkroom, with the safelight on, position the printer frame under the enlarger light beam. Make this slightly out of focus so that any dust particles inside the enlarger are not sharply focused on the contact printer. Now open the frame so that the glass lies on the left-hand side. Lay the transparencies to be

Speed. Original was shot
on Ektachrome 200 with
an 80–200 mm zoom
Nikkor. Duplicates were
then made to increase
contrast and delete some
shadow detail.

copied on the glass so that the top edge of the top three protrudes slightly over the glass edge. Lay the transparency originals so that the emulsion side faces up. Have the box of sheet duplicating film handy on the right-hand side of the bench. Insert the CP2B ultra-violet filter into the filter drawer and, if you think there is a colour cast that would be better removed from the original, insert the appropriate correction filters. You can use Table 17, as a guide, but remember that reversal materials require very little filtration and it may well be better to begin with none at all.

Next, set your enlarger timer to the 'seconds' mode. Select 5 seconds for average well-lit, but not too contrasty, scenes. The f-stop on the enlarger lens should be at f8 – 11, midway between the two. Briefly turn out the darkroom safelight and ensure that all other lights on machinery and instruments are extinguished or taped over. Turn the light back on and find a light-tight box in which to place the exposed film. Keep this handy by the enlarger.

Turn out the darkroom lights. Open the box of duplicating film. You will find that all sheet film is code-notched in one corner. Place the notch in the top right-hand; the emulsion is now facing you. Carefully feel for the raised edge of the foam back of the contact printer, top right corner. Place the film sheet emulsion-side-up in this corner, so that both its top edge and outer edge are aligned with the foam back. Now take the transparencies to be duplicated and align the top edge with the top outer edge of the sheet film. The transparencies should also be emulsion-side-up. Carefully close the glass cover of the printer. Make the 5-second exposure. Open the glass cover and remove the exposed film sheet and place it in the light-tight box. As soon as you have prepared the chemistry, process the sheet of film. Dishes or tanks can be used for this purpose as described in Chapter 2. If you plan to make a regular habit of processing 5 × 4 in sheet film, a tank designed for the job is a good investment. Sheet film can be processed in a cylindrical tank, but with some

difficulty, although Jobo do make a 5 × 4 in sheet film loader for their tank spirals.

Once you have developed the first sheet of film following the chemistry instructions to the letter, you will be able to see exactly where, if at all, any errors have been made. These are most likely to be in the exposure, which is why it is important to choose an original transparency of normal brightness and fairly low contrast. First results from this will provide a duplicate master from which subsequent exposures can be adjusted.

To make enlarged duplicates first strip the original of any mount, clean by dusting with a squirrel-hair brush or compressed air. Remove any marks from the back of the original with a well-washed cotton handkerchief dipped in a little carbon tetrachloride (CT). 25 ml bottles of CT are usually available from a good pharmacist or hairdressing suppliers. It is not usually advisable to touch the emulsion side of the slide, unless this is so badly marked and dirty that it cannot be duplicated without cleaning. When you have wiped over the back of the slide with CT, polish it gently with a clean area of cloth and then dust off loose matter. Flick the edge of the slide with a fingernail to discharge any static electricity. Now place the slide emulsion-side-down in the enlarger negative carrier. Make sure the CP2B filter is inserted in the filter drawer.

Normally, I make whole frame 5 × 4 in dupes from the original, but I have also used a 6 × 9 cm roll film back containing Ektachrome 120 format film balanced for tungsten use and made acceptable duplicates. The roll film back is fitted into a jig made up with small aluminium brackets on a small sheet of plywood. This mounted back is held in position on the enlarger baseboard by using a pair of small wood-working cramps. When you make up the jig, remember that the end of the back into which the dark slide is inserted must be kept free. The slide has to be removed and replaced before and after each exposure.

Load the film into the back in the normal way, making sure that the tongue of the film is properly secured in the take-up spool.

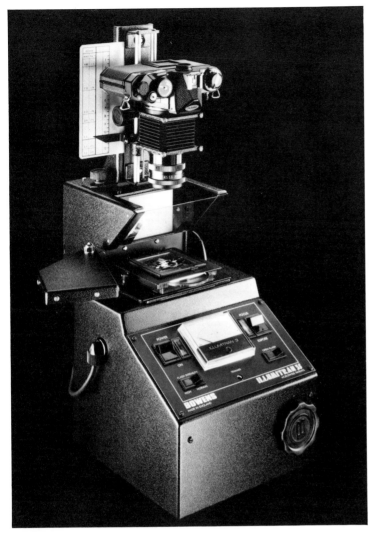

A professional duplicating machine such as the Bowens Illumitran means that contrast and filtration can easily be controlled.

first frame. Re-position the back in the jig and begin making exposures as soon as you are ready.

Using a 5 × 4 in double dark slide film holder, the process is much simplified. First, in total darkness, load up as many sheets of film as you think will be required for a duplicating session. Keep one side of one holder empty and mark the side with a piece of coloured adhesive tape so that you know exactly where it is. Into this side, place a sheet of white paper of approximate film thickness cut to size. This is used as a printing frame to crop and accurately focus the original transparency. The dark slide should always be inserted after use; it keeps the paper clean and ensures that the slide does not get lost or scratched.

A special jig is not required for this process, though individuals may prefer working with one. A normal printing easel is quite sufficient, the two adjustable arms being used to hold the film holder in place. When exposures are being made, short lengths of masking tape are useful to fix the film holder more securely in place. From here on, the procedure is much the same as one might use for making prints from slides.

Crop and focus on the plain white sheet held in the marked holder. When you are satisfied, remove the focus film holder and insert a loaded double dark slide holder into the printing frame. Tape in place if necessary. Extinguish all lights, check for light-emitting diodes (LEDs) and other stray lights. Remove the dark slide and make the exposure. Replace the dark slide and mark the exposed side by placing a short length of masking tape over the centre of the slide. Continue making exposures as required.

If you are using tungsten-balanced film, you will find the exposures required for satisfactory density and contrast level in the duplicates are much shorter than for Ektachrome 6121 duplicating film which has an average time of 10 seconds. Shorter times may be required for contact duplicates. When making enlarged duplicates using tungsten-balanced film, start at 2 seconds with an f-stop of f11.

Wind on a couple of turns, but not as far as the arrow markers on the film backing paper. Before closing the back, cut a thin sheet of white paper 6 × 9 cm and attach it to the black backing of the loaded film where it will close inside the frame aperture. Close the film back and mount in the jig. Using a safelight only for general illumination, position the back on its mount exactly where required under the light beam. Size and focus the original onto the white sheet of paper in the film back. When you are happy with position and focus, gently remove the film back from the jig and wind on the film to its arrow marker position in the normal way. Now insert the dark slide and wind on to the

Duplication of 35 mm originals to larger formats is usually only successful if the original is sharp and not too contrasty. This reproduction is from a 5 × 4 in duplicate made on Ektachrome Type B sheet film. In cases where the original is valuable and unlikely ever to be repeated, duplicates should be made.

6121 film does not normally require an out-of-focus pan mask, but if contrast seems a little on the high side when duplicating without a mask increase exposure marginally and cut the first development time. Start with an increase of half a stop and reduce the first development by 10 per cent. Similar practice can be used with tungsten film, only more exposure and less first development may be required in some instances.

CONTRAST MASKS

The use of duplicating film may obviate the need for a contrast mask. However, normal to high contrast subjects on original material may duplicate more satisfactorily if a mask is used.

The mask is made using high-speed panchromatic film: Tri-X or HP5 are both suitable for this purpose. A wooden contact printing frame is the most suitable carrier for this purpose, but is not essential if you have an ordinary print-contacting frame.

Place the mask film material emulsion-side-up on a clean, flat surface. On top of this

place a glass spacer. An old glass negative plate is ideal. This must first have the emulsion washed off which is simply done by immersing the plate for a few minutes in warm water. Wash and dunk in a solution of photo-flo and hang to dry. You will then have a clear piece of optically flat glass for the spacer.

When the spacer is positioned, place the original transparency on top of the spacer, emulsion-side-down. Make sure the glass cover of the printing frame is cleaned and place the sandwich, transparency at the top, under the frame. Make several exposures using different sheets of film and process normally in Kodak DK 50 diluted 1 + 2 for 4 minutes at 68°F.

The spacer provides a degree of unsharpness on the mask, but this in itself is often not sufficient and use should be made of a point source light of low wattage to expose the film. The light source should be at a distance of at least 4 feet (1.2 m) from the print frame. Alternatively, an enlarger source may be used if the light beam can be diffused by employing a sheet of etched plastic or opal

Duplication of 35 mm originals to larger formats can also be achieved by using the enlarger to expose the transparency directly onto sheet or roll film. Here, a Graflex roll film back was used to make consecutive duplicates on Ektachrome Type B film using the whole and small portions of 35 mm originals sited in the enlarger negative carrier. Some adjustment to overall contrast was effected by slight over-exposure and reduction of the first development.

glass. Ideally, masks should be developed to a gamma of about zero 0.7, but it will pay to make several exposures giving the same development in order to find the most suitable contrast.

Once you have selected a suitable mask, this must be registered with the original. This task is easily accomplished over a light box with the aid of a high-powered optical magnifier. It should be very easy to see where the original and mask are out of register. Once aligned, tape the two together and sandwich between two optical flats (pieces of glass). If a glass negative carrier is used, the sandwich will not be necessary and some newer enlargers, like the Durst, have a pin registration system in the negative carrier which is ideally suited for this purpose as well as for making montages.

Duplicating from low-contrast originals will normally produce very acceptable results using tungsten-balanced film of 50 ISO. Ektachrome 160 Tungsten is a trifle too contrasty for this purpose, although there will be subjects from time to time which will benefit from the increased contrast and apparent colour saturation this emulsion provides. The same principles apply in making copy transparencies from original flat colour prints or artwork. Begin by using the lowest ISO rated film rather than the highest. If necessary, increase exposure and reduce the first development by 30 seconds when using Ektachrome 160. The same procedure applies when using this material to make enlarged duplicate transparencies.

FAULTS

The following is a list of faults which may become apparent after processing using Photo Technology Ltd chemistry.

COLOUR PRINTS FROM NEGATIVES

Prints too contrasty, possibly a yellow cast. Cause: over-development; contamination of pre-heat water with blix.

Prints contrasty, possibly with violet cast, blue stain on borders and in highlights. Cause: developer contamination with blix.

Streaks or urn marks green and/or pink in colour from drum processed prints. Cause: liquid retained in drum or lid which runs across dry paper.

Blue stain or fogged borders and highlights. Cause: contamination of developer with blix; pre-heat water too hot; check safelight is the right type; possibly over-exposure to safelight.

Yellow or orange streaks or patches at corners and edges of paper. Cause: stray light causing paper to fog while in partially opened packet; check darkroom for source.

Under-developed areas on corners and edges of print (white or pale areas). Cause: print not fully immersed in developer.

Red or yellow scratch marks. Cause: abrasion of wet emulsion surface.

Finger marks. Cause: paper handled with damp, contaminated fingers; wash and dry well under air drier.

PRINTS FROM SLIDES

Prints too dark, no contrast. Cause: oxidised first developer.

Prints have poor blue blacks, colours washed out. Cause: oxidised colour developer.

Prints with greenish-grey blacks, contrast low, colours poor. Cause: first developer contaminated with colour developer.

Prints with green blacks, low contrast, poor colours and yellow cast. Cause: first developer contaminated with blix.

Prints with blue blacks, low contrast, poor colours and orange cast. Cause: colour developer contaminated with first developer.

Prints with blue or violet/blue blacks, severely degraded colours and strong overall blue or violet/blue cast. Cause: colour developer contaminated by blix.

TRANSPARENCY PROCESS

Transparencies appear black with little or no image. Frame numbers on edges appear normal. Cause: severe under-exposure in-camera; faulty shutter; film not transported through camera; faulty flash synchronisation etc.

Entire film black. No frame markings. Cause: first developer oxidised or exhausted; colour developer and first developer used in wrong order.

Entire film including film edges transparent; little

or no image. Cause: little or no colour development; chemistry oxidised or exhausted; film fogged by accidental exposure to light as when camera back opened before film rewound.

Dense transparencies but edges and leader normal. Cause: under-exposure; insufficient first development; time and/or temperature incorrect; exhausted first developer; no account of increased time necessary when employing used chemistry.

Very dense transparencies with blue/purple cast. Exposed end of leader blue. Cause: first developer severely exhausted and/or oxidised.

Transparencies too light, otherwise film normal. Cause: film over-exposed in camera; too much first development; wrong time/ temperature; film force-processed inadvertently.

Low density and contrast. Colour saturation poor. Cause: insufficient colour developer; wrong time/temperature; oxidised/exhausted colour developer.

Shadow areas and frame divisions have low density with red/brown cast. Cause: colour developer exhausted/oxidised or made with insufficient Solution B.

Mottled veil-like appearance. Film leader grey. Cause: blix process incomplete; repeat blix with fresh solution and rewash.

Dark or light band entire length of one edge of film. Cause: insufficient coverage by solutions at one or all stages of processing; it may be possible to remedy this by repeating the blix stage if the film is properly developed.

Unprocessed areas of film, irregular patches. Cause: film not properly spooled; doubled up on some grooves causing film to stick together at some points.

Small black spots, irregular pattern. Cause: air bubbles on emulsion during first development; remember to tap tank on bench top during first few seconds of first development; vigorous agitation required initially.

CROSS-CONTAMINATION OF SOLUTIONS

The effect on film will depend largely on the degree of contamination. Severe contamination will produce low-density edges and pronounced colour casts.

First developer contaminated with colour developer. Result: loss of density in shadows and unexposed areas of film. Marked colour changes.

First developer contaminated with bleach-fix. Result: general appearance of over-exposure; cyan/green cast, loss of image density, green edges to film.

Colour developer contaminated with first developer. Result: strong green or yellow/green cast.

Colour developer contaminated with bleach-fix. Result: severe cyan cast.

LIGHTING CASTS

Emulsions balanced for daylight will give strong yellow/orange casts when exposed under tungsten lighting and greenish casts when exposed under fluorescent light. Emulsions balanced for tungsten light give blue casts when exposed under daylight conditions.

All of these possible faults and remedies apply equally when making duplicate transparencies from originals using E-6 chemistry. The biggest cause of all problems is usually cross-contamination of solutions. Wash out and dry tanks thoroughly before starting a fresh process. Where possible, use more than one thermometer and keep the same containers for use with the same chemicals. ALWAYS wash hands after immersing them in one solution.

14
Polaroid Photography

Standing on the roadside with a bucket in one hand and a half-cleared negative in its stainless cut film holder in the other, I began to ponder on the modern marvels of photographic technology, simultaneously wondering whether Fox Talbot had felt any of the emotion I was now experiencing as he carefully developed the wet collodion plates he had just exposed, in a mobile field darkroom. I hoped that he had, reflecting ironically that after nearly 20 years of freelancing in photojournalism, I had at last found a process that made me feel the kind of things I had always thought conventional photography should have made me feel, but never had. It has always seemed to me that the actual process of conventional development and print-making was somehow not connected psychologically with the art of picture-making.

The artist can watch a picture of his subject appear slowly in front of his eyes while viewing that same subject. The photographer is compelled to commit the picture to memory until such time as the exposed image can be developed at another place, at another time. It is a procedure I often find a trifle frustrating. That, combined with the anti-climax on discovering some time later that the pictures developed are not what one had either hoped or expected, has affected the way I think about image-making for some time.

Perhaps I should explain. I had been investigating the various possibilities of conventional colour emulsions and how they could be manipulated to achieve a particular effect. At this time, much had been written in the trade press with regard to manipulative processes to produce results that were far from those intended by the boffins who had spent years perfecting those emulsions. I liked the ideas, but not the results, and anyway am far

too arrogant and conceited to want to utilise someone else's 'discovery' – though I suppose that in itself is a somewhat hypocritical attitude in view of the history of conventional photography. What I was really after was a process that would give me a colour more suited to the very intangible ideas I had been nursing.

To this end I had purchased a plastic Polaroid 1000 camera on the simple theory that instant photography was something I had never seriously dabbled with, nor had any need for. In fact, in the past, viewing the results of Polaroid Instant colour had only confirmed my suspicions about the apparently awful quality of colours reproduced, and nothing I had read anywhere seemed to allay those fears. Armed with a pack of SX70 type colour film, I began making a few simple exposures. A pillar-box red garden swing on a green lawn had caught my eye.

Not knowing precisely how the film was balanced (except for daylight) I could not have known how it would react to the bright backlighting of a cold December morning. The first print was rushed indoors and held

This is a magnified image of part of one eye, and clearly shows the linear colour grid which at normal 10 × magnification in print form is not noticeable.

Polaroid film has long been used by many professionals as a medium for checking exposure and colour balance, set design and picture composition, before the final picture is committed to conventional emulsions. But Polaroid materials have their very own distinctive character and, in some instances, use of these emulsions might be better suited to the end product requirement than conventional materials. Polachrome, which is available in 35 mm format only, uses the additive linear grid screen to form colours, which when properly exposed give brilliantly saturated results. Notice that in this photograph, no large white areas are visible adjacent to other colours. This is a key to the successful use of the material. (Courtesy Polaroid [UK] Ltd.)

over a radiator for the recommended developing period. As if to confirm my suspicions, the print developed with a ghastly blue cast over everything. My bright pillar-box red was a soggy pink and the green lawn had turned to sea water.

What if the film, like conventional reversal materials, was balanced for a very high Kelvin value? Any cast resulting from the actual colour of the light would be far more pronounced on a print than on a transparency. For the next exposure, I positioned a pale amber 81C filter over the lens and fired the magic button. Much better! There was a very pronounced improvement in rendition of both reds and greens, but I could have done better with a more powerful filter, which unfortunately was not available. But that was it. In spite of the simplistic nature of my new toy, Polaroid has given my imagination a kick in the pants and a renewed interest in many other photographic techniques I had long since forgotten.

And that is, more or less, how I came to be standing in the roadside holding a bucket in

one hand and wet negative in the other. The gallon plastic bucket contained a dilute working solution of sodium sulphite, mixed earlier in the darkroom from 500 g of anhydrous salts. This stuff was essential for the proper clearing of the negative I hoped to get from the Polaroid 665 black-and-white positive/negative film exposed in the Hasselblad. Unable to obtain sodium sulphite the day before, I had used plain water in my impatience to 'try' out a few exposures. It cleared the opaque backing from the emulsion OK, but prolonged overnight storage in the water had softened the emulsion so much that the negatives scratched too easily.

The beauty of this emulsion is that it provides the photographer with a usable negative, one from which prints can be made on conventional papers, in addition to a print, straight out of the camera. The type 665 Positive/Negative film is a film pack with an ISO of 75 and a development time of 30 seconds under ideal temperature conditions. However, it is not quite the plain sailing one might imagine, and how the film is exposed depends very much on the ultimate requirement.

In order to produce a fully exposed and developed negative, I found that the rated speed of the film was a trifle optimistic, especially when used outside in low temperatures. My first efforts were grossly under-exposed, so I kept reducing the effective ISO until I had reached a point where the prints were over-exposed by a full stop after development. Type 55 film has a rated ISO of 50, but this also needs considerable reduction in the field in cold conditions. Further, in both types, you will find the print material a little faster than the negative, a difference of probably EI20.

Working in the open like this requires a little ingenuity in maintaining a fairly high temperature level for processing. I had been running the car for a while, so the radiator was quite warm. By holding the exposed film pack close to its surface, I was able to keep development within 90 seconds. The alternative would have been an under-the-arm job, which I did not relish because of the risk of damaging both print and negative, or a portable heater of some description. An empty biscuit tin inverted over the car radiator and in which the film was held during the development time might have been more reliable.

You can use plain filtered water to remove the opaque backing from the negative, but, as I found in my impatience, this produces a rather soggy negative from which not all of the developing agent is removed and which is easily scratched or abraded. It is better to have the right chemicals in the first place. The negative will clear after a few minutes of rapid agitation. To harden the negative, prepare a solution of 28 per cent acetic acid by mixing 250 ml with 500 ml of water at 21 °C (70 °F). Add to this solution 16 g of potassium alum and top up the mix with water to make 1 litre. Immerse with gentle agitation for about 2 minutes in this solution. A thorough wash is then required before dunking in photo-flo solution and drying. The wash should be in running water for not less than 20 minutes.

The emulsion thickness of Polaroid 665 negative material is very much thinner than conventional Estar-based sheet films, which makes it very floppy and prone to the slightest possibility of accidental damage. If you value your negatives, make sure that they are placed in a glassine bag as soon as they are dry.

Out in the field, negatives can be kept in a sodium sulphite solution for a period of up to 72 hours if it is not possible to return immediately to base where running water and drying facilities are available. The industrious photographer will no doubt arrange for a field kit to be made up which can be easily transported in the boot of a vehicle; one cannot travel far or very fast with buckets of solution slopping about in the back!

Polaroid used to manufacture a field kit which comprised a plastic bucket with sealed lid and space on a rack for several negatives. I understand that these units are no longer available, but it may be possible to track one down through the classified columns of a trade magazine. The company also supplies sachets of pre-measured anhydrous sodium sulphite for mixing small quantities of the solution.

The Polaroid back for use on the Hasselblad has an optical flat over the frame aperture, and it is essential that this be cleaned before a film pack is inserted for use. Any foreign matter on the glass will show up as black specks on the negative when it is developed. Quite a number of medium-format cameras are available with off-the-shelf polaroid backs: apart from the Hasselblad just mentioned, the Kowa Super 66, Bronica models SQA and GS1 and the very latest Mamiya 645 with interchangeable backs, plus of course the Mamiya RB67, all offer a Polaroid facility.

There is a Polaroid back available for the Nikon F2 and F3 made by Marty Forscher of New York. It has a special fibre optic block which allows the image at the normal film plane of the camera to be carried back to that of the Polaroid back. In addition, the back has a facility for exposing two frames independently on the same sheet of film.

Using the 'O and ER' Express enlarging easel under a conventional enlarger it is possible to make direct colour prints onto Polaroid materials, or to make black-and-white negatives and/or prints. This equipment is manufactured in the United States by Optical and Electronic Research Inc., and is available in the UK from distributors George Elliott. (Photo courtesy O and ER.)

Naturally, because this piece of equipment is produced in fairly limited quantities, it is expensive and would hardly be considered as anything other than a professional aid to better pictures. If you want to know exactly what that 2,000 mm lens is going to put on the frame before you shoot the Kodachrome, a Polaroid back could prove invaluable.

That is exactly what many professionals using larger formats use their Polaroid backs for; to check exposures, to check the studio set, to check on the ability of a certain lens to produce the right result. But, for me, instant photography does not end here. It is just a beginning, and with a great deal of help from Polaroid UK Ltd I have been able to explore just a few of the possibilities.

One of the most recent developments to come from the Cambridge, Massachusetts,

Corporation was the introduction of a range of 35 mm emulsions in both colour and black-and-white which made their debut at the *Photokina* exhibition in 1982. Polachrome, Polapan and Polagraph are all compatible with any camera employing the 35 mm format, are packaged in distinctive white labelled cassettes with swaged-over end caps. The manufacturer thoughtfully provides an ingenious tin plate device for extracting leaders which have been inadvertently wound-in after exposure. This device comes with the 'Darkroom in a Box' which provides all the equipment one needs to process a film within minutes of its exposure. Fox Talbot would have loved it and I cannot imagine anyone who has used the system who would not feel similarly disposed.

Each film is provided with its own cartridge of processing chemical which is released from a pod in the cartridge and is transferred to a 'vehicle' film of thin polyester sheet and mated with the exposed film via a set of lightly sprung rollers. Both cartridge and film are easily inserted into the magic 'box' and anchored onto a take-up drum. The box is closed and, by depressing a lever, the caustic jelly-like developing agent is released from its capsule inside the cartridge ready to be carried to mate with the exposed film on the 'vehicle'. A few quick turns of the winding handle (there is also a motorised version) pulls the film and vehicle out of their respective cassettes and winds them onto the drum. After the relevant number of seconds has elapsed, development is complete, the lever released and each film wound back into cassette and cartridge. On opening the box, both vehicle film and exposed film are detached from the drum. Discard the developing cartridge. Over a light box, gently pull out the processed film for inspection, et voilà!

POLACHROME

Until the fairly recent advent of Fujichrome 50, I had always stocked Kodachrome 25 and used it for all of the important 'eventing' around the world. Its main attraction is the inherently fine granular structure which allows fine resolution of detail and, in the hands of a good photo-mechanical processor, excellent reproduction. Nothing else can touch it. Fuji's E-6 film is fine-grained too, using a different manufacturing and colour coupling process, but allows user processing; a great advantage for professionals dealing with the news media and requiring a rapid turn-around period between exposure and street reproduction. Good as both these emulsions are, however, I was never convinced that colour for colour's sake was either important to me or necessarily a good thing for the reader. After all, we are surrounded, nay virtually bombarded, by media colour in a variety of forms until the mind is drowned in its whirlpool.

I have no 'formal' training in photography or art, but my instinct seems to tell me what is worth a second look. Black-and-white has been the mainstay of my photographic career probably more because the end product assimilates more easily with my feelings for art, nostalgia, adventure, human endeavour and the impact of disaster. Communicating any of those feelings through photography to the viewer is somehow easier without the complication of colour.

Colour in the conventional photographic form lacks immediacy. No matter what the subject, it is rarely capable of giving the viewer a sharp smack between the eyes which says, 'Wake up, look at me; I am doing something which should affect your senses.' Colour in photography has got to make me feel the same kind of things I feel when I look at a painting; admiration for the person who painted it because of the technique used; a feeling of the whole being acceptably right because subject and composition have been well chosen and balanced on the canvas in a way that my brain can easily digest; a feeling that the actual coloured pigments used are not artificial but closer to those created by nature.

Suddenly, by accident more than design, I have found a colour emulsion that makes me feel some of these things, even if there is room for mechanical improvement in the way in which that colour is reproduced on

the emulsion. A good eye can easily pick out the filter rulings without the aid of a lupe, though in web-offset reproduction the effect is largely lost in the screening process. Polachrome has the ability to render most colours in a highly saturated form. Reds, orange, blues, browns, blacks, yellows and pinks are rich, vividly bright. It definitely does not like the presence of ultra-violet light, nor subjects which reflect white or near-white. It has a low ISO (40) and very little latitude in exposure, having characteristics similar to the original Kodachrome where exposure was critical. Ambient temperature makes no apparent difference to

This is a Polachrome copy of an original oil painting with Kodak Colour control patches. The colours are very close to the original painting, although some detail has been lost in the darker brown/black areas.

Compare colour of the top picture, which was shot on Fujichrome 50, with colour of the tangerine in the bottom one. The latter was exposed on Polachrome using a 180 mm lens with 27 mm extension tube, a custom-made malleable-clear acrylic filter, and processed using a Polagraph processing cartridge for 2 minutes. The combined effect of using a filter and a high-contrast developer increases the apparent effect of colour saturation while bleaching lighter areas.

In a conventional darkroom, negatives are washed and dried and can then be printed in the normal way on bromide or RC papers. The first picture shows the full negative area. The second is a print on original Polaroid material. The third is a print on conventional resin coated paper.

either contrast or colour rendering when exposures are being made, but development temperature must be within the range recommended by the manufacturer. Best results are obtained at 21 °C (70 °F).

What are rulings? Polachrome colours are achieved by the additive process of combining very fine rulings of the three 'additive' primary colours, red, green and blue in a grid pattern layed over the emulsion. When viewed by a very strong white light, the combining effect of minute specks of these colours on the eye and brain is such that we see colours of the image in much the same way as when looking at the printed colour picture on a page. Colour television works on the same principle. When viewed against a point source light with a magnifying glass, Polachrome transparencies appear to defract the light into its spectral sources and this gives a very clear indication of how the additive screen process works.

Polachrome is certainly unique, even if its development is somewhat loosely based on the findings of a certain Dr John Joly of Dublin who, as far back as 1893, had devised a three-colour linear-ruled plate. Louis Dufay also produced an additive-based colour motion picture film in the 1930s known as Dufaycolor. There was also a Dufaycolor reversal processed still format film, which sank into oblivion when Godowsky and Mannes produced the first subtractive-based Kodachrome.

Polachrome's main attraction for me is its richness of colour, and when transparencies are viewed on a white beaded screen with the full power of a projector bulb colours are stunning. There is little evidence of the 'television' type line effect. From colour prints produced with an 8 × 10 in Polaprinter using Polachrome originals, the richness of colour is retained, but because prints are viewed by reflected light some of the original transparency brilliance is lost. In reproduction, I imagine that the finest mechanical processes available would produce impeccable results.

Polachrome used under normal daylight shooting conditions shows up the weaknesses of the film. Whites are bleached, while little or no detail is evident in shaded areas. Colours under an overcast sky, however (left), are well saturated.

Polachrome's best asset is its ability to reproduce vibrant and brilliantly saturated colours. To this end it must be used under fairly controlled conditions, although in both of these examples, which were processed normally using the Polachrome pod, exposures were made using daylight and fill-in reflectors.

I am not certain, however, that what I have seen in the way of printed reproductions using standard web-offset printing, such as is used for the printing of many of the world's magazines, is capable of doing the product justice. I shall be as interested as the reader to see just how well or indifferently the illustrations in this chapter have fared in the photo-mechanical process.

Because of the fragile nature of 35 mm Polaroid it is important to observe one or two conventions. When developed film is extracted from the cassette, scratches and abrasions are more easily avoided if the film is pulled with one felt flap against the anti-halation backing. Hold the cassette in the right hand so that the exit gate of the cassette is turned slightly upward from the horizontal; pull the film in a downward fashion against the lower felt pad. Use the special cutter/mounter first of all to mount processed transparencies before viewing. This helps to avoid unnecessary scratches caused by a lupe being held on the metallic silver image. Use masking or transparent adhesive tape to remove ragged edges of the black developer layer which is not completely separated from the film during processing. Lay the processed film emulsion-side-up on a cleaned light box. Place adhesive tape on the film edge and, while holding one end of the processed film securely, rapidly peel off the tape. The black layer will come away easily and cause no damage to the film base or exposed frames. Excessive amounts of developer layer remaining on the processed film is usually caused by not rewinding the film fast enough after the development time has elapsed.

The 'Darkroom in a Box' is small, lightweight and could be taken on any assignment into the field where transportation is available, or for that matter in a backpack. Aviation specialist Richard Cooke has used' Polachrome successfully while airborne to establish formation patterns while working with aerobatic teams. Polachrome gives more or less instant access to information, often much needed by the roving photojournalist, and I think I would be wary now of going off on a major project without having a few rolls of film and the processor handy.

A Polaroid film pack back for medium-format work and the Polaroid 405 back for use with the 5 × 4 in format have established themselves in my camera cases as standard equipment. Use of the various materials available has already helped to broaden the scope of my photography and encouraged me to attempt assignments I probably would have found dull or uninteresting before because I did not have the means or access to an instant result.

POLAROID MATERIALS AND EQUIPMENT

Listed in Table 18 are the main specifications of the three 35 mm format emulsions available, followed by a general list of materials and equipment produced by the Polaroid Corporation.

FILMS

Polaroid instant films are available in six formats. They may be used in a variety of Polaroid film holders sold through professional photographic dealers, or in Polaroid camera backs sold by over 150 other manufacturers of photographic and scientific equipment.

SIZES

8 × 10 in. Individual positive sheets and negatives, 15 to a box. For use with 8 × 10 in view cameras, graphic arts reproduction cameras, computer graphic cameras etc. There are three colour films including Polacolor ER Type 809, Polacolor 2 Type 808, Colorgraph Type 891 for overhead projection quality transparencies.

4 × 5 in. Individual film packets, 20 to a box. For use with 4 × 5 in cameras and instruments that accept Polaroid's Model 545 film holder. There are six film types including Polacolor ER Type 59 and Polacolor 2 Type 58 film, both of ISO 80. Black-and-white; Type 57 High Speed Film ISO 3000, Type

55 Positive/Negative ISO 50, Polapan Type 52 ISO 400 and Type 51 High Contrast ISO 320 daylight/125 tungsten.

4 × 5 in. Eight-exposure film pack. For use with 4 × 5 in cameras and instruments that accept Polaroid's Model 550 film holder. There are two film types including Polacolor ER Type 559 ISO 80, and Polapan Type 552 ISO 400 for black-and-white.

3.25 × 4.25 in. Series 100 or 600 professional film. Eight-exposure film pack. For use with cameras and instruments equipped with

Model CB101 or CB102 camera backs or 4 × 5 in cameras and instruments that accept the Model 405 film holder; also for use with Polaroid 3.25 × 4.25 in pack film format cameras. There are seven film types including. Polacolor ER Type 669 and Polacolor 2 Type 668, both with ISO 80. There are five instant black-and-white films including Type 667 High Speed ISO 3000, Type 665 Positive/Negative Film ISO 75, Type 612 Ultra High Speed Instrument Recording Film ISO 20,000, Type 611 Video Image Recording Film and Type 084 High Speed CRT recording Film ISO 3000.

3.25 × 4.25 in. Eight-exposure film rolls. For use with cameras and instruments equipped with CB40 camera backs (no longer manufactured). Also for use with Polaroid 3.25 × 4.25 in roll film format cameras (no longer manufactured).

$3\frac{1}{4} × 3\frac{3}{8}$ *in.* Series 80 film. Eight-exposure film pack. For use with cameras and instruments equipped with the Model CB80 camera back; also for use with Polaroid 3.24 × 4.25 in pack film format cameras.

SX-70. Ten-exposure film pack. For use with cameras and instruments equipped with the CB71 camera back; also for use with Polaroid cameras that accept SX-70 film.

CAMERAS AND SLIDE PRINTERS

A complete range of products is available from the Polaroid Corporation in Cambridge, Massachusetts, USA, and from Polaroid (UK) Ltd., in St Albans, Hertfordshire, England. In addition to a range of automatic instant cameras, Polaroid also market the Polaroid 600 and 600SE cameras. These two cameras are based on the Mamiya Universal Press camera and, in fact, the lenses for both models are made by Mamiya, as is, I suspect, the rest of the camera. The 600SE has interchangeable lenses with a full range of shutter speeds from B and 1 second to 1/500 second. The camera accepts an interchangeable Polaroid film back. The 600 model has a fixed

Table 18: CHARACTERISTICS OF POLAROID EMULSIONS

Characteristics	Polachrome CS (colour transparency film)	Polapan CT (continuous tone black-and-white transparency film)	Polagraph HC (high-contrast transparency film)
Balance	daylight	panchromatic	panchromatic
Speed: ISO	40	125	400
Exposure latitude	$+1\frac{1}{2}$ stop	±1 stop	$\pm\frac{1}{3}$ stop
Reciprocity behaviour: 1-second exposure	$+\frac{2}{3}$ stop	$+\frac{2}{3}$ stop	$+\frac{2}{3}$ stop
10-second exposure	$+1$ stop	$+1$ stop	$+1$ stop
Contrast (gamma)	2.0	2.0	4.0
Emulsion resolution (line pairs/mm)	90	90	90
Grain	medium	fine	fine
Colour fidelity	high	—	—
Colour saturation	high	—	—
Processing time*	5 minutes	5 minutes	5 minutes
Developing time	60 seconds	60 seconds	120 seconds
Processing temperature latitude	15–29 °C (60–85 °F)	15–29 °C (60–85 °F)	15–29 °C (60–85 °F)
Projected brightness base density	0.7	0.2	0.05
Frames per cassette	12 and 36	36	12

*Includes loading, development and unloading of AutoProcessor.

Printing slides from Polachrome or conventional transparencies using Polaroid print materials requires more skill than normal because of the inherently low brightness range of the material. The original shot on Fujichrome (left) produces an acceptable print using the 10/8 Polaprinter technique, but with marked loss of greens, reds and shadow detail. Low-contrast originals will make better prints. Right: nearly all texture detail in the suit of HRH Princess Michael of Kent has had to be sacrificed in order to retain detail in the hair and visage.

127 mm lens with the same shutter speeds as the 600SE. The film back is interchangeable also and both cameras accept 665, 107C and type 108 film packs.

Another interesting piece of equipment is the Polaprinter 8 × 10 Instant Slide Printer which is used for making prints from slides, either full frame or cropped on Polacolor ER type 809 film. The printer can also be used for making overhead projection transparencies from original or duplicate

35 mm transparencies on Polaroid Colorgraph Type 891 film.

The Polaprinter 8 × 10 System consists of the Polaprinter Model 3580 for previewing the slide and making the exposure, the Polaroid 8 × 10 in film holder, the loading tray and the Polaroid universal 8 × 10 in film processor. The system is powered by 220/240 volt AC power source and can be used in normal room lighting.

The Polaprinter slide printer is a much

smaller version of the 8 × 10 in Polaprinter, and is designed primarily for making instant prints from 35 mm slides in black-and-white or colour using standard 3.25 × 4.25 in film packs. Slides are previewed on the built-in editing screen, and contrast and exposure controls are adjustable. Vivitar also manufacture and market a slide instant printer which utilises Polaroid materials. Both of these machines are ideal for the photographer interested in providing a rapid proofing service to customers in a hurry. Picture libraries who need to supply potential clients with a good positive image of the original slide, and anyone with a large collection of black-and-white or colour slide originals who needs to keep a handy record of important work to hand for easy viewing will find the Polaprinter invaluable.

NEW DEVELOPMENTS

Polaroid are constantly working on improvements and new inventions in instant photography. When Dr Edwin H. Land retired in 1982, he held more than 500 patents. Critics of the first Polaroid instant black-and-white film launched in 1947 firmly believed that Land's attempts to create a professional quality film capable of instant development would not only fail but would never capture the public imagination. Polaroid's sales in 1984 reached a staggering $1.3 billion. By the time this book is off the presses, the range of 35 mm emulsions will have been extended to include two new 35 mm formats; Polablue and Polalith. There is also to be an interesting departure into the realms of conventional silver-image photography with the introduction of a new professional-quality colour-reversal material in sheet form which is processed in E-6 chemistry. The new Polachrome is made by Fuji and is packed in individual sheets for use in 5/4 Polaroid backs. Also in the wings is a new fully automated AutoProcessor for the 35 mm emulsions, an illuminated slide mounter and viewer and a Palette for use in conjunction with the BBC Master series micro computers. This device enables screen graphics to be photographed directly onto 35 mm formats for the production of audio-visual slides.

Polaroid's demonstration of the then new Polacolor process in 1960 was a unique and outstanding contribution to modern photography; probably the most significant advance in photographic science that this century has seen so far. Those early peel-apart instant pictures have steadily improved in quality to a point where, now, there cannot be much further to go. As the popularity of 35 mm instant photography grows, so too will the demands for improved quality and faster ISO speeds. The fully automated daylight darkroom is not as far away as one might imagine.

15
Other Processes and Techniques

The knowledgeable amateur may find that this book does not include discussion of some common manipulative techniques. In my opinion, techniques which are used to produce *Sabattier*, *Posterisation*, *Bromoil*, *Gum bichromate* and other effects based on fairly vintage recipes are not *Essential Darkroom Techniques*. That is not to say that they may not produce effective results or that they may not be essential to some technicians. One or two of these devices for the enhancement of what would otherwise be fairly boring pictures are time-consuming and quite complicated to prepare; others are relatively simple, requiring only as much as the striking of a match during print or film development. Other books by other authors are available which describe the various processes in detail and they are nearly all contained in the earlier-mentioned book published by Kodak entitled *Creative Darkroom Techniques*.

This last chapter is used more as a listing for the odd items which I do consider essential, and a brief description of each process and its purpose follows.

COLOUR TO BLACK-AND-WHITE

There are various reasons for wanting to make black-and-white prints from colour materials. The most usual is for purposes of reproduction in newsprint or a magazine.

Colour negatives are the most common source of original material and these will normally print acceptably on a grade 3 or 4 paper. There may, however, be some change in tonal rendition of original colours due to the way in which colours are recorded on colour-negative materials. The complimentary colours contained in the negative tend to absorb the blue component of white light, to which most conventional black-and-white

materials are most sensitive. Consequently, items of the subject which would normally be rendered blue are yellow in the negative and, as the yellow acts as a safelight, these tones in the print will be lighter than normal. Lighter colours of the subject will print darker and so on. To correct these tonal differences, use a panchromatic paper which is specially designed to overcome the problem, such as Kodak's Panalure II RC paper. It should be used in conjunction with a No.13 (amber) safelight.

Panalure is a fast paper easily processed in the tray or machine using Dektol or other suitable RC paper developers. Stop bath, fixing and washing are compatible with conventional black-and-white paper processing. Colour negatives may be filtered using CP or CC acetate and gelatin filters to produce just the right tonal effect and contrast.

BLACK-AND-WHITE FROM TRANSPARENCIES

There are several ways in which black-and-white prints are obtained from slides. Prints can be made directly from the slide using a panchromatic reversal paper. Tetenal paper and chemistry are available from professional photographic dealers.

The most commonly used method is to make a black-and-white internegative from the original slide using a medium-speed panchromatic film such as FP4. Slower emulsions like Pan F or Agfapan 25 may be more useful when making contact internegatives. Faster ISO speeds may be necessary when enlargements of a segment of the original slide is to be made. Use the same procedures as for slide duplication with sheet film or a roll-film back. With FP4, which is a good all-rounder for this purpose, an enlarger light source of 75w and an aperture of f5.6 give an exposure of 2 seconds for an EI60. FP4 is normally rated at 125 ASA, but because of the increase in contrast which would result if the film were exposed and processed normally a fairly big cut in development is necessary to compensate for the over-exposure. Make several trial exposures and begin by reducing normal development by 30 per cent.

With contrasty original transparencies in which large areas of blue sky predominate, use filters to correct the tonal rendition in the internegative in the same way as when black-and-white film is exposed in camera.

If your enlarger column and head bracket can be converted for use as a copying stand, black-and-white internegatives can be easily made using a bellows focusing unit and the standard lens for 1 : 1 reproduction. A simple diffused light source is all that is required to light the transparency. A sheet of opal perspex, an electronic flash gun or photoflood light source in reflector, plus two empty shoe boxes, are all that is required.

Use the shoe boxes, stood on edge on the enlarger baseboard, as pillars for the perspex sheet. Place the electronic flash in the space under the perspex (or photoflood). Lay the transparency to be copied on the perspex sheet. Adjust the column height of the copying camera and fine focus the image. Cameras with TTL metering will be useful when the photoflood is the preferred light source. To establish the correct exposure with flash, set the ISO speed on the 'auto' mode dial and select the smallest aperture setting. Make a series of bracketed exposures on a short length of film and process using Table 1.

The handy person will not find it difficult to construct a small reflex light source with flashed opal perspex top.

MOUNTING

There are several methods and different types of materials available for the photographer who wishes to mount pictures for exhibition, copying or framing. Resin-coated papers do not adhere well to mounting boards when a liquid paste is employed. The paper base is waterproof and little or no adhesion will form when the material is brought into contact with the mount.

For general-purpose use where archival properties of the mounted picture are not considered, double-sided self-adhesive tape is as good as anything. Simply apply the tape to the four sides of the trimmed print to be mounted, align one edge with relevant marks on the card and then peel off the outer tape protector on the side of the print to be fixed in place by gently holding the print in position on the card with a cloth wad. When one edge is secured, hold the print off the mount by the opposite edge and peel off the remaining three tape protectors. Gently lay the print out from the edge already secured.

A more convenient adhesive, if the print is required to lay completely flat on its mount, is 3M Scotch which is available in aerosol cans. Several types of this adhesive are made; one allows for repositioning, another is formulated for more permanent requirements. Spray the back of the print to be mounted by placing it face down on sheets of newspaper. Shake the can contents well and then, with the nozzle at a distance of approximately 9 – 12 in (23 – 30 cm), begin spraying in parallel bars across the picture from left to right. Repeat the action from top to bottom to give an even spread of adhesive, but do not move the print off the newspaper until both directions are complete and the adhesive has dried.

To mount, hold the print by its top right-hand corner and gently align the lower left and bottom edge at the corner. Apply light pressure at this point and then secure the bottom right-hand corner in the same way. Using a cloth wad, gently curl the print down, while simultaneously applying a light pressure with the cloth wad to remove any air bubbles which may form. Quite large prints can be successfully mounted in this way but you must take care at every stage to ensure absolute cleanliness, otherwise foreign matter may be deposited on the adhesive side of the print, which will cause unsightly marks in the finished product.

Seal commercial dry-mounting press for the proper mounting of all photographs and artwork. (Photo courtesy of Pelling & Cross.)

Use a lint-free cloth lightly damped to prepare the back of the print ready to accept the paste. Apply the paste with a soft-haired brush in an even pattern. Carefully align the edges to the mount and squeeze out air bubbles using another cloth working from the centre of the print outward. Be very careful when you get to the edges to ensure that no paste is brought back onto the print. Unless your prints are for important exhibition purposes and are expected to remain in service for many years, the use of self-adhesive tapes or sprays is to be recommended. Paper and Linen archival tapes are also available.

The most common method of mounting prints on board uses a 'dry-mount' tissue adhesive. This requires a heated press to effect a professional finish. An ordinary domestic iron can be used, but I have never found the use of such implements very successful.

Lay the mount tissue (Lamatec) on the back of the print and gently tack in place with the tip of a medium/hot iron. About nine different tack spots is ideal in a three-up/three-down pattern. Cut off excess tissue around the edge of the print. I usually do this before tacking in place using a sharp knife on a cutting board of thick card with a metal rule. Cut the tissue about an eighth of an inch smaller than the print to be mounted. That way there is no risk of a 'spread' from under the print as it is mounted. When you have tacked the tissue to the back of the print, align on the mount marks. Cover the print with a sheet of heavy-gauge brown wrapping paper. This is used to protect the print from the iron. Tack each corner in place with the nose of the iron with a gentle pressure for about 10 seconds. Remove the protective brown paper and check that the print is correctly positioned. Replace the paper if all is well and begin ironing from the centre of the print outward with a widening circular motion. 20 seconds should be sufficient to get proper adhesion with a fibre-based print. Resin-coated papers will need a very low temperature and mount tissue of low melting temperature.

A high throughput of mounting will best be served by the installation of a custom-

Aerosol adhesives are fairly expensive. However, I have found that this is the most convenient mounting method for photographers who only have an occasional need. Prints can be mounted quickly onto virtually any surface once the mount area has been marked out and there is little or no mess. Newspapers can be discarded as soon as the sprayed print has dried ready for mounting. I still have prints I mounted using this method well over a decade ago and they are as good today as others which were dry-mounted using tissue and a hot press on the same occasion. Neither is there any noticeable deterioration in print colour or tone.

Fibre-based prints can be mounted using conventional pastes such as those made from rice starch. These should be of low or neutral acidity to prevent 'foxing' and other unsightly stains caused by chemical reactions with residues of chemistry left in the print or contained in the mount board. Atlantis Conservation Board is an acid-free archival mounting board which is available in a variety of textures and colours. (See also the black-and-white section under paper listings on p. 113–16.)

Wet-mounting can be a messy and tedious business and does not work well with prints that have been hot-dried on a glazing machine or flat-bed drier. Prints should be completely flat and undistorted – no curl.

built press such as the Commercial 210M or Jumbo 160M made by Seal.

With the use of Daler picture mount board, a sharp cutting knife such as an adjustable model-making type, or a scalpel, prints can be effectively mounted on the kitchen table. It is better if you have a large work bench on the dry side of the darkroom, so that all tools and materials are easily to hand when needed. Small prints will benefit from having a *window* mount which is cut from a second piece of card with a picture framer's 45°-angled cutting knife. These gadgets are usually obtainable at little cost from good artists' supply stores. The 45° edge to the window mount helps add a little depth to any photograph and gives a more professional finish than the usual straight edge cut. (See Alto Bevel Cutter, below.)

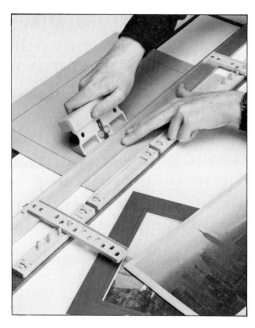

Alto bevel edge mount cutter gives a neater finish to picture surround when framed for hanging.

PROFESSIONAL PHOTO-MOUNTING MATERIALS AND EQUIPMENT

PERMA-MOUNT

Water-based spray adhesive suitable for all paper base types. It is non-flammable and allows re-positioning on the mount board. It is available in an aerosol 12.2 oz can.

PROTECT-ALL

Gloss print lacquer with built-in ultra-violet protection which absorbs harmful light rays. It increases light fastness and seals print from foreign matter.

PHOTO-FINISH

Matt finish print lacquer similar to the above. It incorporates UV protection. It is ideal for spraying onto glossy prints which need camera copying. Excellent results can be obtained from sprayed colour print originals copied onto Ektachrome 160 Tungsten.

SEAL PLATE CLEANER COMPOUND

Specially formulated for cleaning the platen

on a dry-mounting press to which bits of print and dry-mount tissue have adhered.

FUSION 4000

100 per cent thermoplastic adhesive without paper support. It flows freely when heat is applied. It has very tough adhesion; ideal for mounting prints to metals and laminated plastics.

RELEASE PAPER AND RELEASE FOLDER

Silicone-treated materials which prevent thermoplastic adhesives from adhering to print materials or mounting platen. The folder is single-sided and has a longer life span. It can be re-used.

TEMPERATURE INDICATOR STRIPS

These are impregnated with coloured heat-sensitive wax patches. One will melt at 93 °C (200 °F), the other at 99 °C (210 °F). They are ideal for accurate control of platen temperatures.

SEALECTOR TACKING IRON

This has a built-in adjustable thermostat. It is

Seal tacking iron for use in dry mounting.

Teflon-coated. It is used for tacking adhesive in place on print.

PRINT MOUNTING POSITIONER

A calibrated 'T' square specially designed for print mounting. There is no neeed for pencil marks or lines and it comes with comprehensive instructions.

ALTO BEVEL CUTTER

This device comprises a cutting jig which is adjustable to give frame borders of between $1\frac{1}{2}$ and $6\frac{1}{2}$ in (3.8 − 16.5 cm) in steps of an eighth of an inch (3 mm) and a special cutter which produces a 60° bevel. It cuts up to 31 in (79 cm) long, and materials up to an eighth of an inch thick are accommodated. It is an ideal device for making window mounts.

TONING

Sepia toning has always been the most popular form of reducing the harsh impact of pure black-and-white in prints. Before the advent of colour-negative materials for general use, and particularly in studio portrai-ture, the high-street photographer automatically toned every print that came out of the wash, a process also used as a preliminary stage to hand-colouring. Sepia colours vary from a reddish-brown to pale brown and are achieved by converting the black areas of the print using a ferricyanide bleach followed by redevelopment in a dilute solution of sodium sulphide. The latter should not be used in an unventilated space and preferably not in the darkroom where its vile-smelling vapours will fog any unprotected light-sensitive materials. Mix the solutions A and B in a well-ventilated space. The bleach can be re-used if kept in stoppered Winchester-type bottles. The dilute sodium sulphide should be discarded after use well diluted.

Mix chemicals in the following proportions:

1) Solution A (Bleach): potassium ferri-cyanide 100 g + potassium bromide 100 g dissolved in 1 litre of filtered water.
2) Solution B (Tone Developer): sodium sulphide 50 g dissolved in 1 litre of filtered water.

Then, to make working solutions:

1) Dilute 1 part of A with 10 parts filtered water and pour into first dish.
2) Dilute 1 part of B with 10 parts filtered water and pour into second dish.

METHOD

Prints which are to be toned should have received more than the normal amount of washing; a minimum of 50 per cent longer is usual and wet prints are easier to tone than dry ones.

Immerse the print in the bleaching solution A and begin a process of gentle agitation, continuing until the deep shadows are only just visible. Mid-tones and highlights should have disappeared, but different tonal effects can be obtained, depending on the strength of tone of the original and how much new tone is required.

When the correct level of bleaching has

been obtained, remove the print from solution A and wash thoroughly in running water for a minute. A ragged-ended sponge dish-washing utensil is ideally suited to removing excess ferricyanide.

Drain the print from the wash and immerse in solution B. After a few minutes of gentle agitation, the print will have been redeveloped and stained. Wash and dry in the normal way.

STAINING SOLUTIONS

Various proprietary staining solutions prepared in liquid form are available from most photographic dealers if you cannot easily obtain the dry chemicals required for this process. Kodak manufacture and supply the following.

KODAK RAPID SELENIUM

Effect: cold brown tones. Slight increase in print contrast. Dilute stock 1 + 3. Wash for 1 hour.

KODAK POLY-TONER

Effect: Warm to cold sepia tones. Dilute stock 1 + 4 or 1 + 24. Wash for 30 minutes.

KODAK SEPIA

Effect: sepia tone. Use with most papers. Follow maker's instructions using 'A' + 'B' solutions. Wash RC papers for 4 minutes, others for 30 minutes.

KODAK BROWN

Effect: sepia tone. Use with most papers. Toner contains poisonous fumes, so use only in a well-ventilated space. Immersion normally 15–20 minutes at 20 °C (68 °F). Wash: same as for Kodak Sepia toner.

FARMER'S REDUCER

This is a bleaching bath which was invented by the English chemist E.H. Farmer in 1883 and which has long been used for reducing the silver-image content of highlights and shadows. The action on negatives is quite rapid and needs careful application. Prints can be more easily controlled depending on the dilution of chemicals.

The formula for solution A is: potassium ferricyanide 20 g + 250 ml water.

The formula for solution B is: sodium thiosulphate (hypo) 250 g + water to make 1 litre.

METHOD

30 ml of solution A + 120 ml of solution B mixed with 1 litre of water is used for negative reductions. 3 ml of solution A + 12 ml of solution B mixed with 1 litre of water is used for print reduction. For example, prints in which the highlight areas need 'whitening' are immersed in a working solution and agitated gently for several minutes. The tray should be placed in a good light where the action of the reducing agent can be seen. As soon as the brightest highlights begin to lose their greyish tones, remove the print and wash for 30 minutes and then dry.

Negatives to be reduced should ideally be immersed in a small dish which is placed over a strong light source. A sheet of flashed opal perspex let into a bench under which the light is mounted is ideal for this purpose. The rebate for the perspex should be generously applied with waterproof mastic or bedding compound to prevent accidental splashes of liquid reaching the light source.

Stock solutions can be further reduced if the reducing action is found to be too rapid.

Index